# How to Start, Run, and Stay in Business

**Other Books by Gregory and Patricia Kishel**

*How to Start and Run a Successful Consulting Business*
*Start, Run, and Profit from Your Own Home-Based Business*
*Start and Succeed in Multilevel Marketing*

# How to Start, Run, and Stay in Business

## Third Edition


*Gregory F. Kishel*
*Patricia Gunter Kishel*

John Wiley & Sons, Inc.

New York • Chichester • Weinheim • Brisbane • Singapore • Toronto

This book is printed on acid-free paper. ♾



Published by John Wiley & Sons, Inc.

Published simultaneously in Canada



***Library of Congress Cataloging-in-Publication Data:***

Kishel, Gregory F.
How to start, run, and stay in business / Gregory F. Kishel, Patricia Kishel. – 3rd ed.
p. cm.
Includes index.
ISBN 0-471-24773-1 (paper : alk. paper)
1. Home-based businesses. 2. New business enterprises.
I. Kishel, Patricia Gunter. II. Title.
HD62.7.K58 1998
658'.041–dc21 97-51304

Printed in the United States of America

10 9 8 7 6 5 4 3 2 1

# Contents

**Preface** ix

**1 Getting Started** 1

What's in It for Me? / Do I Have What It Takes? / Goal Setting / What Kind of Business? / Starting versus Buying a Business / Checklist for Going into Business

**2 Preparing Your Business Plan** 16

When to Use a Business Plan / The Plan / Guidelines for Successful Planning / Planning Checklist

**3 Determining the Best Location** 27

Choosing the Community / Choosing the Site / The Environment / Making a Traffic Count / Geographic Information Systems Mapping / Rating the Site

**4 Your Building** 38

Looks / Livability / Layout / Amenities / Rating Your Building

**5 Structuring the Business** 47

Sole Proprietorship / Partnership / Corporation / Limited-Liability Company / Government Regulation / Structuring the Business Checklist

**6 Recordkeeping and Taxes 71**

The Value of Good Records / Recordkeeping Systems / Taxes / Tax-Related Decisions / Recordkeeping and Taxes Checklist

**7 Financial Statements 83**

Summarizing Financial Data / The Importance of Financial Statements / The Balance Sheet / The Income Statement / Interpreting Financial Data / Financial Ratio Checklist

**8 Obtaining Capital 94**

Determining Your Initial Investment / Sources of Capital / SBA Business Plan Questionnaire / Financing Checklist

**9 Controlling Your Inventory 113**

The Optimum Level of Inventory / Purchase Discounts / Merchandise Turnover / Universal Product Codes / Just-in-Time Management / Inventory Shrinkage / Inventory Checklist

**10 Setting the Price 122**

Pricing and Customers / Pricing and Competition / Pricing and the Economy / Pricing and Profit / Pricing Methods / More about Markups / Pricing Strategy / Pricing Strategy Checklist

**11 Staffing 133**

Analyze Each Job / Prepare Job Descriptions / Check Recruitment Sources / Use Application Forms / Conduct Interviews / Verify Information / Make the Hiring Decision / Staffing Checklist

**12 Managing and Motivating 146**

Developing Your Own Management Style / Knowing When to Delegate / Finding Ways to Motivate / Developing a Corporate Culture / Leadership Checklist

**13 Developing Your Promotional Strategy 156**

Advertising / Publicity / Preparing an Advertising Budget / Promotional Strategy Checklist

**14 Selling and Servicing 176**

A Positive Approach to Selling / Maintaining Good Customer Relations / Customer Service Checklist

**15 Safeguarding Your Business 189**

Risk Management / Types of Insurance Coverage / Recognizing Warning Signals / Insurance Checklist

**16 International Marketing 201**

Why Go Global? / Evaluating Foreign Markets / Utilizing Market Research Data: Secondary versus Primary Data / Sources of Information / Choosing Your Entry Strategy / International Marketing Checklist

**17 Franchising 216**

The Definition of Franchising / The Price / The Advantages and Disadvantages of Franchising / The Franchise Agreement / How to Find Franchise Opportunities / Evaluating a Franchise / Franchising Checklist

**18 Getting Help 227**

Sources of Outside Help / Accountants / Advertising Agencies / Attorneys / Bankers / Chambers of Commerce / Colleges and Universities / Government Agencies / Insurance Agents / Libraries / Management and Marketing Consultants / Temporary Help Services / Trade Associations / Publications / SBA Field Offices / Small Business Development Centers (SBDCs) / Small Business Resource Websites

**Index 256**

# Preface

Starting and running your own business is one of the most exciting and potentially rewarding activities in which you can engage. In terms of your standard of living, as well as your level of personal satisfaction, there's no limit to what you can achieve through private enterprise. To increase the probability of your success, our book provides the practical information every business owner needs–and presents it in a way that's easy to understand and ready to be used.

Many features make *How to Start, Run, and Stay in Business* equally suited for both prospective and present business owners:

*Handbook format.* Each stage of business operations–from selecting the right kind of business to financing, insuring, and promoting it–is covered on a chapter-by-chapter basis.

*Checklists.* Included throughout the book are checklists, so that you can measure your progress and monitor any areas of your business that need improvement.

*Graphic examples.* Whether you need a financial statement, a job application, or a press release, you can *see* what it looks like.

*Approach.* The book's real-world approach to running a business gives you the information you want when you need it.

Here are a few questions explored in the following chapters:

- How can I raise enough money to get started?
- What's the right kind of business for me?
- Which is better–a sole proprietorship, a partnership, or a corporation?
- How much insurance should I have?
- What's the best way to find good employees?

- How much should I charge?
- How should I promote my business?
- How complex should my bookkeeping system be?
- What's involved in purchasing a franchise?
- What if I get stuck and need outside help?
- How can I use the Internet to build my business?
- How can I expand into foreign markets?

Whether you're thinking about starting your own business or you're already running one, you'll find the answers you've been looking for in these pages.

Tens of thousands of readers used the earlier editions of our book to start or build businesses of their own. Many took the time to thank us for writing the book and to share their stories with us. For this we are grateful. One entrepreneur told us that she kept the book next to her cash register and had used it so many times that the pages were falling out!

Now, with this updated and expanded edition of *How to Start, Run, and Stay in Business,* we look forward to helping the next generation of entrepreneurs. We wish you much success . . . and hope that our book finds a place next to *your* busy cash register.

Gregory F. Kishel
Patricia Gunter Kishel

# 1

# Getting Started

In any successful business operation the secret ingredient is planning. The adage that failing to plan means planning to fail is especially true of running a business. Without good plans, a business is totally at the mercy of fate, ruled by laws based on random probability rather than sound judgment. In this situation, instead of you running your business, it runs you. The way to avoid this is by taking the time to formulate your objectives *before* starting your business. This entails analyzing your reasons for wanting to go into business in the first place, rating your abilities in different areas, and determining what kind of business best suits you.

## What's in It for Me?

"What's in it for me?" is the first question you should ask yourself. Starting and running your own business requires investments of money, time, and energy. In exchange for the opportunity of owning your own business, you give up the benefits that employees take for granted: job tenure, a regular paycheck, paid holidays, vacations and sick leave, and a company insurance plan, as well as the ability to leave your job behind at the end of the day. It's only logical that you should want to know what to expect in the form of a return on your investment–not just in dollars, but in satisfaction.

### The Advantages of Owning a Business

The number of new businesses started in the United States each year is currently growing at a faster rate than the population–clear evidence that owning a business is perceived as offering certain advantages. The ones mentioned most often include these:

- *Control.* The authority to make decisions rests with you. As the boss, you have the power to direct all the activities of your business.

- *Creative freedom.* Without the restriction imposed by set policies and the need to go through channels, your ideas and talent can be freely expressed.
- *Profits.* The more successful your business is, the more money you can make. Whereas employees' salaries generally depend on budget approvals and cost-of-living increases, yours is directly linked to your performance.
- *Job security.* Because it's your business, you can't be fired, laid off, or forced to retire.
- *Pride.* You gain the satisfaction that comes from knowing you have built your business into a successful operation through your own efforts.

## The Disadvantages of Owning a Business

Being the boss isn't without its disadvantages. Among those most frequently mentioned are these:

- *Risk of investment.* If the business fails, you could lose your entire investment. In addition, your personal assets may be jeopardized.
- *Long hours.* Keeping your business going is rarely just a 9:00 to 5:00 proposition, especially in the beginning. Be prepared to put in many 12-hour days to make it work.
- *Income fluctuation.* Instead of reliably receiving a steady paycheck, you depend on income subject to the ups and downs of the business.
- *Responsibility.* The freedom to make decisions carries the burden of standing by them. If anything goes wrong, ultimately you're the one who's responsible.
- *Pressure.* There's always the pressure to please your customers, meet your payroll, and satisfy your creditors' demands.
- *Regulations.* You must abide by federal, state, and local laws, as well as the safety stipulations imposed by your insurance carrier.

Do the advantages of owning a business outweigh the disadvantages? That's something only you can determine. Just as some individuals can be happy only when working for themselves, others prefer to work for an employer. In planning your own business, it's important that you keep sight of your own needs and wants. Will owning a business enable you to satisfy them at a price you're willing to pay?

## Do I Have What It Takes?

Do you have what it takes to own and operate your own business? It isn't a matter of how smart you are; it's more a matter of personality and behavior. Researchers have found that individuals who possess certain characteristics are more likely to succeed as business owners than those who lack these characteristics. Although there's not total agreement as to the characteristics that are the most important, those frequently cited include

- *Motivation.* The drive (mentally and physically) to succeed, to accomplish the tasks of your own choosing, on your own terms
- *Confidence.* The firm belief in your own capabilities and your chances of success
- *Willingness to take risks.* The readiness to sacrifice your own security, if need be, in order to accomplish your goals
- *Ability to make decisions.* The skill to analyze complex situations and draw the conclusions that will make your business succeed
- *Human relations skills.* The ability to get along with others, to inspire cooperation, confidence and loyalty
- *Communications skills.* The talent to express yourself, to understand others, and to share ideas
- *Technical ability.* The expertise to produce the goods and services of your business

To rate yourself in these areas and to get some additional input regarding your suitability for the entrepreneurial role, read the following rating scale, and answer the questions as objectively as you can.

### Rating Scale for Personal Traits Important to a Business Owner

*Instructions:* After reading each question, circle the letter of the answer that fits you best. Be honest with yourself.

1. Are you a self-starter?
   a. When something needs to be done, I do it. Nobody has to tell me.
   b. If someone gets me started, I keep on track.
   c. Easy does it. I don't put myself out unless I have to.

2. How do you feel about other people?
   a. I like people and can get along with just about anybody.
   b. I have plenty of friends. I don't need anyone else.
   c. People, in general, tend to irritate me.
3. Can you lead others?
   a. I can get most people to follow me without much difficulty.
   b. I can give the orders as long as someone tells me what to do.
   c. I usually let someone else get things moving, then I join in if I want to.
4. Can you take responsibility?
   a. I like to take charge and see things through.
   b. I can take charge if I have to, but I'd rather let someone else be responsible.
   c. Go-getters always want to show off. I say let them.
5. Are you a good organizer?
   a. I like to have a plan before I start. I'm usually the one to get things lined up.
   b. I'm pretty good unless things get too complicated. Then I quit.
   c. I just take things as they come. It's easier that way.
6. Are you a good worker?
   a. I can keep going as long as necessary. I don't mind working hard.
   b. I'll work hard up to a point, but when I've had enough, that's it.
   c. I can't see that hard work gets you anywhere.
7. Can you make decisions?
   a. I can make up my mind when I need to, and my decisions usually turn out okay.
   b. I can if I have plenty of time. Otherwise I end up second-guessing myself.
   c. I don't like to be the one who decides things. There's too much pressure.
8. Can people trust what you have to say?
   a. They sure can. I don't say things I don't mean.
   b. I try to be on the level, but sometimes I just say what's easiest.
   c. I don't worry about the truth if the other person doesn't know the difference.

9. Can you stick with it?
   a. If I make up my mind to do something, I don't let anything stop me.
   b. I usually finish what I start.
   c. If a job doesn't go right, I bail out. Why beat your head against a wall?
10. How good is your health?
   a. I never run down.
   b. I have enough energy for most things I want to do.
   c. I'm okay as long as I don't try to do too much.

Where did most of your circles go? Ideally, letter *a* should have been your choice for each question. If it wasn't, then you have one or more weak spots to consider. It's up to you to find ways to bring about improvements in these areas, either by changing your personal habits and attitudes or by staffing your business with people whose strengths can augment yours.

## Goal Setting

One way to improve your chances for success is to set goals for accomplishing the various tasks associated with forming and operating your own business. For each goal, you should indicate your plan of action and specify the target date for the goal's achievement. Then, as each target date arrives, you can compare your actual performance with your intended performance. Whenever you reach a goal, set a new goal for yourself. In this way you can keep both your momentum and your motivation going at a steady pace. For example, your list of goals might look like this:

**Month 1**

- Read *How to Start, Run, and Stay in Business.*
- Visit the Small Business Administration (SBA) and gather information on starting a business.
- Do research in the public library and on the Internet.
- Talk to business owners to get their input.

**Month 2**

- Decide on the type of business to start.
- Collect as much information as possible on this type of business.
- Attend one of the SBA's Prebusiness Seminars and any other relevant seminars.

**Months 3–5**

- Decide whether to start a business from scratch or to buy an existing business or franchise.
- Prepare a plan of action to obtain funds, locate, and furnish business.
- Go over the plan with a counselor at the local Small Business Development Center.

**Month 6**

- Open business.

**Year 1**

- Have business break even.

**Year 2**

- Make a 15 percent profit on sales.
- Determine ways to improve or expand business.

**Years 3–5**

- Open additional stores.

For the goal-setting process to work, the goals that you set for yourself should be (1) measurable, (2) scheduled, (3) realistic, and (4) written.

1. *Measurable.* It isn't enough just to say that you want to "do well" or to "be a success." You have to have a way to measure your goals. In other words, if you want to be a recognized leader in your field within three years, think of the criteria for judging whether you have attained the goal–memberships in specific organizations, write-ups in newspapers and magazines, sales volume, profits, and so on. Unless there is some standard of measurement you can use to determine what constitutes a recognized leader, there's no way to know whether you are one.

2. *Scheduled.* Each goal that you set for yourself should have a specific time frame for its completion. If you have to move a date forward or push it back, you can, but having a completion date to shoot for will make it easier for you to schedule the work needed to accomplish your goal and to monitor your progress. Are you on schedule, behind schedule, or ahead of schedule?

3. *Realistic.* If you set unrealistic goals for yourself, you set yourself up for failure. Few people become "overnight" millionaires or earn enough to retire within six months of starting their business. Look at what other business owners in your field have accomplished, and find out how long it took them to do it. Then compare their situations to your own circumstances, and set your goals accordingly. Keep in mind, too, that the closer your business goals are to your personal goals, the greater the likelihood that you will achieve both.

4. *Written.* A goal that isn't in writing isn't a goal, as management experts will tell you. By writing down the things you want to accomplish, you start to realize them. Putting your goals in writing not only clarifies them, but also enables you keep them in focus as you work toward attaining them.

## What Kind of Business?

Perhaps you have already selected the kind of business you would like to start. Instead, you may be considering several alternatives. In either case, how can you tell whether you've picked a winner? Will your proposed business be able to support you both materially and emotionally? The answer depends on such difficult-to-predict factors as the economy, the competition, the available resources, and the political environment–all of them forces beyond your control. In addition, however, it depends on another factor that you *can* control–yourself. Be sure to consider this factor as carefully as the others. A business that's right for a friend of yours may not be right for you. Unless you select a type of business or a field that genuinely appeals to you, the odds on your winning are so slight that you're better off not leaving the starting gate.

To shift the odds in your favor, the first thing you should do while planning your business is to think about what you really want to do. Try to come up with ideas for businesses that you would actually enjoy running, not just to make money but to have fun doing it. The more ideas the better. As you come with each idea, *write it down.* Once you start digging into your own background, experience, education, and hobbies for inspiration, you may be surprised at how many different businesses appeal to you.

After you've expanded your list as much as you can, your next step is to narrow it down, focusing on those business opportunities that most closely match your own qualifications. For instance, if you have a fear of heights and have never jumped out of a plane, a skydiving school is probably a poor choice for you. If, on the other hand, you're talented at drawing and have computer skills, a graphic-design business may be an excellent choice.

If you're determined to start a specific business, even though you know very little about it, what can you do to minimize your risk? Find out as much as possible about your intended business before attempting to open it. You can do this by getting additional education, taking a job in someone else's business, researching the business in the library, talking to people in the field, and so on. Even though this step may make you postpone opening your doors, the delay will be worth it. Once your doors are open, you'll be in a better position to *keep* them open.

As for those uncontrollable factors that also affect your business, the best way to cope with them is to stay tuned in to what's happening in each area. Some new business owners get so caught up in their own affairs that they fail to keep track of events that may have a direct bearing on their operations. You can avoid this mistake by reading newspapers and magazines, listening to what people have to say, and observing the changes in your environment.

## Starting versus Buying a Business

Once you've selected the kind of business that is best for you, you face another important decision: whether to start your business from scratch or to buy an existing business. Neither method is better than the other. It's a matter of choosing the one that best fits your own needs, circumstances, and financial situation. For example, if speed is of the essence–you want to open your doors in time to capitalize on a key selling period or to take advantage of favorable lending terms–then buying an existing business that's already up and running may be the answer. If, however, the existing business is in a bad location or its facilities are deteriorating and in need of extensive repairs, you could end up with major problems.

Thus, in comparing the two choices, you should pay close attention to the pros and cons of each method.

### Starting from Scratch

**Pros**

- You start with a clean slate–the business is your vision.
- You choose everything–from the location, design, and layout to the merchandise, supplies, and equipment.
- You hire the employees you want.
- You control the business's image.
- There aren't any old problems to resolve.

**Cons**

- It takes time to do everything necessary to start the business.
- Lenders and investors may be reluctant to put money into an unknown business.
- It's hard to find good employees.
- You have to build customer awareness.
- You don't have the input of a previous owner to help you.

### Buying a Business

**Pros**

- It's already a going concern.
- It's known in the community.
- Supplier and distribution agreements are in place.
- It has an established customer base.
- Credit can be more easily obtained with a proven business.

**Cons**

- The business may be overvalued.
- The location or facilities may be bad.
- The inventory, supplies, or equipment may be outdated.
- It may be operating inefficiently.
- There may be unforeseen debt or legal problems.

### Additional Considerations

Other factors to keep in mind are

- Your own preferences
- The availability of a suitable business to buy
- The costs associated with each method
- The profit projections for each method

Your comparison should also include a thorough background check into the history of any business you consider buying. This entails

1. Looking at a minimum of three years of its tax returns
2. Getting an estimate of its worth and its credit rating from Dun & Bradstreet or another financial-information services company
3. Talking to its employees, suppliers, distributors, and competitors
4. Getting the opinions of current and former customers
5. Checking with government and consumer organizations to determine whether any complaints or legal actions have been filed against the business

## Checklist for Going into Business

Now that you have thought about your reasons for going into business, examined your temperament, considered the opportunities open to you, and set goals for your business, the following checklist should help you to get started. The questions in it relate to both the formation and the actual operation of your own business. Answer each question yes or no. Be as honest with yourself as you can. This will help you find areas of weakness that need improvement and topics that you need to research further.

| Before You Start | Answer Yes or No |
|---|---|
| **About You** | |
| Are you the kind of person who can get a business started and make it go? | ________ |
| Do you want to own your own business badly enough to keep working long hours without any guarantee that it will succeed? | ________ |
| Have you ever worked in a business like the one you want to start? | ________ |
| Have you ever worked as a supervisor or a manager? | ________ |
| Have you had any business training in school? | ________ |
| Have you researched your proposed business and tried to learn as much about it as possible? | ________ |

| Before You Start *(continued)* | Answer Yes or No |
|---|---|
| **About Money** | |
| Have you saved any money to invest in a business? | ______ |
| Do you know how much money you will need to get your business started? | ______ |
| Do you know how much credit you can get from your suppliers–the people you will buy from? | ______ |
| Do you know where you can borrow the rest of the money you need? | ______ |
| Have you figured out what your annual net income (salary plus profits) will be? | ______ |
| Can you live on less than this amount, if necessary? | ______ |
| Have you talked to a banker about your plans? | ______ |
| **About a Partner** | |
| If you need a partner with the money or the know-how that you don't have, is there someone available you could work with? | ______ |
| Do you know the pros and cons of going it alone, having a partner, or incorporating your business? | ______ |
| Have you talked to a lawyer about your options? | ______ |
| **About Customers** | |
| Have you identified a niche for your business in the marketplace? | ______ |
| Is there a need for your particular product or service? | ______ |
| Do you know who your customers will be? | ______ |
| Do you understand their needs and wants? | ______ |
| Will your product or service offering be competitive in all aspects–price, quality, and so on? | ______ |
| Have you chosen a location that is convenient for your customers? | ______ |

*(continued)*

| Getting Started *(continued)* | Answer Yes or No |
|---|---|
| **Your Building** | |
| Have you found a suitable building for your business? | ________ |
| Will you have enough room when your business grows? | ________ |
| Can you fix the building the way you want it without spending too much money? | ________ |
| Will there be adequate parking, maintenance, security, or other necessary support services? | ________ |
| Have you had a lawyer check the lease and zoning for the facility? | ________ |
| **Equipment and Supplies** | |
| Do you know what equipment and supplies you need and how much they will cost? | ________ |
| Can you save money by buying secondhand equipment? | ________ |
| Have you compared the difference between buying and leasing? | ________ |
| **Your Merchandise** | |
| Have you decided what merchandise to carry? | ________ |
| Do you know how much inventory you will need on opening day? | ________ |
| Have you found suppliers who will sell you what you need at a good price? | ________ |
| Have you compared the prices and credit terms of different suppliers? | ________ |
| **Your Records** | |
| Have you chosen a recordkeeping system that will keep track of your income and expenses, assets, and liabilities? | ________ |

| Getting Started *(continued)* | Answer Yes or No |
|---|---|
| Have you worked out a way to keep track of your inventory so that you will have enough on hand for your customers, but not more than you can sell? | ______ |
| Have you figured out how to maintain your payroll records and take care of tax reports and payments? | ______ |
| Do you know what financial statements you should prepare? | ______ |
| Do you know how to use these financial statements? | ______ |
| **Your Business and the Law** | |
| Do you know what licenses and permits you need? | ______ |
| Do you know what business laws you have to obey? | ______ |
| Do you know a lawyer who can give you advice and help with legal papers? | ______ |
| **Protecting Your Business** | |
| Are you aware of the various risks that you should guard against? | ______ |
| Have you talked with an insurance agent about what kinds of insurance you need? | ______ |
| Have you made plans for protecting your business against thefts of all kinds–shoplifting, robbery, burglary, employee thievery? | ______ |
| **When Buying a Business** | |
| Have you made a list of what you like and don't like about buying a business that someone else has started? | ______ |
| Are you sure you know the real reason the owner wants to sell the business? | ______ |
| Have you compared the cost of buying the business with the cost of starting a new business? | ______ |

*(continued)*

| Getting Started *(continued)* | Answer Yes or No |
|---|---|
| Is the inventory up-to-date and in good condition? | ________ |
| Is the building in good condition? | ________ |
| Will the owner of the building transfer the lease to you? | ________ |
| Have you talked with others in the area to see what they think of the business? | ________ |
| Have you talked with the company's suppliers? | ________ |
| Have you talked with a lawyer about the purchase? | ________ |

| Making It Go | Answer Yes or No |
|---|---|
| **Advertising** | |
| Have you decided how you will advertise (newspapers, magazines, direct mail, radio, etc.)? | ________ |
| Do you know where to get help with your ads? | ________ |
| Have you observed the types of promotion used by your competitors? | ________ |
| **Pricing** | |
| Do you know how to calculate what you should charge for each item you sell? | ________ |
| Do you know what other businesses like yours charge? | ________ |
| **Buying** | |
| Do you know what suppliers you intend to buy from? | ________ |
| Will your plan for keeping track of your inventory tell you what and when to buy? | ________ |
| **Selling** | |
| Do you know what selling techniques to use? | ________ |

| **Making It Go** ***(continued)*** | **Answer Yes or No** |
|---|---|
| Have you thought about why people buy the products or services you offer and how you can convince customers to buy from you? | ________ |
| Are you fully aware of the benefits associated with the products or services you will sell? | ________ |
| **Your Employees** | |
| If you need to hire someone to help you, do you know where to look? | ________ |
| Do you know what kind of person you need? | ________ |
| Do you know how much to pay such a person? | ________ |
| Do you have a plan for training your employees? | ________ |

| **A Few Extra Questions** | **Answer Yes or No** |
|---|---|
| Will owning a business enable you to achieve your goals? | ________ |
| Have you talked it over with your family and gotten their support? | ________ |
| Are you willing to make the commitment to "be the boss"? | ________ |
| Are you ready to begin developing your business plan? | ________ |

For every *yes* answer you gave, think of yourself as one step closer to turning your business dream into a reality. Each *no* answer represents an area to work on–a temporary roadblock, yes, but a dead end only if you let it be.

# 2

# Preparing Your Business Plan

Given the rapid changes occurring in the marketplace and the increasing levels of competition that all businesses face, you can't afford to proceed blindly, hoping that hard work alone will be enough to make your business a success. To succeed, a business must have clearly defined objectives and a fully developed strategy for achieving them. In short, what's needed is a business plan.

Far from viewing a business plan as a luxury reserved for big businesses or as something created solely to impress the financial community, entrepreneurs should see it for what it is–one of the most important tools a business can have. Just as an organization chart shows the working relationships of the people within a business, a business plan shows the purpose of the business and what it intends to accomplish. A good business plan helps to give form and substance to an entrepreneurial vision, providing a mechanism that enables owners, managers, and workers alike to function effectively. The better the business plan, the better equipped your business will be to recognize and assess the opportunities and risks that lie ahead.

## When to Use a Business Plan

Much like a Swiss Army knife, with its multitude of tools and utensils, your business plan can serve many purposes. Among the times that your business plan should be of the greatest use to you are when you're

1. Starting your business
2. Expanding your business
3. Developing new products
4. Obtaining financing

5. Making management decisions
6. Maintaining control

### Starting Your Business

During the start-up stage of a business, the existence of a sound business plan can mean the difference between success and failure. Rather than pursuing conflicting goals or allowing the business to develop haphazardly, you can use the plan to keep your business on track.

Some of the questions your plan should answer are

- What business am I in?
- What are my products or services?
- Who are my competitors?
- Who is my target market?
- What's the best marketing strategy?
- How should my resources be utilized?
- What is the business's profit potential?

Even though you may not be able to work out all the answers in advance or may find that they change later, the important thing is to have a set of assumptions about the business and its environment that you can share with other people. This will make it easier for you to enlist their support in launching your business and in working as a cohesive unit to carry out their respective tasks.

### Expanding Your Business

Your business plan can also help reduce the added risks involved in expanding your business. A plan is especially critical during an expansion phase because this is one of the most dangerous times for a business. If a business tries to expand too quickly, before mastering its current level of activity, the quality of its products and services often suffers. On the other hand, if it waits too long, the market could already be saturated with similar product offerings and the opportunity may be lost.

By addressing such issues as *timing*, the *rate* of expansion (should the business grow at an annual rate of 5 percent or 20 percent?) and the *type* of expansion (a bigger building? additional locations? new products?), your plan can help you to make the right choices. In this way, instead of being overwhelmed by growth, you should be able to manage it.

### Developing New Products

For most businesses the need to develop new products is a fact of life brought about by the continuing challenge to satisfy their customers. To remain competitive, your business must be able to anticipate and respond to customers' changing needs and to make effective use of new technologies. The way to accomplish this is by developing new products and services or by improving existing ones. The company that developed the electronic lightbulb knew this; they invented a product that lasts years longer than traditional incandescent and fluorescent bulbs and is more energy-efficient, too.

Unless a business has a plan to guide it, though, the chances of its coming up with profitable ideas for new products, product modifications, or improvements are minimal. To make the most of your resources as your business grows, you must have a systematic plan for developing new products and managing your current ones.

### Obtaining Financing

Commercial lenders, such as banks and finance companies, expect to see a business plan as a matter of course before they will lend money to a business. The same holds true for government lenders. Even when there is sufficient collateral to pledge as security for the loan, a business plan is still likely to be required because it shows where the business is going and how the money will be used.

A business plan is even more important if you're seeking investment capital. Investors, especially venture capitalists, tend to be more demanding than lenders because their risks are greater. Unless a plan can convince them that financing a business will enable them to earn a substantial return on their investment, the standard response is, "No go. No dough." This puts the burden on you to demonstrate through your business plan that the investment will be worth their while.

### Making Management Decisions

Perhaps the most valuable use of a business plan is in making management decisions. By stating what the business wants to accomplish and assessing both its internal and external environments, a business plan shows the "big picture." This gives entrepreneurs a real advantage. Instead of operating in the dark or looking at just one aspect of a problem, they can consider it from all points of view and make the decision that is in the best overall interests of the business.

Along with this, your business plan can also help you to maintain your objectivity, enabling you to see the business as an outsider would. Putting sentiment aside, you can then focus on what needs to be done to achieve your goals, making hard decisions when necessary.

### Maintaining Control

Another key use of a business plan is as a control device. Are you meeting your goals? Did sales reach their target? Is production capacity increasing according to schedule? Are costs staying in line? Is the business doing what it set out to do?

You should be able to get the answers to these questions and more by examining your business plan. Then, by carefully rating your performance against your goals, you can determine whether you're moving ahead or merely moving in place. If a method or strategy isn't working, or if you find that the business is going in a different direction, you can act quickly to bring things back in line or to chart a new course.

## The Plan

Once you've made up your mind about what kind of business to start and have done your preliminary research, you're ready to begin preparing your business plan. Much as you may be tempted to skip this step or hire someone else to do the work for you, *don't.* The effort you put into it will be more than compensated later when your business is operational. Also, the knowledge you gain from creating the finished, written plan will be invaluable.

Although every business plan is different, reflecting the ideas and intentions of the person who wrote it, certain elements, or sections, are common to all plans. As shown in the following Business Plan Outline, your plan should be organized so that it provides essential information in a concise and logical format.

### Business Plan Outline

- Title Page
- Table of Contents
- Executive Summary

- Business/Industry Description
- Product or Service Description
- Organizational Data
- Marketing Strategy
- Competitive Analysis
- Operations Plan
- Financial Information

### Title Page

The title page should include the name of your business, its address, contact numbers (phone, fax, and e-mail) and the names of all owners. If your business is still at the idea stage, then use your own address and phone number for the time being. The important thing is to provide prospective lenders, investors, and others who see the plan with a means of contacting you.

### Table of Contents

A table of contents is absolutely essential. It not only provides an overview of what's in your plan, but also enables readers to quickly find what they're looking for without having to thumb through all the pages. This makes for a more "reader-friendly" plan, which will, in turn, help to generate a favorable response.

### Executive Summary

The executive summary is the single most important element of a business plan. Because it has the power to make or break your plan, it should provide a concise, but clear, picture of your business–within a maximum of two pages. Designed to stimulate a busy reader's interest, the executive summary's job is to convince the reader to take the time to go over the rest of the plan in detail.

Among the points that you should cover in the executive summary are

1. The current status of your business, indicating when it was started or when it is expected to commence operations
2. A description of your products or services

3. Information about your target market and your means for reaching it
4. The strengths inherent in your business that will enable it to achieve its objectives (i.e., experience, a unique idea, good location, product quality, and so on)
5. Your short-term and long-term plans
6. Financial projections
7. The amount of money, if any, you're currently seeking

Condensing all this data to a two-page summary isn't easy. By staying focused on the key facts, however, you can do it. Also, even though the summary comes *first* in your business plan, write it *last*. That way you'll have the business in perspective and the information you need in hand.

### Business/Industry Description

This section should begin with a statement of your business's goals and objectives, defining what your business does (or will do) and its purpose. This is the place to put background information about the founding of your business, its ownership and legal structure, the nature of its industry, and the role you intend for your business to play in that industry. You should also include any data you have about changes in the marketplace that will lead to an increased demand for what your business has to offer. As you can imagine, investors are particularly attracted to growth industries.

### Product or Service Description

Explain what your business sells or proposes to sell, describing your products or services in detail: their features, quality and performance levels, functions, and so on. Here it's important to point out what separates them from competitors' product offerings and what benefits customers will derive from them. In other words, what makes your products or services unique or gives them the edge? If you are using a trade secret (such as a recipe or formula) or have (or expect to receive) patent protection, state that, too.

### Organizational Data

In this section, outline the duties and responsibilities of the people involved in your business. Make it clear who does what (in production, sales, accounting, and so on) and who reports to whom. If you're currently an organization of one, describe the tasks you will be carrying out, and estimate your future personnel needs. To further illustrate how your business is set up, include an *organization chart* in this section, along with *résumés* showing each person's qualifications.

### Marketing Strategy

The main reason for starting a business is to sell something. That's where marketing strategy comes in. The primary objectives in this section of your business plan are to

1. Define your *target market*, describing your potential customers and why they buy
2. Estimate the total *market size* and determine what share of it you can realistically hope to obtain
3. Develop a *pricing structure* that will ensure you maximum profitability
4. Determine what combination of *advertising and publicity* to use to promote the business
5. Outline a *distribution strategy* that will enable you to reach customers in the most efficient way possible

In spelling out these objectives, try to be as specific as you can, basing your marketing strategy on facts, rather than on wishful thinking. Much of the information you'll need to formulate your strategy can be obtained through books, magazines, government reports, trade associations, and your own observations and research.

### Competitive Analysis

Your competitive analysis should identify the key players in your industry and explain how your business can compete with them. Focusing on your strengths and advantages (as noted in your product or service description), you want to show how you can capitalize on them to gain your desired market share. Your purpose isn't to belittle the competition. Rather, it's to point out (1) the customers whose needs they are failing to serve properly, if at all; and (2) the limitations (such as being too large or having dated technology) that keep them from doing what you can do.

### Operations Plan

This is the nuts-and-bolts section of your business plan–the place to describe how your product or service will actually be produced or delivered to the customer. All information about facilities, equipment, and supplies goes here. You should also explain what technologies, skills, and processes are required to do the job.

### Financial Information

Last is the section of your plan that lenders and investors often consider to be the "heart" of it. This section describes the financial data relevant to your business venture, including your current financial statements (if the business is already established), as well as a projected

- Income statement
- Balance sheet
- Cash-flow statement

These projections, covering a period of one to three years, are meant to provide a financial picture of your business, showing its expected revenues and expenses, assets and liabilities.

Doing the work to come up with the financial data you need takes time, but with practice, you'll be surprised at how adept you become at "number crunching." To find out more about financial statements and how to prepare and use them, see Chapters 7 and 8.

## Guidelines for Successful Planning

The following guidelines should help you to master the planning process and to become more proficient at preparing, updating, and using business plans.

1. *Set aside time for planning.* Recognizing the need to plan is one thing; allocating the time to do it can be another. Call it "planning phobia" or simply "procrastination." Whatever the case, for your business to succeed, you must spend sufficient time on planning.

2. *Determine in advance what you want to accomplish.* What is the purpose of your planning effort? To prepare a business plan for a new venture? To update an existing plan? To obtain financing? By identifying

your specific goals for planning, you can focus your attention on the key issues or activities that need to be addressed.

3. *Make sure you have access to the necessary facts.* Information is what fuels the planning process. To plan effectively, your information must be relevant, accurate, and up-to-date. This means having access to *internal information,* such as accounting records and sales reports, and *external information,* such as industry trends, consumer buying habits, and so on.

4. *Coordinate your planning efforts with the efforts of others.* Make sure that each person involved in the planning process knows what everyone else is doing. To avoid working at cross purposes–with you pursuing one planning objective while a partner or employee is pursuing another–you must coordinate efforts. This is the only way to maintain harmony and ensure that the various goals set for the business are compatible.

5. *Keep an open mind.* To achieve the best results as a planner, avoid getting locked into one approach to a problem or situation. Give different strategies a chance to develop, and explore various possible courses of action. Above all, let yourself be creative. Rather than starting out with a preconceived idea of what your business should or should not do, take the time to consider the alternatives.

6. *Solicit input from others.* Don't be afraid to ask for advice and to get other people's viewpoints. As your business grows, these diverse insights will become increasingly important. The planning process works best when the people responsible for creating the business plan collaborate with those who will be called upon to implement it.

7. *Review your business plan.* Once you complete your business plan, go over it to see that it clearly depicts your business and adequately states your intentions for the business. Before implementing it, make sure that it will help you to achieve your objectives.

8. *Update the plan.* Business experts often recommend updating a business plan every six months. That way you can determine whether the plan is continuing to meet the needs of your business. As circumstances change or as new information becomes available, update the plan accordingly.

9. *Make the plan accessible.* All too often, business plans are kept from the very people who need to see them. Keeping proprietary information from your competitors makes sense; keeping it from your own people does not. For key employees to fully contribute their talents and

abilities to the business, they must know what it stands for and where it's going.

10. *Use the plan.* Most important of all, *use* your business plan. A plan that's gathering dust on a shelf or that's buried in a filing cabinet can't do you any good. If your plan really *is* going to be the blueprint for a successful business, then you must put it to work.

## Planning Checklist

To evaluate how your planning efforts are going and to identify those areas that need work, answer these questions.

| Planning Checklist | Answer Yes or No |
|---|---|
| 1. Have you developed a clear concept of what you want your business to be? | ________ |
| 2. Have you learned as much as possible about your business and its industry? | ________ |
| 3. Do you have the necessary information (financial data, marketing research, production requirements, and so on) to put together a business plan? | ________ |
| 4. Have you looked at other business plans (available at your local library or Small Business Development Center) to see how they were written? | ________ |
| 5. Are you willing to put in the necessary time to prepare a business plan? | ________ |
| 6. Have you talked about your plan with the people whose support you'll need, and have you solicited their help with it? | ________ |
| 7. Have you taken steps to make the planning process inclusionary, rather than exclusionary, so that everyone involved in your business can contribute to it? | ________ |

*(continued)*

| **Planning Checklist *(continued)*** | **Answer Yes or No** |
|---|---|
| 8. Is planning an ongoing part of your business activities? | ________ |
| 9. Do you place as much importance on planning as you do on taking action? | ________ |
| 10. Is your mind open to new ways of doing things and new opportunities? | ________ |
| 11. Have you allowed yourself to be creative in forming a business vision that is uniquely your own? | ________ |
| 12. Do you update your business plan at least once a year? | ________ |
| 13. Do you currently have a business plan that you are satisfied with? | ________ |
| 14. Are you really using your plan as a tool in making management decisions and in shaping your business? | ________ |

# 3

# Determining the Best Location

The location for your business is too important to be chosen casually or solely on the basis of personal preference. To do so is to invite disaster. Major corporations are well aware of this. When seeking to relocate or expand their facilities, big business leaders sometimes spend years weighing the pros and cons of various locations. In your case, spending that much time is probably not feasible or even advisable. However, the same scientific approach that works for big business can work for you.

## Choosing the Community

When evaluating a particular community, ask yourself the following questions:

1. Is there a need for my product or service?
2. How many customers are there?
3. How strong is the competition?
4. Is the community prosperous enough to support my business?
5. What is the community's growth potential?
6. What kinds of people live there (age, income, interests, occupations)?
7. What are the restrictions on my type of business (licenses, zoning, local ordinances)?
8. Will my suppliers have ready access to me?
9. Is the local labor force both adequate and affordable?
10. Do I like the community enough to live and work in it?

1. *Is there a need for my product or service?* A generally approved business strategy is to find a need and fill it. Will your new or preexisting

business be able to fill a need in the community? If not, a change must be made–either in the type of business you're considering or in the community.

2. *How many customers are there?* Is the number of potential customers large enough to justify locating your business in the community? The closer you are to your main market, the easier it will be to serve it.

3. *How strong is the competition?* Having determined that there is a market for your product or service, it's important not to overlook the competition. Do any businesses already have a foothold in the community? How many? What can you offer that will set your business apart from the rest? If yours is to be the first such business in the community, why haven't others already located there? Perhaps there is some drawback you may have overlooked.

4. *Is the community prosperous enough to support my business?* To determine the community's level of prosperity, take a close look at its economic structure. Is it based on manufacturing, retail, services, or a combination of these? Who are the major employers in the town? What kind of work do the employees perform? How much unemployment is there? Could layoffs in one sector result in an economic collapse–if a plant closes down, for example?

5. *What is the community's growth potential?* Are people moving into the community or leaving it? Some positive indicators of growth are land-development projects, the presence of department stores and other major businesses, well-kept homes and storefronts, active citizens' groups such as a chamber of commerce and PTA, and adequate public services (health, education, safety, transportation).

6. *What kinds of people live there?* In addition to the size of the community's population, you should be concerned about its makeup. Is the average age 52 or 22? How much does a typical worker earn? What percentage of the community is married, single or divorced? What's the average number of children per household? This type of statistical information–called *demographics*–can be obtained from local census tracts and chambers of commerce.

For an even more complete profile of the local residents, you might examine their lifestyles, as well. What do they like to do in their spare time? Read? Ski? Garden? Travel? Spend time with their families? Are they politically conservative or liberal? Data of this nature–known as *psychographics*–tell about the inner workings of people, focusing on their activities, interests, and opinions. Such information can be obtained through questionnaires, interviews, and your own observations.

7. *What are the restrictions on my type of business?* Each community has its own unique restrictions, instituted to either promote or discourage different types of businesses. In selecting your location, make sure that you are aware of these restrictions. Otherwise, you may find yourself prohibited from obtaining business licenses, expanding your facilities, receiving deliveries, or maintaining certain hours of operation. By finding out ahead of time what to expect, you can avoid unpleasant surprises later.

8. *Will my suppliers have ready access to me?* If you are considering a remote, out-of-the-way locale for your business, your privacy may come at a price. Unless your suppliers have ready access to you, you could end up unable to obtain necessary shipments or paying premium shipping costs. This will, of course, have a bearing on the merchandise you carry and the prices you charge for it.

9. *Is the local labor force both adequate and affordable?* Whether labor is available and affordable depends on your type of business. If you are opening a diner, there's probably not much to worry about. Short-order cooks are fairly well distributed geographically. Finding the right chef for an exclusive French restaurant could be more of a problem, however. The more specialized or technical the work tasks are, the greater the difficulty in hiring the right people. This difficulty also increases as the number of workers you need to employ increases. As for wages, these vary with the community's standard of living. Will your budget demand that you locate in a community where labor costs are low?

10. *Do I like the community enough to live and work in it?* Regardless of your answers to the first nine questions, if you can't say yes to this one, keep looking. Relying on personal preferences alone can be disastrous, but ignoring them altogether can be equally so. The location that is best for your business must also be right for you and your family.

Once you've answered these questions, you'll be in a much better position to rate a particular community's attractiveness. You'll also quickly see that an ideal location for one business can be totally wrong for another. A seaside resort, for instance, might just be the place to sell bathing suits, but a bad choice for a furniture store.

Selecting the community where you wish to locate is only half the location process. The second and equally important step is to select a site within the community.

## Choosing the Site

Regardless of the type of business you are planning to start, be it a retail, wholesale, manufacturing, or service establishment, site selection will play an important role in its development. Evidence of this was found in a major study conducted by General Foods. The company wanted to know why certain grocery stores achieved greater profitability than others, so it compared seemingly identical stores carrying the same merchandise and utilizing the same operating and promotional procedures. Management effectiveness was also considered. Surprisingly enough, the stores that stood head and shoulders above the rest weren't always the best managed. Another factor was needed to explain this discrepancy: the sites of the various stores. Because of errors in site selection, some of the stores, though well managed, could never hope to achieve the success of the stores with the better locations. Such liabilities as competition, declining neighborhoods, and inadequate parking space were just too much to overcome.

The success of Wal-Mart can largely be attributed to the company's recognition of the importance of site selection. Instead of locating its stores in the already overcrowded downtown areas of large American cities, where other retailers were focusing their efforts, Wal-Mart decided to open its stores in the small, rural southern and midwestern communities that had been neglected by the major retailers. In this way, Wal-Mart was able to grow virtually unnoticed without having to go head-to-head with the competition.

## The Environment

The site for your business could be

- Your home
- The downtown business district
- A shopping center or mall
- A major street
- A side street
- A site near a highway access ramp

- An industrial/commercial park
- A business incubator
- Cyberspace

Each site has its own unique characteristics, which you will want to consider. Then, given your particular business, you can select the environment that will best suit its needs.

**Your Home** Depending on the type of business you run and where you live, you may find that the best site is right under your own roof. The home, once viewed primarily as a location just for sideline or cash-strapped businesses, is rapidly growing in favor with entrepreneurs who want the convenience and comfort it provides. Those businesses best suited to a home location generally (a) can operate in a small amount of space; (b) are clean, safe, and quiet; and (c) don't disturb the neighbors. This includes businesses in the medical, legal, accounting, and consulting fields and a wide variety of other businesses, such as architecture and design firms, cleaning services, furniture-repair shops, mail-order retailers, and import/export operations. To find out more about locating your business at home, see our book *Start, Run, and Profit from Your Own Home-Based Business.*

**The Downtown Business District** The downtown business district is the part of town where finance, business, and industrial concerns generally have their headquarters. Depending on the community in which you've decided to locate, this area can range in size from a few square blocks to many square miles. In this environment, a high percentage of your customers will be employees of the neighboring businesses. Also, although they may commute great distances by car to reach their jobs, they will generally confine any shopping to what's within walking distance of their workplaces. Peak shopping times, not surprisingly, are during lunch and before and after work. In the evenings and on weekends, sales are likely to drop off. The businesses most likely to flourish in a city's downtown areas are restaurants, shoe stores, bars, department stores, gift stores, bookstores, clothing shops, coffeehouses, and any other enterprises that cater to the working person.

**A Shopping Center or Mall** The development of planned shopping centers and malls changed forever the way people shop. Shoppers could now do their shopping in a controlled environment without having to leave, drive long distances between stores, or repeatedly search for parking places. Retail and service establishments could attract customers into their places of business simply by being in a popular shopping center or mall.

Shopping centers clearly seemed to be the way to go–but not all centers and not for all businesses. Before you locate in one, take the time to find out all the terms of occupancy. What does your rent cover? Are there additional or hidden charges for shared facilities or services, such as parking, landscaping, public rest areas, special programs, and joint advertising? What restrictions will you need to abide by? Will your business have to be open during specific hours on certain days? Will your assigned space be in a good location in relation to the surrounding businesses, as well as to the flow of customer foot traffic, or will your business be off by itself at the end of a side corridor, where customers won't even notice it?

Some other things to be aware of in evaluating a shopping center are these:

- The caliber of management operating it
- The mix of businesses represented (Are they compatible or competitive? What quality of goods or services do they offer?)
- The number of magnet stores (department stores) drawing customers to the center
- The vacancy rate

Locating your business in a shopping center or mall can be expensive. Furthermore, not all businesses derive any real advantage from a shopping-center location. Shoe-repair shops and cleaners, which provide essential services, generally do as well, maybe even better, on a major street where their expenses are less. The businesses that most benefit from a shopping center or mall location are the ones that cater not only to working people but also to nonworking adults and to teenagers who like to gather at the mall. Among these are department stores, clothing and shoe stores, record stores, bookstores, gift stores, restaurants, snack stands, ice cream parlors, candy stores, jewelry stores, and toy stores.

If you feel that a mall location is right for you, but the cost is just too high, an alternative to consider is renting a *kiosk* or *cart* in a mall. More than 80 percent of the enclosed shopping malls in America now have kiosks or carts as part of the tenant mix. The advantage such businesses offer to the mall include the reduced risk because only a short-term lease is involved, the color and diversity these "temporary tenants" offer, and, of course, the added revenue. The business owner, on the other hand, gets prime mall space at a fraction of the going start-up cost or monthly rental rate. Kiosks have become so popular of late that many entrepreneurs, who once used kiosks as stepping-stones to fixed-location stores, are now opening more kiosks and expanding from mall to mall.

**A Major Street** Major streets have the heaviest flow of automobile traffic. Though perfect for fast-food restaurants, shoe-repair shops, cleaners, and other stop-and-shop businesses, heavily trafficked streets can have drawbacks. Getting people to stop is one of them. If your business will depend on foot traffic or window shoppers, scouting a location will require more than just counting the cars passing by. What is your assessment of the array of businesses located there (antique shops or auto-repair shops?), the desirability of the neighborhood, and the availability of parking? Does the street have a character that will make your potential customers feel at ease there?

If you've decided that locating on a major street is the way to go for your business and you've found the right street, the selection process still isn't over. Which *side* of the street is best? According to marketing experts, the going-home side of the street is better. Because people do their shopping on their way home from work rather than on their way to work, businesses on the going-home side of the street tend to have bigger sales. Furthermore, when given a choice of shopping in sun or shade, shoppers generally choose shade. This means that businesses on the shady side of the street also have bigger sales. If the going-home side and the shady side do not coincide, you might compensate for a lack of shade by erecting an awning.

**A Side Street** Side streets are out of the way and less frequently traveled. They may intersect or run parallel to a main street, but for one reason or another less traffic flows there. The main advantage of locating on a side street is lower rent. However, you also have lower visibility, which makes it difficult to attract potential customers.

For a retail business to succeed on a side street, it must be able to draw customers to it on the basis of its reputation. Sometimes this can be accomplished through word-of-mouth or advertising. The businesses most likely to prosper on a side street are seamstress and tailor shops, nursery schools, industrial suppliers, small manufacturers, and others that don't depend on a high traffic flow for sales.

**A Site Near a Highway Access Ramp** The businesses most likely to benefit from locations near highways are those that cater to the driving public by providing food, lodging, and automobile servicing. Amusements and tourist attractions also thrive on the steady flow of automobile traffic. To make the most of this location, your business must be visible from the highway and easily reached by access ramps. As a rule, travelers don't want to stray far from the highway to find you. However, a less visible location can sometimes be improved by means of a large sign that draws attention to your establishment or by means of billboard advertising that includes directions (e.g., "Take Frontage Road exit 2 blocks west").

**An Industrial/Commercial Park** The number of industrial/commercial parks being built continues to increase. These sites are designed and built exclusively for businesses that engage in "business-to-business" selling or in industrial sales. Located on the outskirts of cities or in the suburbs where large parcels of land are available, these "parks" are often chosen by businesses for their headquarters or manufacturing operations. Among the advantages of this type of location are space, parking, desirable zoning laws, and attractive leasing rates. Because most industrial/commercial parks are off the beaten track, though, retail and service businesses that cater to the general public should normally avoid them, opting for more visible locations.

**A Business Incubator** Business incubators are specially designed facilities for new or fledgling businesses. Created to provide entrepreneurs with affordable space and a support system (reception/secretarial services, computers, fax, duplicating equipment, and so on), incubators provide a nurturing environment in which to grow a business. Protecting new businesses at the time when they are most vulnerable, incubators often sponsor workshops and seminars for their entrepreneur tenants on such subjects as financing, marketing, and management. For more information on incubators, contact the National Business Incubation Association, 20 E. Circle Drive, #190, Athens, Ohio 45701.

**Cyberspace** With the continued growth of the Internet, more and more businesses are opting for electronic locations, rather than physical ones. That's not to say that you don't need a place to work or to store supplies and inventory. But the overall business operation is conducted on the World Wide Web portion of the Internet, with customer interaction and transactions occurring in cyberspace via websites and cyber malls. Once limited to technology-related businesses, cyberspace is now host to every type of business imaginable, from gourmet food brokers to sports-equipment distributors. The key to making this location work is to have a well-designed, interactive website that showcases your products or services with appealing graphics. It's also important to be listed on the right sites and to make use of hyperlinks that connect your business to other sites. For more information on Internet marketing, see Chapter 13.

## Making a Traffic Count

One way to gauge the potential sales volume of a site is to do a traffic count. This involves more than simply counting each car or person passing by. It requires that you *analyze* the flow of passersby to determine which are *your* customers. For instance, if you're planning to operate a women's health club, you're not interested in counting the number of men who walk or drive by. Furthermore, if this club is to be very expensive, you can also rule out women who obviously would not be able to afford membership. The accuracy of your traffic count depends on your ability to assess who your potential customers are. So, prior to doing the count, you'll want to spend some time drawing up a profile of your customers to help you recognize them when they pass by.

Having determined whom to count, the next thing to do is decide the *scope* of the count. Will it encompass just the area directly in front of your store, or will it include nearby or cross traffic? Are you going to count people as they enter the area or as they leave it? If you count them at both times, there's a good chance you will be counting some people *twice.* To guard against double counting, it's essential that you set up strategic checkpoints where your count is to be conducted.

The *timing* of your count must also be carefully planned to coincide with a normal or typical period. If you conduct your count during a peak holiday such as Christmas or Easter vacation, it will be too high. Counting on Fridays or on the first day of the month could throw your tally out of balance, too, because these are the times when many people receive paychecks and social-security checks.

After you've chosen the time for your count, the final step is to divide the day into half-hour intervals. In this way, you can get both a total count of the day's traffic flow and subtotals for the flows at various intervals during the day. These subtotals will tell you when to expect the heaviest sales each day, which should help you plan your hours of operation. For additional information, many business owners find it helpful to do more than one traffic count and compare the data for the various days.

## Geographic Information Systems Mapping

Another way to evaluate a potential community or site within it is to put geographic information systems (GIS) mapping technology to work. By using a CD-ROM computer program that combines ZIP code and demographic information into a geographic database, you can create maps that identify where specific target markets live, the routes people travel on their daily commutes, the locations of competitors' stores, underserved areas, and more. At one time, GIS mapping technology was limited to major corporations that could afford to pay GIS technicians to design specialized programs for them, but it is now available in budget-friendly PC versions for use in small businesses. Some of the leading companies that produce CD-ROM mapping technology software are Environmental Systems Research Institute, Inc.; MapLinx Corp., and MapInfo Corp.

## Rating the Site

You should find it easier to determine a site's desirability if you set up a rating system of some kind against which you can judge each site. The following score sheet is one example. Depending on the specific needs of your business, you may wish to modify it.

### Site Evaluation Sheet

| | Grade | | | |
|---|---|---|---|---|
| Characteristics | Excellent | Good | Fair | Poor |
| 1. Centrally located to reach my market | | | | |
| 2. Merchandise/raw materials availability | | | | |
| 3. Nearby competition | | | | |
| 4. Convenient and affordable transportation availability | | | | |
| 5. Parking facilities | | | | |
| 6. Adequacy of utilities (sewer, water, gas, electricity) | | | | |
| 7. Traffic flow | | | | |
| 8. Taxation burden | | | | |
| 9. Quality of police and fire protection | | | | |
| 10. Environmental factors (schools, cultural and community activities) | | | | |
| 11. Quantity of available employees | | | | |
| 12. Prevailing rates of employee pay | | | | |
| 13. Housing availability for workers and management | | | | |
| 14. Local business climate | | | | |
| 15. Conditions of neighboring buildings | | | | |
| 16. Personal feelings about area | | | | |

# 4

# Your Building

Whether you plan to lease an existing building or construct a new one, take care to ensure that the building is appropriate for your specific business. Require the building you finally select to do more than just keep the rain out. It should also promote your business and help it to function properly. Call these elements "looks" and "livability" if you will. Does the building have the looks to get a second glance from your potential customers and, better yet, to make them want to come inside? As for livability, how suitable is the building for your various business activities–selling, manufacturing, administration, shipping, receiving, storage? Unless your building gets a passing rating in both looks and livability, you're in for problems–the most common ones being lost sales, operations headaches, and remodeling costs. In addition, the layout and the amenities of a building will influence its utility for your business.

## Looks

Forget what you've heard about not judging a book by its cover. Right or wrong, this is precisely what people do every time they pass a building. Even those who never come inside and know next to nothing about your business will form opinions about it on the basis of its outside appearance–its looks alone. Thus, you should think of the exterior of your building as a communications medium, capable of transmitting messages about your business. If you aren't careful, though, it's easy to transmit the wrong message. For instance, it would be a mistake for a store selling discount housewares and appliances to be in a building with a polished marble front and brass handles. Potential customers would take one look at the marble and brass and automatically assume that the store had high prices. A brick or stucco exterior, on the other hand, would elicit a positive reaction, encouraging people to associate the store with economy and practicality.

### Retailing

Nowhere do looks exert a greater influence on the success or failure of a business than they do in retailing. Not only must your store's exterior accurately identify the nature of your business–an exclusive shop, for example–but it must also be inviting enough to draw people inside. Achieving both ends–identification and invitation–requires planning and attention to detail. For best results, your store's architectural style, building materials, exterior colors, display windows, and signs should all be part of a coordinated effort. Ideally, each element complements the others and serves to reinforce your store's overall image. More than money, what's needed here is imagination and a clear idea of the kind of store you want. Once you know that, it's easier to communicate the right message to others.

### Manufacturing

Manufacturing establishments have a little more room for error in the looks department than do retailers. This is because they depend less on their ability to draw customers inside their places of business. Customers generally don't see the plants of the companies they do business with. Orders are usually placed through wholesalers and sales representatives or by mail. Potential customers who do visit a plant are generally more interested in examining the production facilities than in admiring the building. Although the looks of your building take a back seat to its livability, this isn't to say that looks should be ignored. The exterior of your building makes a statement about the quality of the products you sell, your company's policies, and the level of success it has achieved. A rundown, unattractive building can only reflect badly on your business.

### Services

Depending on the service you offer, the importance of looks can vary. Some services are so specialized that their clients actually seek them out and go to some trouble to find them (consultants, automobile repair shops, cooking schools, landscape artists). Others, such as shoe-repair shops and cleaners, are frequented so regularly that customers hurry in and out, barely even noticing how the facilities look. These places don't have to use looks to pull customers in because they are coming in already. Not all services find it this easy to attract customers, however. Restaurants and hotels, for instance, rely a great deal on drop-in customer traffic. The more inviting their buildings are, the better it is for business.

## Livability

Conforming to the local building codes is not enough to make a facility suitable for any and all businesses. The difference between a livable building and one that's impossible depends on what you intend to do with it. The same building that's a dream come true for an automobile repair shop would probably be a nightmare for a jewelry shop. The best way to avoid settling into the wrong building is to consider the building in terms of its construction, space, design, and accessibility for your particular business.

Is the building's *construction* such that it will be both safe and serviceable for your business? A manufacturer utilizing heavy equipment needs a building constructed of materials that can hold up to heavy wear, reduce noise, and resist fire. Cement and steel win out over wood and glass.

Does the building provide too much *space* or too little? Is there room for expansion later, should the need arise? For optimum operating efficiency, it's important to strike a balance between your present and your future needs for space.

Can you make effective use of the building's *design?* This requires that the relationship between the building's selling, work, and storage areas be compatible with your business activities.

Is the building readily *accessible* to both your customers and your delivery personnel? Steps, entrances (their number and location), and loading facilities all play an important role in your day-to-day operating efficiency.

## Layout

*Layout* refers to the physical setup of furniture and fixtures, equipment, merchandise, and supplies within your building. The better your layout, the easier it is for workers to do their jobs and for customers to shop. Conversely, a bad layout can be the cause of inefficiency and lost sales.

To arrive at the right layout, you must do more than just move things around and hope for the best. You must arrange things in a way calculated to derive the maximum benefit from the space available. Your objectives are to display merchandise and services to their best advantage, conserve time and motion, and fully utilize equipment. For retail businesses, this translates into increased customer traffic and sales. For manufacturing and service businesses, this means increased productivity and sales.

## Retailing

In retailing, the main function of your layout is to direct the flow of customer traffic throughout your store. This is a two-stage process, first drawing customers into your store and then guiding them from one location to the next within it. Rather than having customers wander haphazardly, or even turn around and walk back outside, an effective layout leads customers where *you* want them to go. Greater exposure to your merchandise en route increases the number of purchases made. It sounds easy–and it is, if you apply a few tested principles.

1. *Study your customers' shopping habits.* Find out which items your customers purchase regularly and which ones only occasionally. Your observations should also help you differentiate between impulse items and demand items. *Impulse items* are purchased on the spur of the moment, without any planning. *Demand items* are purchased deliberately, according to plan.

Once you know how your customers shop, you can arrange your merchandise accordingly. Take a grocery store, for instance. Where are the meat, dairy, and produce items usually located? At the back of the store or along the side walls, running from front to back. This gets customers to walk deep into the store in order to reach them. Because these are demand items, customers don't mind the inconvenience. What's more, because these are regular purchases, customers can be counted on to seek them out repeatedly. This isn't true of such items as candy, potato chips, and magazines. As impulse items, they have to be seen in order to sell. Unless they are in highly visible locations–next to the checkout counter, for example–their sales will drop.

2. *Create visually appealing merchandise displays.* Unless your displays have eye appeal, customers will ignore them. How important is this? According to a group of independent retailers surveyed by the National Retail Merchants Association, one out of every four sales can be attributed to merchandise display. Other stores have credited displays for as much as 50 percent of their sales.

To improve your displays, notice the displays in other stores, read trade magazines, and ask your merchandise suppliers for tips. Many manufacturers will provide retailers with ready-made displays of their product at little or no charge.

3. *Keep merchandise displays fresh.* Even the most dramatic display starts to look commonplace when it's been left up too long. Don't let yours become permanent fixtures.

4. *Coordinate merchandise displays.* Merchandise that goes together should be displayed together. In this way, customers are stimulated to purchase more than a single item. A customer purchasing a man's shirt is likely to buy neckties to go with it. Displaying sunglasses, suntan oil, and beach towels together is a good way to increase the sale of all three items.

5. *Create a pleasant shopping environment.* Make your store an enjoyable place in which to shop. In addition to being clean and attractive, it should have appropriate lighting and adequate temperature controls and ventilation. Conveniently located drinking fountains and rest rooms are also a plus.

6. *Utilize space according to its value.* Space directly in the path of customer traffic has the greatest sales potential and therefore the greatest value. The most valuable space of all is directly in the front of the store where customer traffic is the heaviest. The space having the least value is farthest from the traffic flow, generally in the back of the store.

Given these differences in value, you should differentiate between your selling and your nonselling activities and allocate your least valuable space to nonselling activities (administration, shipping and receiving, storage, and customer service). This allows more valuable space to be utilized to generate sales. In so doing, impulse items should be located as close to the traffic flow as possible (preferably at the front of the store), and demand goods can be located farther away, in space having less value.

The chart of Retail Store Floor Values shown here illustrates how the space in a store with a single entrance might be valued. Note that the space to the right of the entrance has a higher value than the space to the left. This is because more customers turn to the right on entering a store than to the left, so there is greater traffic flow on that side.

7. *Determine which type of layout to use—grid or free flow.* A *grid layout* is made up of merchandise aisles arranged in straight, parallel lines, while a *free-flow layout* consists of merchandise groupings clustered throughout

| | | |
|---|---|---|
| 2% | 5% | 4% |
| 5% | 8% | 6% |
| 6% | 12% | 10% |
| 10% | 18% | 15% |

Retail Store Floor Values (Total Value = 100%)

the selling area. The advantage of a grid layout is that it forces customers to move in a linear fashion from one point to the next throughout the store and has clear sight lines that make it easy to monitor customer activity. The disadvantage of a grid layout is that it's less esthetically pleasing and doesn't encourage browsing. Grid layouts are commonly used by supermarkets, drugstores, and hardware stores.

The advantage of a free-flow layout is that it allows customers to discover merchandise on their own and to go at a more leisurely pace throughout the store, browsing at will. The disadvantage is that customers may miss things, and it's harder to keep track of their movements throughout the store. Free-flow layouts are often used in gift stores, boutiques, and specialty shops.

### Manufacturing

In a manufacturing establishment the main function of your layout is to increase productivity. Whereas in retailing a layout directs the flow of customer traffic throughout the store, here it directs the flow of raw materials throughout the production process. An effective layout provides for the most efficient utilization of personnel and equipment with minimal unnecessary movement of materials.

The two most commonly used are the product layout and the process layout. A company that produces a steady flow of standardized products, such as a manufacturer of machine parts, would use a *product layout.* Here, equipment is arranged in an assembly-line format that corresponds to the sequence of production steps for each product. Raw materials are then located at the points where they are needed and added to the line as the unfinished products pass by.

A company (such as a clothing manufacturer) that produces nonstandardized products or varying quantities of products, according to customer orders, is unable to operate this way. Instead, it would use a *process layout.* Here, separate processing departments are maintained, and each product passes through only those processing stages it requires. Unlike the product layout, this involves additional movement of unfinished goods and leaves some equipment idle, while other equipment struggles to function at peak capacity. These problems can be partially remedied through efficient scheduling; proper maintenance of equipment; and watchful monitoring of production activities to streamline them wherever possible.

### Services

Service establishments fit into two categories: those oriented toward merchandising (beauty salons, restaurants, hotels) and those oriented toward processing (automobile-repair shops, cleaners, plumbers). Layouts for merchandise-oriented businesses normally are similar to those of retail operations, whereas processing services tend to follow manufacturing layouts. The reason for these differences stems from their respective goals: to increase customer traffic or to increase productivity.

## Amenities

In evaluating the suitability of a building for your business, don't overlook the amenities that are included with it. These little things may not seem important at first, but they can add greatly to the building's comfort and convenience for you and your customers. Following are some of the key amenities:

- *Security.* Have the building managers taken adequate measures to protect the safety of the building's tenants and customers? These might include using electronic surveillance systems, security guards, building entry codes, alarms, and so on.

- *Maintenance.* Is someone on hand to perform basic maintenance and repair duties, as needed?
- *Reception.* Is there a comfortable place for your customers and other visitors to be greeted and to wait until you are able to see them?
- *Landscaping.* What kind of landscaping is there? The presence of plants and flowers outside the building and in the common areas inside can enhance your environment and can help to put workers and customers in a positive frame of mind.
- *Business Services.* Is there a business-services center on the premises to handle your word processing, duplicating, telecommunications, delivery, travel planning, and other business-related functions?
- *Food Service.* Is there someplace to eat in the building–a restaurant, food court, or vending-machine area? Can food service be provided for meetings with employees or customers?

Depending on what type of business you run, some of these amenities will be more important than others. The ones to look for are those that save you time or enable you to better serve your customers.

## Rating Your Building

The following Building Evaluation Sheet can help you to get a better idea of a building's ability to meet the specific needs of your business. This can be useful both in selecting the building in which you want to locate and in designing your layout for optimum efficiency.

**Building Evaluation Sheet**

| | Grade | | | |
|---|---|---|---|---|
| **Characteristics** | **Excellent** | **Good** | **Fair** | **Poor** |
| 1. Physical suitability of building | | | | |
| 2. Type and cost of lease | | | | |
| 3. Overall estimate of quality of site in 10 years | | | | |
| 4. Provisions for future expansion | | | | |
| 5. History of building | | | | |
| 6. Exterior of building in promoting your business | | | | |
| 7. Safe environment for customers and employees | | | | |
| 8. Conformity to all zoning requirements for your type of business | | | | |
| 9. Ready accessibility to customers | | | | |
| 10. Effectiveness of merchandise displays | | | | |
| 11. Pleasantness as a place to shop | | | | |
| 12. Quality of lighting | | | | |
| 13. Utilization of space according to its value | | | | |
| 14. Layout in facilitating movement of employees and materials | | | | |
| | | | | |

# 5

# Structuring the Business

The type of legal form that you select for your new business can be crucial in determining its success. Your ability to make decisions rapidly, compete in the marketplace, and raise additional capital when needed relates directly to the legal structure of your business.

The three main legal forms to choose from are sole proprietorship, partnership, and corporation. No one form is better than another. Each has its advantages and disadvantages. The important thing is to ascertain the legal form of business that will work best for you. Following are some questions you should ask yourself when making this decision:

- What do I already know about this type of business?
- In what areas of the business will I need help?
- How much money will I need to get started?
- What sources of money will be available to me later?
- What kinds of risks will I be exposed to?
- How can I limit my liability?
- What kinds of taxes will I be expected to pay?

## Sole Proprietorship

Close to 75 percent of all businesses in the United States today are *sole proprietorships.* This means that they are owned by just one person. More often than not, that person is directly involved in the day-to-day operation of the business.

As a sole proprietor, you're in the driver's seat. In addition to having total control over your business, you have total responsibility for it. Just as all profits from its operation will be yours, so will all its debts and liabilities be yours as well.

## Advantages of a Sole Proprietorship

***You're the boss*** As a sole proprietor, you have the freedom to run your business in any legal way you choose. You can expand or contract your business, add or drop products or services, and hire, promote, and fire personnel. This ability to make decisions quickly, without having to wait for committee approval, lets you take advantage of timely opportunities. If you are looking for maximum control and minimum government interference, the sole proprietorship could be just the thing.

***It's easy to get started*** The sole proprietorship is by far the simplest legal form you can choose. There's no legal expense or red tape in getting started. All you need to do is obtain the assets and commence operations. In some instances, local or state licenses may required, such as if food or beverages are to be sold. More often, however, it's just a matter of hanging out your shingle.

***You keep all profits*** All profits from a sole proprietorship go to the owner. You are not obligated to share them with anyone else. It's up to you whether to keep them for your personal use or reinvest them in the business.

***Income from the business is taxed as personal income*** The government considers income derived from a sole proprietorship to be part of the owner's income. As such, you will have no separate income tax to pay. Furthermore, losses incurred by the business can be deducted from your personal income tax.

***You can discontinue your business at will*** Should you decide you want to go on to something new, dissolving your business is quite simple. Without the necessity to get second opinions, divide up shares, or process paperwork, you need only cease operations.

## Disadvantages of a Sole Proprietorship

***You assume unlimited liability*** A sole proprietor is responsible for all business debts or legal judgments against the business. In the event that these exceed the assets of the business, your own personal assets–home, automobile, savings account, investments–can be claimed by creditors. In other words, your financial liability is not limited to the amount of your investment in your business, but extends to your total ability to make payment. This unlimited liability is the sole proprietorship's worst feature. (Methods for protecting yourself are discussed in Chapter 15.)

***The investment capital you can raise is limited*** The amount of investment capital available to your business is limited to the money you have or are able to borrow. Unlike partnerships or corporations, which can draw on the resources of others, sole proprietors have to provide the total investment for their businesses.

***You need to be a generalist*** Anyone who starts a sole proprietorship must be prepared to perform a variety of functions, ranging from accounting to advertising. Most new sole proprietorships can't afford the luxury of hiring specialists for these tasks. Even if you can, you still have to understand what they're doing because you're the one who will be held liable for their actions.

***Retaining high-caliber employees is hard*** You may have difficulty holding onto your best employees because they want more than you are offering them–namely, part ownership in your business. For these employees, a good salary and bonuses often won't be enough. Your only recourse is to let them go or to convert your sole proprietorship to another legal form.

***The life of the business is limited*** The death of the owner automatically terminates a sole proprietorship, as does any other unforeseen occurrence (long-term illness, for example) that keeps the owner from operating the business. Because there is no one else to carry on, the business just ceases to function.

## Partnership

A *partnership* exists when two or more people share in the ownership of a business. By agreement, they determine the amount of time and money each partner will invest in the business and the percentage of the profits that each will receive. The extent of each partner's authority and liability must also be made clear.

To avoid misunderstandings later, the partners should put in writing everything to which they have agreed, preferably with the assistance of an attorney. The importance of a written partnership agreement cannot be overemphasized. In the absence of such a document, the courts can resolve any disputes that arise, but the outcome might not please one or more of the partners–and it will be expensive to reach.

Here is some of the information to include in your partnership agreement:

- Each partner's responsibilities and authority
- The extent of each partner's liability
- The amount of capital each partner is investing in the business
- How profits and losses are to be shared
- How disputes between the partners are to be resolved
- Arrangements for the withdrawal or admission of partners
- How assets are to be distributed, should the business be dissolved

### Advantages of a Partnership

***Two heads are better than one*** In a partnership you have the advantage of being able to draw on the skills and abilities of each partner. Ideally, each partner's contributions to the business complement those of the other partners. For instance, one partner oversees accounting functions, another is in charge of production, and another handles sales.

***It's easy to get started*** Starting a partnership is relatively easy. Although it entails additional cost and more planning than a sole proprietorship (selecting partners, preparing the partnership agreement, and so on), red tape is minimal.

***More investment capital is available*** Your company's ability to increase capital can be enhanced by simply bringing in more partners. Unlike a sole proprietorship, which can draw on the financial resources of only one individual, in a partnership, you have the combined resources of the partners.

***Partners pay only personal income tax*** Partnerships are taxed the same as a sole proprietorship. The total income of the business is considered to be the personal income of the partners. This means there is no separate business income tax to pay, and business losses are deductible from each partner's income tax.

***High-caliber employees can be made partners*** Partnerships are able to attract and retain high-caliber employees by offering them the opportunity to become partners. This method of employee motivation has been particularly successful in the legal and accounting professions.

### Disadvantages of a Partnership

***Partners have unlimited liability*** Like sole proprietors, partners are responsible for all debts or legal judgments against the business. This liability is even worse for partners than it is for sole proprietors because, as a partner, you are responsible not only for your own debts but also for those of your partners. Should they incur liabilities, you could be left holding the bag. And remember that even though your investment in the business may be minimal, your losses could be substantial. Your liability extends beyond the amount of your investment to include your personal assets as well.

***Profits must be shared*** All profits resulting from the partnership must be distributed among the partners in accordance with the partnership agreement. What percentage of the profits is to be reinvested in the company must be decided by the partners. Your wishes in this matter represent only one viewpoint.

***The partners may disagree*** Disputes among partners can literally destroy a partnership. One partner's desire to expand the business can go against another partner's goal of cutting costs. Should your money be spent on improving your product or on promoting it? When key decisions must be made, the feelings of trust and admiration that drew you together as partners can disintegrate. To avoid this outcome, you must give your full attention to selecting partners and drawing up the partnership agreement. Foresight in the planning stage can pay off later.

***The life of the business is limited*** As with a sole proprietorship, the life of a partnership is limited. Should one of your partners withdraw from the business or die or become too ill to carry on, the partnership is automatically dissolved. Though it is possible for the remaining partners to reorganize the business, the financial interest of the departing partner must first be paid. Furthermore, any time a new partner is admitted to the business, dissolution of the partnership is mandatory. A new partnership, reflecting the addition of the new partner, must be formed.

### Limited Partnerships

Because of the unlimited liability to which partners are subject, you may be reluctant to assume the risk. One way around this is to form a limited partnership. In a limited partnership there are two kinds of partners–general and limited. *General partners* assume unlimited liability for the business. The liability of *limited partners* is confined to the amounts of their investments. However, in exchange for this limited liability, limited partners are restricted from taking an active role in the company's management. The withdrawal of a limited partner from the business does not necessarily dissolve the partnership, should others wish it to continue.

In a limited partnership the risk can be shifted from one partner to another. It cannot be avoided entirely, though, because every limited partnership must have at least one general partner. If you decide to set up a limited partnership, you must give public notice to this effect, stating that one or more partners have limited status. Otherwise it is assumed that a general partnership exists, in which all partners have unlimited liability.

### Other Partners

Within the scope of the partnership format, there are four other types of partners you may wish to consider.

1. *Silent partners* invest money in a business but take no active role in its management, nor do they share liability. They are primarily interested in getting a return on their investment.
2. *Secret partners* are active in the management of the business but are not known to be partners. Although they want to participate in running the business, they don't want the public to know about their involvement.
3. *Dormant partners* are neither active in the business nor known to the public. Like silent partners, they are concerned with getting a return on their investment. Like secret partners, they want to maintain their privacy.
4. *Nominal partners* aren't partners at all, but by their behavior they lead the public to believe that they are. An example of this is the person who permits his name to be associated with a business in exchange for a fee.

Depending on your company's needs, one or more of these kinds of partners may be right for you.

### Joint Venture

The kinds of partnership just described all share the intention of being ongoing businesses. A joint venture differs from these in that it is a partnership set up for a specific purpose of limited duration. For example, suppose you and a friend decided to buy, renovate, and resell a house together. Your joint venture would start when you purchased the house and end when you sold it. As for your taxes, joint ventures are taxed the same as partnerships.

During the life of such a joint venture, each partner is subject to unlimited liability, so the same caution should be exercised in selecting a joint-venture partner as in selecting any other partner. Similarly, you can avoid many problems by consulting an attorney and putting the terms of your joint-venture agreement in writing.

## Corporation

A corporation differs from other legal forms of business in that the law considers it to be an artificial being, possessing the same rights and responsibilities as a person. Unlike a sole proprietorship or a partnership, a corporation has an existence separate from its owners. As such, it can sue and be sued, own property, agree to contracts, and engage in business transactions. Additionally, because a corporation is a separate entity, it is not dissolved with every change in ownership. As a result, corporations have the potential for unlimited life.

### The Corporate Charter

To form a corporation you must be granted a charter by the state in which your business resides. Each state sets its own requirements and fees for the issuance of charters. The cost for incorporating a small business usually ranges from $1,500 to $4,000. Generally, your charter must include such information as:

- Your corporation's name
- Names of principal stockholders
- Number and types of shares to be issued
- Place of business
- Type of business

### Stockholders

Each person who owns stock in your corporation is a co-owner with you in the business. This does not mean that every stockholder will actively participate in your company's management, or even be associated with it in any way, other than by purchasing shares of the corporation's stock.

Even so, they are still guaranteed the right to vote on the members of the corporation's board of directors and on certain major corporate policies.

Enabling people to become co-owners in a business in this way benefits both the corporation and the stockholders. The corporation is able to obtain investment capital, and the stockholders can share in whatever profits the corporation earns. These profits are distributed to stockholders in the form of dividends. Furthermore, because stock is transferable, stockholders are free to sell their stock at any time and receive the current market value for it.

### The Board of Directors

The board of directors represents the stockholders and is responsible for protecting their interests. Board members are elected annually, usually for one-year terms, which can be renewed indefinitely by means of the election process. Because the number of votes that stockholders can cast is related to the number of shares they have, major stockholders can virtually elect themselves to the board.

The board of directors generally concerns itself with determining corporate policies, rather than taking care of day-to-day operations. To handle these, the board appoints the chief executive officer and other top corporate officers–vice presidents, secretary, treasurer, and so on. They, in turn, see that the policies stipulated by the board of directors are implemented.

### Advantages of a Corporation

***Stockholders have limited liability*** One of the most attractive advantages of the corporate form of business is that the owners have limited liability. Investors are financially liable only up to the amounts of their investments in the corporation. This limited liability ensures that creditors of the corporation cannot touch the personal assets of owners.

***Corporations can raise the most investment capital*** You can increase the investment capital in your corporation simply by selling more shares of stock. Whereas sole proprietorships and partnerships are limited in the number of owners they can have, a corporation can have any number of owners.

***Corporations have unlimited life*** Because of its status as a legal entity, a corporation has its own identity. Unlike sole proprietorships and partnerships, with life spans linked to those of their owners, it is possible for your corporation to exist indefinitely. The withdrawal of stockholders, corporate officers, or employees will not terminate its existence.

***Ownership is easily transferable*** Ownership in a corporation is easily transferable from one person to another. Investors can buy and sell shares of stock as they please without seeking the prior approval of anyone. In addition to providing investors with maximum control over their investments, this fluid ownership enables your corporation to go on operating without disruption.

***Corporations utilize specialists*** Because of the separation of ownership and management, the corporate form of business can most effectively utilize the services of specialists. Unlike sole proprietorships and partnerships, which tend to rely on the skills and abilities of the owners to perform each function, corporations employ specialists. The availability of specially trained personnel leads to higher productivity and increased efficiency.

### Disadvantages of a Corporation

***Corporations are taxed twice*** Unlike sole proprietorships and partnerships, corporations and their owners are taxed separately. In what amounts to double taxation, both the income your corporation earns and the income you earn as an individual are taxed. This is the primary drawback to the corporate form.

***Corporations must pay a capital stock tax*** In addition to paying a corporate federal income tax, corporations must pay a *capital stock tax.* This is an annual tax on outstanding shares of stock, which is levied by the state in which the business is incorporated.

***Starting a corporation is expensive*** More expense is involved in starting a corporation than is involved in starting any other legal form of business. There are the costs for legal assistance in drawing up your charter, state incorporation fees, and the purchase of record books and stock certificates. All these require expenditures not only of money but also of time.

***Corporations are more closely regulated*** The government regulates corporations much more closely than it does any other form of business. Numerous state and federal reports must be filed regularly. Each year,

**The Advantages and Disadvantages of Each Legal Form of Ownership**

*Sole Proprietorship*

**Advantages**

1. You're the boss.
2. It's easy to get started.
3. You keep all the profits.
4. Income from business is taxed as personal income.
5. You can discontinue your business at will.

**Disadvantages**

1. You assume unlimited liability.
2. Your ability to raise investment capital is limited.
3. You need to be a generalist.
4. You may have trouble retaining high-caliber employees.
5. The life of your business is limited.

*Partnership*

**Advantages**

1. Two heads are better than one.
2. It's easy to get started.
3. More investment capital is available.
4. Partners pay only personal income tax.
5. High-caliber employees can be made partners.

**Disadvantages**

1. Partners have unlimited liability.
2. Profits must be shared.
3. The partners may disagree.
4. The life of the business is limited.

*Corporation*

**Advantages**

1. Stockholders have limited liability.
2. Corporations can raise the most investment capital.
3. Corporations have unlimited life.
4. Ownership is easily transferable.
5. Corporations utilize specialists.

**Disadvantages**

1. Corporations are taxed twice.
2. Corporations must pay capital stock tax.
3. Starting a corporation is expensive.
4. Corporations are more closely regulated.

corporations are required to prepare, print, and distribute an annual report summarizing the company's activities during the preceding year. Often, specialists are retained on staff solely for the purpose of providing the data for these reports.

### S Corporation

If you are interested in forming a corporation but hesitate to do so because of the double taxation, there is a way to avoid it. You can do this by making your business an *S corporation.* The Internal Revenue Service permits this type of corporation to be taxed as a partnership rather than as a corporation. However, to qualify for S status, your business must meet the specific requirements set forth by the IRS. These include limits on (1) the number and type of shareholders in the business, (2) the stock that is issued, and (3) the corporation's sources of revenues. For more information on forming an S corporation, ask the IRS for its free publication, *Tax Guide for Small Business*, publication number 334.

## Limited-Liability Company

Still another way to avoid double taxation is to form a limited-liability company (LLC). The newest of the legal forms available, an LLC combines the best features of a corporation with those of a partnership, much the way that an S corporation does, but it doesn't have the restrictions on ownership that S corporations have, and it offers greater freedom in the allocation of profits and losses. Rather than owning shares of stock, members of an LLC have a "membership interest" in the business, which entitles them to receive distributions. Brought into existence at the state level, rather than the federal level, LLCs initially needed to gain acceptance on a state-by-state basis and to resolve potential conflicts between state and federal tax laws. They've since become one of the fastest-growing legal forms. For more information on LLCs, contact the Association of Limited Liability Companies in Washington, D.C. Its website (www.llc-usa.com/resources/assoc./html) has a lot of information.

## Government Regulation

Depending on what you sell and where your business is located, you will also have to consider various permits and paperwork, as well as trademarks, patents, and copyrights. To protect your business's legal standing in the community, it's important to find out which local, state, and federal regulations apply to it.

### Local Regulations

At the local level, regulations pertaining to businesses are primarily concerned with taxation, public health and safety, and zoning. Although each community is different, the most typical forms of regulation are

- Business taxes and permits
- Fictitious business name statements
- Zoning restrictions
- Other regulations

**Business Taxes and Permits** Commonly referred to as a *business license*, a permit is issued by the city and/or county in which a business is located and is usually valid for one to two years. The fee for it, which is based on the gross sales of your business, can range from less than $50 to more than $250. To find out whether a business license is necessary in your particular circumstances and which agency issues it, check the White Pages of your telephone directory under City of ———, Business Tax Division, Business Licenses, or City Clerk.

**Fictitious Business Name Statement** If you're planning to operate your business under a name other than your own, such as B&G Enterprises or Midtown Realty Company, then you'll probably need to file a fictitious business name statement with the county clerk's office. The purpose of this statement is to inform the public of your identity and the identities of any others who are co-owners in the business.

Providing this public notice is a two-part process that involves (1) filing the statement with the county clerk and (2) having the statement published in a newspaper of general circulation. You can usually eliminate the first part, though, by going directly to the newspaper that's going to run your statement. As a convenience to their customers, most newspapers keep fictitious business name forms on hand (see page 59) and will file the completed statement for you. The total cost for filing and publishing the statement should be somewhere between $30 and $90.

**Zoning Restrictions** Just as some people are more entrepreneurially inclined than others, so are some communities. Whereas one city may encourage businesses to locate there, another may not. Typically, local

SEE REVERSE SIDE FOR INSTRUCTIONS — NOT VALID UNLESS CLERK'S ENDORSEMENT APPEARS BELOW

**REMINDER**
1. Submit original and 3 copies.
2. Filing fee $24.00 for one business name.
   $5.00 for each additional business name.
   $5.00 for each additional partner after first two.
3. **Provide return stamped envelope if mailed.**

☐ New Fictitious Business Name Statement

☐ Refile

**GARY L. GRANVILLE, COUNTY CLERK**
**PUBLIC SERVICES DIVISION**
**211 W. SANTA ANA BOULEVARD**
**POST OFFICE BOX 22013**
**SANTA ANA, CA 92702-2013**

THIS STATEMENT WAS FILED WITH THE COUNTY CLERK OF ORANGE COUNTY ON DATE INDICATED BY FILE STAMP BELOW.

## FICTITIOUS BUSINESS NAME STATEMENT

File No. ____________ THE FOLLOWING PERSON(S) IS (ARE) DOING BUSINESS AS: (TYPE ALL INFORMATION)

| | | | | |
|---|---|---|---|---|
| 1. | Fictitious Business Name(s) | | | |
| 2. | Street Address, City & State of Principal place of Business in California | | | Zip Code |
| 3. | Full name of Registrant | (if corporation—show state of incorporation) | | |
| | Residence Address | City | State | Zip Code |
| | Full name of Registrant | (if corporation—show state of incorporation) | | |
| | Residence Address | City | State | Zip Code |
| | Full name of Registrant | (if corporation—show state of incorporation) | | |
| | Residence Address | City | State | Zip Code |
| 4. | (CHECK ONE ONLY) This business is conducted by ( ) an individual ( ) a general partnership ( ) a limited partnership ( ) an unincorporated association other than a partnership ( ) a corporation ( ) a business trust ( ) co-partners ( ) husband and wife ( ) joint venture ( ) other—please specify ) | | | |
| 5. | THE REGISTRANT(S) COMMENCED TO TRANSACT BUSINESS UNDER THE FICTITIOUS BUSINESS NAME(S) LISTED ABOVE ON: DATE: | **NOTICE: THIS FICTITIOUS NAME STATEMENT EXPIRES FIVE YEARS FROM THE DATE IT WAS FILED IN THE OFFICE OF THE COUNTY CLERK. A NEW FICTITIOUS BUSINESS NAME STATEMENT MUST BE FILED BEFORE THAT TIME. THE FILING OF THIS STATEMENT DOES NOT OF ITSELF AUTHORIZE THE USE IN THIS STATE OF A FICTITIOUS BUSINESS NAME IN VIOLATION OF THE RIGHTS OF ANOTHER UNDER FEDERAL, STATE, OR COMMON LAW (SEE SECTION 14400 ET SEQ., BUSINESS AND PROFESSIONS CODE).** | | |
| 6 | Signature ____________ <br> ____________ (TYPE OR PRINT NAME) | If Registrant is a corporation sign below: <br> Corporation Name ____________ <br> Signature & Title ____________ <br> ____________ | | |

FILE NO ____________

FO182-266.13 (7/92)

FILE WITH COUNTY CLERK

Fictitious Business Name Statement

regulations apply to the types of businesses that are acceptable, the size and placement of signs, exterior displays of merchandise, inventory storage, parking, and hours of operation. Because the main purpose of zoning restrictions is to protect the rights of people and property, a business that is noisy, smelly, or unsightly can expect to run into trouble. To find out the zoning restrictions for your community, contact your local planning department.

**Other Regulations** Depending on the nature of your business, other local regulations may also apply. For instance, if you are engaged in food preparation, processing, or serving (mail-order cheesecakes, pizza restaurant, catering), you must stay within the county health department codes. Antique dealers often find that a permit from the police department is a prerequisite for doing business because stolen goods are sometimes sold through such dealers. Other departments that have jurisdiction over businesses include the fire and sanitation departments.

### State Regulations

At the state level, regulations pertaining to businesses center around taxation and the monitoring of specific professions. Each state sets its own standards in these areas, but the most common regulations involve the issuing of seller's permits and occupational licenses.

**Seller's Permit** Many states require anyone who buys and sells merchandise to obtain a seller's permit. This permit (1) exempts you from paying sales tax on the merchandise you purchase for resale through your business and (2) authorizes you to collect sales tax from your customers.

Usually there is no fee to obtain a seller's permit, but, depending on your estimated gross sales for the year, you may be required to post a bond. This is to ensure that you collect and remit to the state all sales tax due. To find out more about the seller's permit and whether you should have one, check your telephone directory White Pages under State of —— Taxes.

**Occupational License** To maintain set standards of performance and protect the safety of consumers, most states regulate entry into specific occupations or professions, such as those in the health services, cosmetology, accounting, and real-estate fields. If your business is in a regulated field, you must first meet the standards set forth by the state licensing board governing your occupation. Once you have demonstrated your competence, you will be issued a license, which is usually valid for a period of one to two years and is renewable. To determine whether an occupational license is required for your business activity, check with your state's Department of Consumer Affairs.

### Federal Regulations

At the federal level, regulations pertaining to businesses focus on taxation, employer responsibilities, consumer protection, and the registration of trademarks, patents, and copyrights.

**Employer Identification Number** If you employ one or more persons in your business, the federal government requires you to have an employer identification number. This enables the government to verify that you are paying all appropriate employer taxes and withholding the proper amounts from employee paychecks. Even though you may not have any employees in the beginning, it's still advisable to obtain a number, especially if you sell to businesses, because customers often need it for their records. Also, if you should decide to hire someone later, take in a partner, or incorporate, you will need the number for tax purposes. Obtaining your identification number is an easy matter. What's more, there is no fee for it. Just fill out IRS form number SS-4 (shown on page 62) and submit it to the Internal Revenue Service.

**Consumer Protection Regulation** To protect the rights of consumers, the federal government regulates practices in a variety of areas. Businesses that engage in mail-order sales or sell their products in more than one state are subject to regulation by the Federal Trade Commission, Interstate Commerce Commission, and the U.S. Postal Service. The Federal Trade Commission also oversees product packaging and labeling, product warranties, and advertising claims. With nutritional supplements, health-care products, or cosmetics, the Food and Drug Administration steps into the picture. Financial services businesses may come under the jurisdiction of the Securities and Exchange Commission. To familiarize yourself with the regulations that apply to your type of business, write to the Federal Trade Commission, Washington, DC 20580.

Form **SS-4** (Rev. April 1991) Department of the Treasury Internal Revenue Service

# Application for Employer Identification Number

**(For use by employers and others. Please read the attached instructions before completing this form.)**

EIN

OMB No. 1545-0003 Expires 4-30-94

Please type or print clearly.

1 Name of applicant (True legal name) (See instructions.)

2 Trade name of business, if different from name in line 1

3 Executor, trustee, "care of" name

4a Mailing address (street address) (room, apt., or suite no.)

5a Address of business (See instructions.)

4b City, state, and ZIP code

5b City, state, and ZIP code

6 County and state where principal business is located

7 Name of principal officer, grantor, or general partner (See instructions.) ► ____

**8a** Type of entity (Check only one box.) (See instructions.)

☐ Estate ☐ Trust

☐ Individual SSN ____ ☐ Plan administrator SSN ____ ☐ Partnership

☐ REMIC ☐ Personal service corp. ☐ Other corporation (specify) ____ ☐ Farmers' cooperative

☐ State/local government ☐ National guard ☐ Federal government/military ☐ Church or church controlled organization

☐ Other nonprofit organization (specify) ____ If nonprofit organization enter GEN (if applicable) ____

☐ Other (specify) ► ____

**8b** If a corporation, give name of foreign country (if applicable) or state in the U.S. where incorporated ► | Foreign country | State

**9** Reason for applying (Check only one box.)

☐ Started new business ☐ Changed type of organization (specify) ► ____

☐ Hired employees ☐ Purchased going business

☐ Created a pension plan (specify type) ► ____ ☐ Created a trust (specify) ► ____

☐ Banking purpose (specify) ► ☐ Other (specify) ►

**10** Date business started or acquired (Mo., day, year) (See instructions.)

**11** Enter closing month of accounting year. (See instructions.)

**12** First date wages or annuities were paid or will be paid (Mo., day, year). **Note:** *If applicant is a withholding agent, enter date income will first be paid to nonresident alien. (Mo., day, year)* . . . ►

**13** Enter highest number of employees expected in the next 12 months. **Note:** *If the applicant does not expect to have any employees during the period, enter "0."* . . . ►

| Nonagricultural | Agricultural | Household |
|---|---|---|
| | | |

**14** Principal activity (See instructions.) ►

**15** Is the principal business activity manufacturing? . . . ☐ **Yes** ☐ **No**

If "Yes," principal product and raw material used ►

**16** To whom are most of the products or services sold? Please check the appropriate box. ☐ Business (wholesale)

☐ Public (retail) ☐ Other (specify) ► ☐ N/A

**17a** Has the applicant ever applied for an identification number for this or any other business? . . . ☐ **Yes** ☐ **No**

**Note:** *If "Yes," please complete lines 17b and 17c.*

**17b** If you checked the "Yes" box in line 17a, give applicant's true name and trade name, if different than name shown on prior application.

True name ► Trade name ►

**17c** Enter approximate date, city, and state where the application was filed and the previous employer identification number if known.

| Approximate date when filed (Mo., day, year) | City and state where filed | Previous EIN |
|---|---|---|
| | | |

Under penalties of perjury, I declare that I have examined this application, and to the best of my knowledge and belief, it is true, correct, and complete

Telephone number (include area code)

Name and title (Please type or print clearly.) ►

Signature ► Date ►

**Note:** *Do not write below this line. For official use only.*

| Please leave blank ► | Geo. | Ind. | Class | Size | Reason for applying |
|---|---|---|---|---|---|
| | | | | | |

**For Paperwork Reduction Act Notice, see attached instructions.** Cat. No. 16055N Form **SS-4** (Rev. 4-91)

Application for Employer Identification Number

**Trademarks, Patents, and Copyrights** In addition to protecting the rights of consumers, the federal government also protects the rights of entrepreneurs. In this case, it protects your right to use and profit from your own name (or business or product name), inventions, and artistic creations.

The following information should give you a better idea of the protection provided by trademarks, patents, and copyrights, as well as how you can use them to your advantage.

- *Trademarks.* By definition, a *trademark* is any word, name, symbol, device, or combination of these used to identify the products or services of a business and to distinguish them from those of other enterprises. Often one of a business's most valuable assets, a trademark can help to define the business's image, increase consumer awareness, and stimulate repeat purchases. Although a business isn't required by law to register its trademark, doing so is advisable because it offers the greatest protection (see application form on pages 64 and 65). Once a trademark is registered, the holder's right to use it extends for a period of ten years, at which time registration is renewable. For more information on trademarks, write the U.S. Department of Commerce, Patent and Trademark Office, Washington, DC 20231, and ask for the pamphlet "Basic Facts about Trademarks."
- *Patents.* In granting a *patent* to a business, the federal government gives it the right to exclude all others from making, using, or selling the patented invention in the United States. Patents for new and useful products or processes are valid for 20 years from the filing date. A design patent, covering only the style or appearance of a product, is valid for a period of 14 years from the date granted.

If you develop a product, process, or design you believe has commercial possibilities, obtaining a patent may be advisable, given the protection it affords. The government recommends that inventors not attempt to prepare their own patent applications without the help of a registered attorney or agent skilled in patent procedures. Taking this into consideration, when legal fees are added in, the total cost of obtaining a patent runs between $2,000 and $5,000.

To get the facts on obtaining a patent, read "Basic Facts about Patents," published by the U.S. Department of Commerce, Patent and Trademark Office, Washington, DC 20231.

| TRADEMARK APPLICATION, PRINCIPAL REGISTER, WITH DECLARATION (Partnership) | MARK *(identify the mark)* |
|---|---|
| | CLASS NO. *(if known)* |

TO THE COMMISSIONER OF PATENTS AND TRADEMARKS:

NAME OF PARTNERSHIP

NAMES OF PARTNERS

BUSINESS ADDRESS OF PARTNERSHIP

CITIZENSHIP OF PARTNERS

The above identified applicant has adopted and is using the trademark shown in the accompanying drawing[1] for the following goods: ________________________________________

________________________________________,

and requests that said mark be registered in the United States Patent and Trademark Office on the Principal Register established by the Act of July 5, 1946.

The trademark was first used on the goods[2] on ____________ *(date)* ; was first used on the goods[2] in ____________ *(type of commerce)* commerce[3] on ____________ *(date)* ; and is now in use in such commerce.

4

The mark is used by applying it to[5] ________________________________________

________________________________________

and five specimens showing the mark as actually used are presented herewith.

6

________________________________________ *(name of partner)*,

being hereby warned that willful false statements and the like so made are punishable by fine or imprisonment, or both, under Section 1001 of Title 18 of the United States Code and that such willful false statements may jeopardize the validity of the application or any registration resulting therefrom, declares that he/she is a partner of applicant partnership; he/she believes said partnership to be the owner of the trademark sought to be registered; to the best of his/her knowledge and belief no other person, firm, corporation, or association has the right to use said mark in commerce, either in the identical form or in such near resemblance thereto as may be likely, when applied to the goods of such other person, to cause confusion, or to cause mistake, or to deceive; the facts set forth in this application are true; and all statements made of his/her own knowledge are true and all statements made on information and belief are believed to be true.

________________________________________
*(signature of partner)*

________________________________________
*(date)*

Form PTO - 1477 (4 - 82) *(Instructions on reverse side)* Patent and Trademark Office - U.S. DEPT. of COMMERCE

*(over)*

Trademark Application (Front)

**REPRESENTATION**

If the applicant is not domiciled in the United States, a domestic representative must be designated. See Form 4.4.

If applicant wishes to furnish a power of attorney, see Form 4.2. An attorney at law is not required to furnish a power.

**FOOTNOTES**

1 If registration is sought for a word or numeral mark not depicted in any special form, the drawing may be the mark typed in capital letters on letter-size bond paper; otherwise, the drawing should be made with india ink on a good grade of bond paper or on bristol board.

2 If more than one item of goods in a class is set forth and the dates given for that class apply to only one of the items listed, insert the name of the item to which the dates apply.

3 Type of commerce should be specified as "interstate," "territorial," "foreign," or other type of commerce which may lawfully be regulated by Congress. Foreign applicants relying upon use must specify commerce which Congress may regulate, using wording such as commerce with the United States or commerce between the United States and a foreign country.

4 If the mark is other than a coined, arbitrary or fanciful mark, and the mark is believed to have acquired a secondary meaning, insert whichever of the following paragraphs is applicable:

a) The mark has become distinctive of applicant's goods as a result of substantially exclusive and continuous use in ______________________ *(type of commerce)* commerce for the five years next preceding the date of filing of this application.

b) The mark has become distinctive of applicant's goods as evidenced by the showing submitted separately.

5 Insert the manner or method of using the mark with the goods, i.e., "the goods," "the containers for the goods," "displays associated with the goods," "tags or labels affixed to the goods," or other method which may be in use.

6 The required fee of $175.00 for each class must be submitted. (An application to register the same mark for goods and/or services in more than one class may be filed; however, goods and/or services and dates of use, by class, must be set out separately, and specimens and a fee for each class are required.)

Form PTO - 1477 (Rev. 10 - 82) Patent and Trademark Office · U.S. DEPT. of COMMERCE

Trademark Application (Back)

• *Copyrights.* A *copyright* protects the right of an individual to keep others from copying his or her creations. Although most commonly associated with literary works, copyright protection extends to graphic designs, paintings, sculpture, musical compositions, sound recordings, and audiovisual works. A business doesn't have to be in the arts to benefit from this protection. A sampling of the works that come within the broad scope of copyright coverage includes brochures, catalogs and advertising copy, newsletters and books, audiocassettes and videotapes, reports, charts and technical drawings, and computer programs.

Obtaining a copyright is relatively simple. All you need to do is provide public notice of the copyright on the work itself and file an application form (as shown on pages 67 and 68). The fee is currently $20, and, once granted, the copyright is good for up to 50 years after the holder's death. For more information, or a copyright form itself, write to the Copyright Office, Library of Congress, Washington, DC 20559. Be sure to specify the type of work you want to copyright.

# FORM TX
UNITED STATES COPYRIGHT OFFICE

REGISTRATION NUMBER

TX TXU

EFFECTIVE DATE OF REGISTRATION

Month Day Year

**DO NOT WRITE ABOVE THIS LINE. IF YOU NEED MORE SPACE, USE A SEPARATE CONTINUATION SHEET.**

**1**

**TITLE OF THIS WORK ▼**

**PREVIOUS OR ALTERNATIVE TITLES ▼**

**PUBLICATION AS A CONTRIBUTION** If this work was published as a contribution to a periodical, serial, or collection, give information about the collective work in which the contribution appeared. **Title of Collective Work ▼**

If published in a periodical or serial give: **Volume ▼** **Number ▼** **Issue Date ▼** **On Pages ▼**

**2**

a **NAME OF AUTHOR ▼** **DATES OF BIRTH AND DEATH** Year Born ▼ Year Died ▼

Was this contribution to the work a "work made for hire"? ☐ Yes ☐ No

**AUTHOR'S NATIONALITY OR DOMICILE** Name of Country OR { Citizen of ▶ / Domiciled in ▶

**WAS THIS AUTHOR'S CONTRIBUTION TO THE WORK** Anonymous? ☐ Yes ☐ No Pseudonymous? ☐ Yes ☐ No If the answer to either of these questions is "Yes," see detailed instructions.

**NATURE OF AUTHORSHIP** Briefly describe nature of the material created by this author in which copyright is claimed. ▼

b **NAME OF AUTHOR ▼** **DATES OF BIRTH AND DEATH** Year Born ▼ Year Died ▼

Was this contribution to the work a "work made for hire"? ☐ Yes ☐ No

**AUTHOR'S NATIONALITY OR DOMICILE** Name of country OR { Citizen of ▶ / Domiciled in ▶

**WAS THIS AUTHOR'S CONTRIBUTION TO THE WORK** Anonymous? ☐ Yes ☐ No Pseudonymous? ☐ Yes ☐ No If the answer to either of these questions is "Yes," see detailed instructions.

**NATURE OF AUTHORSHIP** Briefly describe nature of the material created by this author in which copyright is claimed. ▼

c **NAME OF AUTHOR ▼** **DATES OF BIRTH AND DEATH** Year Born ▼ Year Died ▼

Was this contribution to the work a "work made for hire"? ☐ Yes ☐ No

**AUTHOR'S NATIONALITY OR DOMICILE** Name of Country OR { Citizen of ▶ / Domiciled in ▶

**WAS THIS AUTHOR'S CONTRIBUTION TO THE WORK** Anonymous? ☐ Yes ☐ No Pseudonymous? ☐ Yes ☐ No If the answer to either of these questions is "Yes," see detailed instructions.

**NATURE OF AUTHORSHIP** Briefly describe nature of the material created by this author in which copyright is claimed. ▼

**NOTE**

Under the law, the "author" of a "work made for hire" is generally the employer, not the employee (see instructions). For any part of this work that was "made for hire" check "Yes" in the space provided, give the employer (or other person for whom the work was prepared) as "Author" of that part, and leave the space for dates of birth and death blank.

**3**

**YEAR IN WHICH CREATION OF THIS WORK WAS COMPLETED** **This information must be given in all cases.** ◀ Year

**DATE AND NATION OF FIRST PUBLICATION OF THIS PARTICULAR WORK** **Complete this information ONLY if this work has been published.** Month ▶ Day ▶ Year ▶ ◀ Nation

**4**

**COPYRIGHT CLAIMANT(S)** Name and address must be given even if the claimant is the same as the author given in space 2.▼

See instructions before completing this space

**TRANSFER** If the claimant(s) named here in space 4 are different from the author(s) named in space 2, give a brief statement of how the claimant(s) obtained ownership of the copyright.▼

**DO NOT WRITE HERE OFFICE USE ONLY**

APPLICATION RECEIVED

ONE DEPOSIT RECEIVED

TWO DEPOSITS RECEIVED

REMITTANCE NUMBER AND DATE

**MORE ON BACK ▶** • Complete all applicable spaces (numbers 5-11) on the reverse side of this page. • See detailed instructions. • Sign the form at line 10.

**DO NOT WRITE HERE**

Page 1 of ______ pages

Copyright Application Form (Front)

EXAMINED BY

FORM TX

CHECKED BY

☐ CORRESPONDENCE Yes

☐ DEPOSIT ACCOUNT FUNDS USED

FOR COPYRIGHT OFFICE USE ONLY

**DO NOT WRITE ABOVE THIS LINE. IF YOU NEED MORE SPACE, USE A SEPARATE CONTINUATION SHEET.**

**5**

**PREVIOUS REGISTRATION** Has registration for this work, or for an earlier version of this work, already been made in the Copyright Office?
☐ **Yes** ☐ **No** If your answer is "Yes," why is another registration being sought? (Check appropriate box) ▼
☐ This is the first published edition of a work previously registered in unpublished form.
☐ This is the first application submitted by this author as copyright claimant.
☐ This is a changed version of the work, as shown by space 6 on this application.
If your answer is "Yes," give: **Previous Registration Number** ▼ **Year of Registration** ▼

**6**

**DERIVATIVE WORK OR COMPILATION** Complete both space 6a & 6b for a derivative work; complete only 6b for a compilation.
**a. Preexisting Material** Identify any preexisting work or works that this work is based on or incorporates. ▼

**b. Material Added to This Work** Give a brief, general statement of the material that has been added to this work and in which copyright is claimed. ▼

See instructions before completing this space.

**7**

**MANUFACTURERS AND LOCATIONS** If this is a published work consisting preponderantly of nondramatic literary material in English, the law may require that the copies be manufactured in the United States or Canada for full protection. If so, the names of the manufacturers who performed certain processes, and the places where these processes were performed **must** be given. See instructions for details.
**Names of Manufacturers** ▼ **Places of Manufacture** ▼

**8**

**REPRODUCTION FOR USE OF BLIND OR PHYSICALLY HANDICAPPED INDIVIDUALS** A signature on this form at space 10, and a check in one of the boxes here in space 8, constitutes a non-exclusive grant of permission to the Library of Congress to reproduce and distribute solely for the blind and physically handicapped and under the conditions and limitations prescribed by the regulations of the Copyright Office: (1) copies of the work identified in space 1 of this application in Braille (or similar tactile symbols); or (2) phonorecords embodying a fixation of a reading of that work; or (3) both.
**a** ☐ Copies and Phonorecords **b** ☐ Copies Only **c** ☐ Phonorecords Only

See instructions.

**9**

**DEPOSIT ACCOUNT** If the registration fee is to be charged to a Deposit Account established in the Copyright Office, give name and number of Account.
**Name** ▼ **Account Number** ▼

**CORRESPONDENCE** Give name and address to which correspondence about this application should be sent. Name/Address/Apt/City/State/Zip ▼

Area Code & Telephone Number ▶

Be sure to give your daytime phone ◀ number.

**10**

**CERTIFICATION*** I, the undersigned, hereby certify that I am the
Check one ▶
☐ author
☐ other copyright claimant
☐ owner of exclusive right(s)
☐ authorized agent of ____________
Name of author or other copyright claimant, or owner of exclusive right(s) ▲

of the work identified in this application and that the statements made by me in this application are correct to the best of my knowledge.

**Typed or printed name and date** ▼ If this is a published work, this date must be the same as or later than the date of publication given in space 3.

date ▶

**Handwritten signature (X)** ▼

**11**

**MAIL CERTIFICATE TO**

**Certificate will be mailed in window envelope**

Name ▼

Number/Street/Apartment Number ▼

City/State/ZIP ▼

**Have you:**
- Completed all necessary spaces?
- Signed your application in space 10?
- Enclosed check or money order for $10 payable to *Register of Copyrights*?
- Enclosed your deposit material with the application and fee?

**MAIL TO:** Register of Copyrights, Library of Congress, Washington, D.C. 20559.

* 17 U.S.C. § 506(e): Any person who knowingly makes a false representation of a material fact in the application for copyright registration provided for by section 409, or in any written statement filed in connection with the application, shall be fined not more than $2,500.

☆U.S. GOVERNMENT PRINTING OFFICE: 1982-361-278/58

Sept. 1982—600,000

Copyright Application Form (Back)

## Structuring the Business Checklist

To make sure that you have selected a legal form that is appropriate for your business and are familiar with the government regulations that apply to it, answer the questions in the following Structuring the Business Checklist.

| Structuring the Business Checklist | Answer Yes or No |
|---|---|
| 1. Do you know the advantages and disadvantages of each of the following legal forms? | |
| Sole proprietorship | ________ |
| Partnership | ________ |
| Corporation | ________ |
| 2. Is it clear to you why you should have a written partnership agreement for any partnership that you form? | ________ |
| 3. Do you know what information to include in a partnership agreement? | ________ |
| 4. Are you aware of the difference between a general and a limited partnership? | ________ |
| 5. Can you describe the characteristics of each of the following partners? | |
| Silent | ________ |
| Secret | ________ |
| Dormant | ________ |
| Nominal | ________ |
| 6. Do you know what a joint venture is? | ________ |
| 7. Do you know what steps are required to incorporate your business? | ________ |
| 8. Have you considered the benefits of forming an S corporation or a limited-liability company? | ________ |
| 9. Are you are of the local, state, and federal regulations that apply to your particular business? | ________ |

*(continued)*

| Structuring the Business Checklist *(continued)* | Answer Yes or No |
|---|---|
| 10. Have you found out what licenses and permits you'll need? | ______ |
| 11. Do you know how to make use of trademarks, patents, and copyrights to protect your business? | ______ |
| 12. Have you estimated the costs involved in structuring your business and complying with government regulations? | ______ |
| 13. Have you consulted with an attorney and obtained the necessary legal advice to set up your business properly? | ______ |

# 6

# Recordkeeping and Taxes

Maintaining accurate and thorough financial records is a necessary part of doing business. The increasing number of government regulations alone makes it virtually impossible to avoid keeping detailed records. Moreover, just as important as the need to keep records for the government is the need to keep them for yourself. The success of your business depends on them.

## The Value of Good Records

An efficient system of recordkeeping can help you to

- Make effective management decisions
- Compete in the marketplace
- Monitor your business's performance
- Keep track of expenses
- Eliminate unprofitable merchandise
- Protect your assets
- Prepare your financial statements

By substituting facts for guesswork and continuity for confusion, day-to-day accounting records enable you to keep your finger on the pulse of your business. In this way, you can quickly detect any sign of financial ill health and take the appropriate corrective action before it's too late. What's more, instead of having to hunt for the financial information you need, or to develop it on the spot, you already have it in hand, waiting to be used. For instance, you can quickly calculate

- Last month's sales total
- Sales commissions paid in the past two weeks

- Overtime charges for the previous quarter
- Advertising expenses for the month
- Percentage of sales made on credit
- Number of customers behind on their bills
- Amount of money tied up in inventory
- Inventory shortages
- Amount of slow-moving merchandise
- Effects of inflation on profits
- Financial obligations coming due
- Total value of your assets

This information and more can readily be obtained from an adequate recordkeeping system. The question isn't whether your business can afford to have one. Rather, it's whether your business can afford *not* to have one.

### Accountants and Bookkeepers

Once new business owners recognize the importance of recordkeeping, they are often quick to delegate full responsibility for their records to an accountant or a bookkeeper. Pleading ignorance ("What do I know about accounting?") or lack of time ("I can either run the business or keep the books"), they dissociate themselves entirely from the accounting function. And why not? After all, that's what accountants are paid for, isn't it? The problem with this tactic is that it gives your accountant free rein to make decisions affecting your business without receiving any input from you. Moreover, there is an even greater reason for you to keep close tabs on your records system: You can't operate efficiently without access to its information.

For the best results, you and your accountant or bookkeeper should work together as a team, supplying each other with timely information. A strategy employed by many business owners is to have an accountant set up the recordkeeping system for the business, prepare the financial statements, and provide advice on tax matters. Then the day-to-day accounting activities are handled by the business owner, an employee, or an outside bookkeeper.

### Computerized Accounting Programs

With the wide variety of accounting software packages available, it's easier than ever for you to get involved in the accounting process. Eliminating much of the time and toil associated with maintaining a business records system, the computer program enables you to enter information quickly, move it from one location to another, perform calculations, and prepare records and financial statements. Some of the more popular accounting packages for business include those from Microsoft, Lotus, Peachtree, and Intuit. Some trade associations and companies also offer industry-specific software packages designed for particular businesses such as restaurants or consulting firms.

## Recordkeeping Systems

The Internal Revenue Service does not stipulate what kinds of records a business owner must keep, only that the records properly identify the business's income, expenses, and deductions. Thus, you may use any recordkeeping system that meets this criterion and is suited to your particular business. For best results, the system you choose should be (1) simple to use, (2) easy to understand, (3) accurate, (4) consistent, and (5) capable of providing timely information.

You can choose from among a number of business recordkeeping systems, ranging from simple to complex. The simplest of these are the single-entry and pegboard systems available at stationery and business-forms stores; the most complex is the double-entry system.

1. *Double-Entry Accounting.* This is the system used and favored by accountants. As the name implies, for every transaction that is recorded, two entries are required. This is because any change in one account automatically results in a change in another account. For instance, if a customer purchases merchandise from you and pays cash for it, the balance in your cash account increases while your merchandise inventory decreases. Both changes must be recorded–one as a debit and the other as a credit. This provides the system's greatest strength–a means of checks and balances to ensure that errors don't occur. For each transaction the total debit amount must equal the total credit amount. If the amounts are out of balance, the transaction has been improperly recorded.

2. *Single-Entry Accounting.* Although a double-entry accounting system offers the greatest degree of accuracy through its use of checks and balances, it can also be a difficult system to maintain for someone without bookkeeping experience. Thus, while your business is still small, you may prefer to use a single-entry accounting system, which is based on your income statement rather than your balance sheet. A single-entry system does not require you to "balance the books" or to record more than one entry for each transaction. Quick and easy to use, it provides a simple way to keep track of your accounts receivable, accounts payable, depreciable assets, and inventory.

Depending on your needs, you can have an accountant or a bookkeeper set up a single-entry accounting system specially tailored to your business, or you can purchase a ready-made system from an office-supply or stationery store.

3. *Pegboard Accounting.* To simplify your recordkeeping even more, you might consider using a pegboard (or "once-write") recordkeeping system. It's a single-entry system, but its design and its method of use put it in a category by itself. An all-in-one system for keeping records, writing checks, and issuing receipts, it derives its name from the fact that the checks and receipts it uses are overlaid, one after another, on top of your record sheets and are held in place by pegs. Whenever you write a check or a receipt, the information is automatically transferred to the record sheet below. This eliminates the most common accounting error of all—forgetting to record an entry. For more information on pegboard systems, which range in price from $75 to $200, check the Yellow Pages under "Business Forms and Systems."

## Taxes

Much as you might wish to avoid them, taxes are an inevitable part of doing business. The better your recordkeeping system is, the easier it will be to deal with them.

### Business Expenses

For starters, the recordkeeping system for your business must provide you with a record of tax-deductible business expenses. For it to do this, you will have to determine which expenses legitimately can be termed "business expenses." In the words of the Internal Revenue Service (IRS), "To be deductible a business expense must be ordinary in your business and necessary for its operation." According to the IRS, "The word *ordinary* refers to the expense that is common and accepted practice in the industry. *Necessary* expenses are those that are appropriate and helpful in developing and maintaining your business." Thus, an expense that meets both parts of this test is deductible. Just a few of the expenses that generally meet these criteria include

- Accounting services
- Advertising
- Attorney's fees
- Automobile used solely or primarily for business purposes
- Business publications
- Charitable contributions
- Club dues
- Consultants' fees
- Credit reports
- Depreciation
- Entertainment of clients
- Freight charges
- Insurance
- Interest on business loans
- Internet server fees
- Licenses (professional or business)
- Maintenance
- Materials
- Messenger service
- Newsletters
- Postage
- Publicity
- Rent
- Safe-deposit box
- Salaries
- Sales commissions
- Stationery
- Supplies
- Taxes
- Travel (business related)
- Utilities

In calculating your business expenses, it's important to separate them from your personal expenses. For instance, travel expenses on a business trip are deductible, but the same expenses on a vacation are not. Taking a customer to lunch is deductible; going to lunch with a friend purely for social reasons is not. In the event that an expense is partly for business and partly personal, only the business part is deductible. For example, if you go on a trip for both business and pleasure, you can deduct only the business portion of the trip. To keep track of your expenses, make sure to record the following information:

- Date the expense was paid
- Name of person or business receiving payment

- Check number
- Amount of check
- Category of business expense

### Home Business Deduction

If your business is located in your home or you maintain a home office, you may be entitled to deduct a portion of the operating expenses and the depreciation on your home (including rent or mortgage payments, insurance, utilities, repairs, maintenance costs). To qualify for this deduction, the IRS stipulates that part of your home must be set aside *regularly* and *exclusively* for the business. In this regard, the space must be used as either (1) your principal place of business or (2) a place to meet and deal with customers or clients in the normal course of your business.

The percentage of your total home expenses that you can deduct depends on how much space the business occupies. For example, if your business takes up 20 percent of your home, 20 percent times a $1,000 home utilities expense equals a $200 business utilities expense. Those expenses that benefit only your business, such as painting or remodeling the specific area occupied by the business, are 100 percent deductible. Expenses that benefit only your home and are in no way related to the business, such as lawn care and landscaping, may *not* be deducted.

To make certain you have accurately defined those expenses that benefit (1) both your home and your business, (2) only the business, and (3) only the home, it's advisable to consult with an accountant. It's also important to note that if you own your home and decide to sell it later, any home-expense deductions you've taken for the business will have a bearing on how and when capital gains on the sale are to be recognized. For more information on the home business deduction or on how it affects the sale of your home, check IRS publication number 587, "Business Use of Your Home" and number 523, "Tax Information on Selling Your Home."

### Automobile Expenses

If you use an automobile or other vehicle in your business, those expenses resulting from the business use of the vehicle are deductible. This includes gasoline, oil, maintenance and repairs, insurance, depreciation, interest on car payments, parking fees, taxes, license fees, and tolls. To calculate your deductible expenses you can either (1) use the IRS's standard mileage rate for all business miles driven or (2) deduct a percentage of the total operating costs of the vehicle, based on the percentage of miles you drive it for business reasons during the year. For more information on calculating your automobile expenses, check IRS publication number 917, "Business Use of a Car."

### Entertainment Expenses

Business entertainment expenses also are tax deductible. To qualify as a deductible item, the entertainment expense must be *ordinary* and *necessary* in carrying on your trade or operating your business. As with home business expenses and automobile expenses, you must separate your business expenses from the nonbusiness ones. Whenever entertainment is for both business and social purposes, only the business part is deductible. For example, if you entertain a group that includes three business prospects and one social guest, you may deduct a portion of the expenses for yourself and the three prospects, but you may *not* deduct any of the amount you spend on the social guest.

In determining whether an entertainment expense is deductible, ask yourself whether the entertainment had a clear business purpose. Was it to get new business or to encourage the continuation of an existing business relationship? If your answer is yes, then you should be able to claim the expense as a business deduction. For example, taking a prospective customer to lunch or dinner is a deductible expense if you discuss business at some time during the meal.

To comply with the IRS rules on entertainment deductions, you should keep a record of all business entertainment expenses along with the receipts or other supporting evidence to back them up. When claiming an expense as a business entertainment deduction, you must be able to prove the following:

1. The amount of the expense
2. The date the entertainment took place
3. The location of the entertainment, such as a restaurant or theater
4. The reason for the entertainment (to make a sale, to discuss your business with a prospective investor)
5. The name and title (or occupation) of each person you entertained

## Federal Taxes

The two best-known taxes that business owners are required to pay are income tax and self-employment tax. If you employ other people in your business, you may also be subject to employment taxes.

**Income Tax** Every business is required by law to file an annual income tax return. The form you use for this depends on whether your business is a sole proprietorship, a partnership, or a corporation.

***Sole Proprietorship*** If your business is a sole proprietorship, you should report your business income and deductions on Schedule C (1040). Attach this schedule to your individual tax return Form 1040, and submit them together. If you own more than one business, you must file a separate Schedule C for each one.

***Partnership*** If you are a partner in a business, your income and deductions from the partnership should be reported on Schedule K-1 (Form 1065) and filed along with your individual tax return. Each of your partners should do the same, accounting for his or her income and deductions in this way. In addition to this, the total income and deductions for the partnership itself must be reported on Form 1065. Limited-liability companies wishing to be taxed as partnerships use the same forms.

***Corporation*** A corporation reports its taxable income on Form 1120. S corporations use Form 1120S. Any income or dividends that you receive from the corporation should be entered on your individual tax return. If you are a shareholder in an S corporation, however, your income and deductions should be reported in the same way that they would be in a partnership. In this instance, you use Schedule K-1 (Form 1120S).

**Self-employment Tax** Self-employment tax is a Social Security tax for people who are self-employed. It's similar to the Social Security tax paid by wage earners, but you pay it yourself instead of having it withheld from your paycheck. As an entrepreneur, you must pay self-employment tax if you have net earnings from your business of $400 or more a year. To find out more about this tax, check IRS publication number 533, "Self-Employment Tax."

**Estimated Taxes** The IRS requires that you pay your income and self-employment taxes each year on a pay-as-you-go basis. Rather than paying them in one lump sum at the end of the tax period, you must estimate them in advance and pay them in installments by these dates:

- April 15
- June 15
- September 15
- January 15 (of the following year)

Using this method, you pay one quarter of your total tax liability on each date until the liability is paid in full. If you discover in, say, August that you are paying too much or too little tax, you can decrease or increase the size of the remaining payments. Remember, though, that you are required to prepay at least 90 percent of your tax liability each year. If you prepay less than this, you may be subject to a penalty. The form you use to estimate your tax is Form 1040-ES, which can be obtained from the IRS.

**Employment Taxes** If you have employees in your business, you will probably need to pay employment taxes. These taxes include

1. *Federal income tax*, which you withhold from your employees' wages
2. *Social Security tax*, part of which you withhold from your employees' wages and the rest of which you contribute as an employer
3. *Federal unemployment tax,* which you must pay as an employer

Report both income tax and the Social Security tax on Form 941, and pay both taxes when you submit the forms. Report and pay the federal unemployment tax separately, using Form 940. For more information about employment taxes and about which ones, if any, you must pay, read IRS publication number 15, "Circular E."

## State and Local Taxes

The types and amounts of state and local taxes you must pay will depend on where your business is located. For instance, businesses in New York and California are subject to higher rates of taxation than those in Pennsylvania and Texas. Some states have income and sales taxes, whereas others don't. All states have unemployment taxes. Just as the states vary when it comes to taxation, so do counties, cities, and towns within the states. Some of the taxes imposed at this level include business taxes, licensing fees, and income taxes. To make sure that your business is meeting its state and local tax obligations, contact the authorities for your locality to determine those taxes for which you are responsible.

## Tax-Related Decisions

Given the bite taxes can take from your profits, it's important to consider the tax implications of each business decision you make. For example, each of the following decisions can raise or lower your tax obligations:

- The legal structure you choose for your business
- Your choice of financing–debt (borrowed funds) versus equity (investment capital)
- Where your business is located
- How research and development costs are treated–as expenses deducted in the current year or as capital costs amortized over a period of years
- Whether income and expenses are reported on a *cash basis* (as they are received and paid) or an *accrual basis* (as they are earned and incurred)
- Which expenses you term "ordinary and necessary" in your business
- How and when earnings are distributed
- How inventory is valued–at the cost of your most recent or of your oldest acquisitions
- How assets are transferred or sold
- How owner and employee benefit programs are set up
- Estate-planning decisions

To protect your assets, there's no overestimating the value of a competent accountant and attorney to assist you in making the best decisions for you and your business.

To find out more about the tax laws and regulations that have an impact on your business, contact the Internal Revenue Service in Washington, DC, or one of its branch offices. For a list of IRS publications on various business taxation matters, see the back of Chapter 18.

## Recordkeeping and Taxes Checklist

To help ensure that your recordkeeping system is meeting the needs of your business and that you are properly dealing with tax matters, answer the questions in the following checklist.

| Recordkeeping and Taxes Checklist | Answer Yes or No |
|---|---|
| 1. Have you determined which records are important to your business? | ________ |
| 2. Have you decided which kind of accounting system to use and set up your books? | ________ |
| 3. Did you get advice from an accountant or a bookkeeper? | ________ |
| 4. Are you familiar with all aspects of your accounting system? | ________ |
| 5. Is new information entered into your system on a timely basis so that the books are kept up-to-date? | ________ |
| 6. Are you able to verify the following? | |
| Cash on hand at the end of the day | ________ |
| All money owed to you by customers | ________ |
| Accounts that are past due | ________ |
| All money owed to suppliers and creditors | ________ |
| Bills that have been paid | ________ |
| Inventory that has been received | ________ |
| Salary and wages paid | ________ |
| All other expenses that have been incurred | ________ |
| 7. Are you keeping track of all tax-deductible expenses? | ________ |
| 8. Are you separating business expenses from personal ones? | ________ |
| 9. Have you determined whether to utilize the home-business deduction and how to calculate it? | ________ |
| 10. Are you using one of the IRS's approved methods for calculating your automobile expenses and keeping detailed mileage records? | ________ |

*(continued)*

| Recordkeeping and Taxes Checklist *(continued)* | Answer Yes or No |
|---|---|
| 11. Are you familiar with the federal, state, and local taxes that apply to your business? | ________ |
| 12. Are you filing the appropriate tax forms and making the required payments in accordance with government regulations? | ________ |
| 13. Do you consider the tax implications of each business decision that you make? | ________ |

# 7

# Financial Statements

The information obtained through your system of financial recordkeeping is only as good as your ability to use it. In addition to compiling your financial data, you must also know how to summarize and interpret it.

## Summarizing Financial Data

Summarizing involves taking the information contained within your ledger accounts and using it to prepare the financial statements for your business. The two most important of these are the balance sheet and the income statement (often referred to as a profit-and-loss statement, or P&L).

The *balance sheet* is a summary of your business's assets, liabilities, and capital on a given day.

The *income statement* is a summary of your business's income and expenses during a specific period (month, quarter, year).

The difference between these two statements can be compared to the difference between a photograph and a motion picture. The balance sheet is like a photograph, depicting your business as it appears in a single instant. The income statement is like a motion picture, depicting your business as it changes over time.

## The Importance of Financial Statements

Unlike day-to-day accounting records, financial statements provide an overview of your business. Instead of telling what you sold on a particular day, or how much a specific inventory item cost, financial statements give you the big picture–comparing what you own to what you owe, what you earned to what you spent. As such, they form the basis for any financial analysis of your business.

Financial statements are absolutely essential for the following:

- *Management planning.* To operate your business in the most profitable way possible, or lay the groundwork for future expansion, you need to know where your business stands and how it got there.

- *Raising capital.* Bankers and investors use financial statements as a way of evaluating your business. If you wish to obtain the support of either group, you must not only supply statements, but also be ready to explain and defend them.
- *Preparing tax returns.* You need the information contained within your financial statements to prepare your tax returns. Furthermore, in the event of an audit by the Internal Revenue Service, you will be expected to produce the relevant accounting records and statements.

## The Balance Sheet

A balance sheet has two main sections: one listing the assets of the business and one listing the liabilities and capital of the business. In accordance with the accounting equation, the two sides are always equal:

$$\text{Assets} = \text{Liabilities} + \text{Capital}$$

This can be readily explained by the fact that all assets in a business are subject to the claims of creditors and owners.

### Assets

An *asset* is anything of monetary value that is owned by the business. Assets are generally classified as being (1) current, (2) fixed, or (3) intangible. The order in which they appear on the balance sheet is determined by their *liquidity*—that is, their ability to be converted into cash.

**Current Assets** These consist of cash and assets that are expected to be converted into cash within the coming year. Included in this category are *accounts receivable* (money owed by customers) and *inventory* (merchandise, supplies, raw materials, and parts).

**Fixed Assets** These consist of tangible property to be used over a period of years in operating the business. Included in this category are land, buildings, machinery, equipment, motor vehicles, furniture, and fixtures.

**Intangible Assets** These consist of items that are usually nonphysical assets. Included in this category are trademarks, patents, copyrights, and goodwill.

**The Print Shop**
**December 31, 2000**

| | | | |
|---|---|---|---|
| | *Assets* | | |
| **Current assets** | | | |
| Cash | | $15,000 | |
| Accounts receivable | $36,000 | | |
| Less allowance for bad debts | (1,500) | | |
| | | 34,500 | |
| Inventory (at cost) | | 46,500 | |
| Total current assets | | | $96,000 |
| **Fixed assets** | | | |
| Furniture and fixtures | 33,000 | | |
| Delivery van | 30,000 | | |
| | | 63,000 | |
| Less accumulated depreciation | | (3,000) | |
| Total fixed assets | | | 60,000 |
| **Total assets** | | | $156,000 |
| | *Liabilities and Capital* | | |
| **Current liabilities** | | | |
| Accounts payable | $27,000 | | |
| Notes payable (due within 1 year) | 12,000 | | |
| Accrued liabilities | 3,000 | | |
| Total current liabilities | | $42,000 | |
| **Long-term liabilities** | | | |
| Notes payable (due after 1 year) | | 12,000 | |
| Total current liabilities | | | $54,000 |
| **Capital** | | | |
| Owner's capital, January 1, 2000 | | 99,000 | |
| Net income for year | 45,000 | | |
| Less proprietor's drawings | (42,000) | | |
| Undistributed income | | 3,000 | |
| Total capital, December 31, 2000 | | | 102,000 |
| **Total liabilities and capital** | | | $156,000 |

### Liabilities

A liability is a debt owed by the business. Liabilities are classified as being either current or long-term.

**Current Liabilities** These consist of debts that are expected to be paid off within the coming year. Included in this category are *accounts payable* (money owed to suppliers and creditors), *notes payable* (money owed to the bank), and *accrued liabilities* (wages, interest, taxes, deposits, and other accounts due but not paid as of the balance-sheet date).

**Long-Term Liabilities** These consist of those debts that are *not* due to be paid within the coming year. Included in this category are mortgages, term loans, bonds, and similar future obligations.

### Capital

The difference between the assets of a business and its liabilities equals its capital:

$$\text{Assets} - \text{Liabilities} = \text{Capital}$$

Capital represents the amount of owner investment in the business, as well as any profits (or losses) that have accumulated.

**Sole Proprietorship or Partnership** In a sole proprietorship or partnership, capital is listed under each owner's name. Increases (or decreases) in capital are also shown there.

**Corporation** In a corporation, capital is listed under the heading "Capital stock." This represents the paid-in value of the shares of stock issued to each owner. Corporate earnings that are not distributed to shareholders are shown here as "Retained earnings."

## The Income Statement

An income statement (or profit and loss statement) can generally be divided into the following sections:

- Net sales
- Cost of goods sold
- Gross margin

- Expenses
- Net income (or loss)

Together, these demonstrate both the extent and the efficiency of the business's ability to generate income during the accounting period covered by the statement.

*Net sales* represents the total sales during the accounting period, *less* sales tax and deductions for sales discounts, returns, or allowances.

*Cost of goods sold* represents the total amount spent by the business to purchase the products sold during the accounting period. Businesses usually compute this by adding the value of the goods purchased during the period (less discounts offered by suppliers) to the value of the beginning inventory, and then subtracting the ending inventory.

*Gross margin* represents the difference between the net sales and the cost of goods sold. It is also frequently referred to as the *gross profit.*

*Expenses* represents costs incurred as a result of operating the business. These can be divided into two categories–*selling expenses* (expenses, such as sales commissions and advertising, that are directly related to the business's sales activities) and *general administrative expenses* (expenses incurred through activities other than selling, such as clerical salaries, rent, and insurance).

*Net income* represents what's left after all relevant expenses have been deducted from the gross margin. When total expenses exceed the gross margin, this is called a *net loss.*

## Interpreting Financial Data

Interpreting financial data involves studying the various relationships that exist among the figures shown on your financial statements. These relationships are expressed in the form of *financial ratios,* comparative measurements that enable you to pinpoint the strengths and weaknesses in your business operations.

What if you needed to know the answer to one or more of the following questions?

- Is there enough ready cash in my business?
- Are current liabilities at a safe level?
- How well could the business weather a financial setback?
- Are customers paying their bills on time?
- Is inventory moving as quickly as it should be?

**Sample Income Statement**
**The Print Shop**
**for the Year Ending December 31, 2000**

| | | | | Percent |
|---|---|---|---|---|
| **Net Sales** | | | $300,000 | 100% |
| **Cost of Goods Sold** | | | | |
| Inventory, January 1 | | $46,500 | | |
| Purchases | $153,300 | | | |
| Less cash discount | (2,400) | | | |
| | | 150,900 | | |
| Available for sale | | 197,400 | | |
| Less inventory, December 31 | | (47,400) | | |
| Cost of goods sold | | | 150,000 | 50 |
| **Gross Margin** | | | 150,000 | 50 |
| **Expenses** | | | | |
| Accounting and legal | | 3,000 | | |
| Advertising | | 7,500 | | |
| Depreciation | | 3,000 | | |
| Insurance | | 3,500 | | |
| Interest | | 2,500 | | |
| Miscellaneous | | 7,500 | | |
| Payroll | | 36,000 | | |
| Rent | | 25,500 | | |
| Repairs | | 1,500 | | |
| Supplies | | 4,500 | | |
| Travel | | 6,000 | | |
| Utilities | | 4,500 | | |
| Total expenses | | | 105,000 | 35 |
| **Net Income** | | | $ 45,000 | 15 |

- Are prices keeping pace with inflation?
- Are profits what they should be?
- Are assets being used wisely?
- How much of my business do I really own?

How could you get your hands on the necessary information? Call your accountant? Sure, if you had the time and the money to spend waiting for an answer. But why bother when the information is already right at hand, in your financial statements? Solving a few quick arithmetic problems is all it takes to find the answers.

Financial ratios can be used to find out a great deal of information about your business, ranging from the trivial to the significant. Among the ratios most closely examined by the owners, investors, and creditors are those pertaining to (1) liquidity, (2) profitability, and (3) ownership.

### Liquidity Ratios

These measure your business's ability to pay its bills and to convert assets into cash. Creditors look closely at these ratios.

**Current Ratio** This ratio, which compares current assets to current liabilities, is used to assess your business's ability to meet its financial obligations within the coming year. The best known and most widely used of the ratios, it's computed by dividing current assets by current liabilities:

$$\text{Current ratio} = \frac{\text{Current assets}}{\text{Current liabilities}}$$

$$\text{Current ratio} = \frac{\$96{,}000}{\$42{,}000}$$

$$\text{Current ratio} = 2.29{:}1$$

The generally acceptable minimum current ratio is 2 to 1. This can vary, though, depending on the specific circumstances of each business.

**Acid-Test Ratio** This ratio is used to assess your business's ability to meet its current financial obligations in the event that sales decline and merchandise inventory cannot readily be converted to cash. Also called the *quick ratio* because it measures only ready assets, it's computed by dividing cash and accounts receivable by current liabilities:

$$\text{Acid-test ratio} = \frac{\text{Cash} + \text{Accounts receivable}}{\text{Current liabilities}}$$

$$\text{Acid-test ratio} = \frac{\$15{,}000 + \$34{,}500}{\$42{,}000}$$

$$\text{Acid-test ratio} = 1.2{:}1$$

An acid-test ratio of 1 to 1 is considered acceptable, given an adequate means of collecting accounts receivable.

**Working-Capital Ratio** This ratio is used to assess your business's ability to meet unforeseen expenses or to weather a financial setback. It's computed by subtracting current liabilities from current assets:

$$\text{Working capital} = \text{Current assets} - \text{Current liabilities}$$

$$\text{Working capital} = \$96{,}000 - \$42{,}000$$

$$\text{Working capital} = \$54{,}000$$

The need for working capital varies from business to business. Frequently, though, lenders will insist that the level of working capital be maintained at or above a minimum level.

**Average Collection Period** This number is used to assess your business's ability to convert accounts receivable into cash. It's computed in a two-step process: (1) divide net sales by the number of days in the year; and (2) divide this figure (the average day's sales) into the accounts receivable:

**Step 1**

$$\text{Average day's sales} = \frac{\text{Net sales}}{\text{365 days}}$$

$$\text{Average day's sales} = \frac{\$300{,}000}{365}$$

$$\text{Average day's sales} = \$822 \text{ per day}$$

**Step 2**

$$\text{Average collection period} = \frac{\text{Accounts receivable}}{\text{Average day's sales}}$$

$$\text{Average collection period} = \frac{\$34{,}500}{\$822 \text{ per day}}$$

$$\text{Average collection period} = 42 \text{ days}$$

What average collection period is acceptable depends on the credit terms.

Generally, it should not exceed $1^1/_3$ times the credit terms. Thus, because the Print Shop offers 30 days credit, its average collection period is slightly higher than it should be ($1^1/_3 \times 30 = 40$ days).

**Inventory Turnover** This calculation compares your cost of goods sold to your average inventory level. *Average inventory level* is calculated as half the total of adding the beginning inventory to the ending inventory. Inventory turnover is used to assess your business's ability to convert merchandise inventory into sales. It's computed by dividing the cost of goods sold by the average inventory:

$$\text{Inventory turnover} = \frac{\text{Cost of goods sold}}{\text{Average inventory}}$$

$$\text{Inventory turnover} = \frac{\$150{,}000}{^1/_2\,(\$46{,}500 + \$47{,}400)}$$

$$\text{Inventory turnover} = \frac{\$150{,}000}{46{,}950}$$

$$\text{Inventory turnover} = 3.2 \text{ times}$$

Normally, the higher your turnover is, the better. This means you're moving the goods. However, as the turnover rate increases, so does the risk of stock shortages. By trial and error and by studying the turnover rates of similar businesses, you can determine what rate is desirable for your business.

### Profitability Ratios

These ratios measure your business's ability to use its assets to make a profit. Investors look closely at these ratios.

*Net profit on sales* is used for assessing your business's ability to turn a profit on the sales it makes. It's computed by dividing net profit by net sales:

$$\text{Net profit on sales} = \frac{\text{Net profit}}{\text{Net sales}}$$

$$\text{Net profit on sales} = \frac{\$45{,}000}{\$300{,}000}$$

$$\text{Net profit on sales} = 0.15 \text{ or } 15\%$$

In this example, the Print Shop makes 15 cents of profit for every dollar of sales. Whether this is an acceptable level of profit depends on your objectives and the standard for your industry.

*Return on investment (ROI)* is used for assessing your business's ability to turn a profit on the assets it holds. It's computed by dividing net profit by total assets:

$$\text{Return on investment} = \frac{\text{Net profit}}{\text{Total assets}}$$

$$\text{Return on investment} = \frac{\$45{,}000}{\$156{,}000}$$

$$\text{Return on investment} = 0.29 \text{ or } 29\%$$

To determine whether this is a good return on investment, you should compare your figures to those of comparable businesses.

### Ownership Ratio

This ratio measures the levels of ownership in the business, comparing owners' claims to those of creditors. *Worth to debt* is used for assessing your business's ability to protect creditors against losses. To compute it, divide net worth by total debt:

$$\text{Worth to debt} = \frac{\text{Net worth}}{\text{Total debt}}$$

$$\text{Worth to debt} = \frac{\$102{,}000}{\$54{,}000}$$

$$\text{Worth to debt} = 1.89{:}1$$

For every dollar lent to the Print Shop the owner has invested $1.89. Usually a ratio of 2 to 1 or better is preferred because this provides creditors with more protection. To improve this ratio, the owner can either invest more money in the business or reduce her or his debt.

As you can see, calculating the financial ratios for your business can be done fairly easily. To make it even easier and to more readily compare one set of ratios with another, there are several financial software programs on the market that you can use.

## Financial Ratio Checklist

Once you have prepared the financial statements for your business, you can pinpoint its financial strengths and weaknesses by computing the ratios in the following Financial Ratio Checklist.

| | Ratio | Satis-factory | Unsatis-factory |
|---|---|---|---|
| **Liquidity** | | | |
| Current ratio | _____ | _____ | _____ |
| Acid-test ratio | _____ | _____ | _____ |
| Working capital | _____ | _____ | _____ |
| Average collection period | _____ | _____ | _____ |
| Inventory turnover | _____ | _____ | _____ |
| **Profitability** | | | |
| Net profit on sales | _____ | _____ | _____ |
| Return on investment | _____ | _____ | _____ |
| **Ownership** | | | |
| Worth to debt | _____ | _____ | _____ |

# 8

# Obtaining Capital

Prior to commencing operations, you will want to estimate as realistically as possible the amount of capital needed to launch and sustain your business during its first three to six months. This is your initial investment. Because it takes a while before revenues exceed or even equal expenses, a financial cushion is essential in your estimate. The cushion can mean the difference between success and failure, enabling you to meet payroll and supplier obligations, make loan payments, and keep your doors open until the business is fully self-supporting.

A common mistake of first-time entrepreneurs is in neglecting to take into account such invisible costs of operating a business as insurance, deposits or bonds, license fees, estimated sales taxes, and membership dues in professional organizations. If added only after the fact, these "incidentals" could easily throw the best of budgets out of kilter.

Your own personal financial needs must also be considered. Not only does your business need capital in order to survive during the first months of operations, but so do you. To be accurate, your estimated initial investment must include an allowance adequate to support yourself while you are establishing your business. This allowance can be in the form of either a salary or drawing account privileges.

## Determining Your Initial Investment

### For a Retail Operation

The first step in determining the amount of your initial investment is to estimate your projected annual sales volume. This is based on such factors as the type and size of your intended business and its location. Any previous related business experience that you may have, combined with the most up-to-date research you can find, will be invaluable here. The more you know about your new business, the more you will know what to expect.

Once you have computed your sales volume for the year, it's easy to work backward to figure out the dollar investment necessary to meet your starting merchandise inventory requirements. You do this by dividing your estimated sales volume by your anticipated inventory turnover (the number of times per year that your merchandise will sell out). For instance, if your estimated annual sales volume is $300,000 and you expect to turn over your merchandise three times per year, then your initial merchandise inventory should last four months and have a retail value of $100,000. At cost, given a 50-percent markup, this would amount to an initial investment of $50,000.

Merchandise inventory turnover varies by industry and by merchandising techniques (high-volume retailer versus specialty store), but you can find out the average turnover for your type of business by referring to Robert Morris Associates *Statement Studies* or Dun & Bradstreet's *Key Business Ratios,* both available at most libraries. For additional information, make it a point to consult with prospective suppliers.

Now that you have estimated your initial merchandise inventory costs, the next step is to estimate the amount of money required to meet all other costs during your first turnover period. These include rent, insurance, furniture and fixtures, supplies, salaries, utilities, and advertising. Remember to cushion your projections. When added to your merchandise inventory costs, these will give you the total initial investment required for your business.

**Initial Investment for a Retail Operation**

| | | |
|---|---|---|
| Starting inventory at cost | | $ 50,000 |
| Furniture and fixtures | | |
| Purchase price (if paid in full) | | 12,000 |
| Cash down payment (if purchased on contract) | | 4,500 |
| Fees for legal, accounting, licenses, and other preopening expenses | | 3,750 |
| Expenses (for 4 months, 1 turnover period) | | |
| Payroll | $ 9,000 | |
| Rent | 8,400 | |
| Other | 16,600 | |
| Total expenses | | 34,000 |
| Contingencies | | 3,750 |
| Total initial investment | | $108,000 |

### For a Nonretail Operation

If you are starting a manufacturing company or service establishment, the method of calculating your initial investment will need certain minor revisions. The major difference between a manufacturer and a retailer is that the bulk of the manufacturer's initial investment doesn't go for merchandise; it goes for machinery, which will be used for several years, and for raw materials, which can be converted into finished goods. Furthermore, a manufacturer must make such key decisions as whether to lease or to buy equipment and whether to manufacture or to purchase the component parts of the product. These decisions will affect the amount not only of your initial investment, but also of your taxes.

In most cases, a service establishment requires neither an extensive merchandise inventory nor a large investment in capital equipment. Skills are the main product. As a result, the service establishment is easier to start than either a retailing or a manufacturing business, and it usually calls for a considerably smaller initial investment. This explains in part why the number of businesses categorized as services is increasing at such a rapid rate. Statistics provided by the Labor Department show that service industries will continue to expand and grow in the coming years.

## Sources of Capital

You can turn to a variety of sources to obtain financing for your business. Which ones you choose will depend primarily on the way in which the money is to be used in the business and the degree of ownership you wish to retain.

**Capital Usage** If a large sum of money is required–such as for the purchase of physical facilities, machinery, or inventory–it's likely that you will want to delay repaying this as long as possible. Conversely, smaller sums of money to cover operating expenses would normally be repaid within the year.

**Debt versus Ownership** Whether you borrow the money you need or solicit it from investors will determine your level of ownership in the business. Once you accept a loan, you have an obligation to repay it with interest, but you transfer no ownership to the lender. Investment capital is just the opposite of this. You neither return the investor's money nor pay interest on it. However, the investor becomes a co-owner with you in the business.

In determining the proper balance of *debt capital* (borrowed money) to *equity capital* (invested money) that's right for you, you should be aware of two drawbacks. In the case of debt capital, if for any reason you are unable to repay your loans on time, you could easily be forced into bankruptcy. Equity capital, on the other hand, though seemingly risk free, presents another problem: control. Unlike lenders, investors have a say in how the business should be run. The greater the amount of equity capital you obtain, the greater the amount of ownership you relinquish.

## Personal Investment

Your first and most likely source of capital is, of course, yourself. The amount of money you decide to invest in starting a business will depend partly on how much money you have readily available, be it in savings, in investments, or in your home equity. It will also depend on how the ownership in the business is to be divided.

Your chances of avoiding investing any of your own money in the business are slim. Because starting a business involves risk, prospective creditors and investors will expect you, the owner, to share in that risk. There are exceptions, however. If you have a unique idea or valuable skills to contribute to the business, these might augment capital or be an acceptable substitute for it.

Should you be planning to finance your business solely from your own personal resources, on the other hand, you may want to reconsider. Instead of putting the money directly into the business, it would be to your advantage to use it as collateral for a loan to the business. Not only would this build up your credit standing, but also, because the interest paid on the loan is a tax-deductible expense, the loan would be virtually cost free.

## Family and Friends

Obtaining money from family and friends, through loans or investments, may also be an alternative. Bear in mind, however, that this can strain both your personal and your business relationships unless you take the proper safeguards.

You should clearly state in writing the provisions for the repayment of such loans including the duration of each loan, the interest rate, and the repayment schedule. In this way, you can minimize future misunderstandings over the nature of the money entrusted to you.

When relatives or friends become investors in your business, the terms of this association should be stipulated in advance. How much of a say will they have in running the business? Do you have the right to buy back their interest in the company? How will the proceeds be distributed? All this should be put in writing. If you answer these questions and others in the beginning, you may avoid problems later.

### Partners

People other than friends and family may be interested in entering into the business with you. These could be business acquaintances, classmates, or simply entrepreneurs looking for a business opportunity. Forming a partnership with one or more of these interested parties could be the way to fulfill not only your capital requirements but also your personnel needs. Remember, though, that in so doing you dilute your ownership and lessen the magnitude of your control.

### Shareholders

Selling shares of stock in a business as a means of raising capital is an option permitted only to corporations. Should you decide to do so, you must first incorporate. Because this involves obtaining a corporate charter from the state in which your business will be based, it is advisable to consult an attorney for assistance in this matter.

Offsetting the red tape inherent in forming a corporation is the corporation's unique ability to accumulate large sums of capital. Aided by such features as limited liability and easy transfer of stock ownership, the corporation is able to draw on the resources of a vast and diverse pool of investors. Brought together by a common goal–to make a profit–these investors, as shareholders, will have the right to influence corporate policy decisions. However, you can retain control by holding onto a majority of the shares of stock.

### Direct Public Offerings

To reduce the cost and red tape involved in selling stocks, most states now permit direct public offerings (DPOs), which allow companies to sell stock themselves, rather than by going through securities brokers. The two most common types of DPOs are: (1) the small corporate offering registration (SCOR), which permits businesses to raise up to $1 million per year without filing with the Securities and Exchange Commission (SEC), and (2) the Regulation A offering of up to $5 million per year, which must be filed with the SEC. An alternative to the Wall Street initial public offering route, DPOs work best when you have a unique product and a loyal following of customers willing to invest in your company. You also have to be prepared to blow your own horn and get the word out about the stock offering. For example, some savvy entrepreneurs have advertised their stock on clothing tags, macaroni-and-cheese dinner packages and bags of coffee, while others have used the Internet to reach investors.

## Bondholders

In addition to selling stock, corporations are permitted to sell bonds. Unlike shares of stock, which represent ownership in the business, bonds represent debt. In exchange for investing in bonds, bondholders are paid a predetermined interest rate over the life of the bond. This interest differs from dividends in that it is categorized as a business expense and therefore is deductible. When the bond matures (usually in 10 to 30 years), the bondholder receives the principal investment back.

Because bonds are a form of long-term debt, they are more often used to finance major business expansion costs such as the purchase of plant and equipment. Before making the decision to sell bonds, though, it's important that you determine your corporation's future ability to pay the annual interest and to retire the bonds when they reach maturity. Furthermore, during the early stages of your business, investors may be understandably reluctant to purchase the corporation's bonds, preferring that you establish yourself first.

## Commercial Banks

Despite what you may have heard about how difficult it is to get a bank loan, banks are a major source of capital for new businesses. Prior to approaching your banker for a loan, though, you should be aware of the criteria on which your request will be evaluated. In banking terminology, there are *six Cs of credit:* capital, collateral, capability, character, coverage, and circumstances.

Your banker will want to know how much *capital* your business has to start with and what percentage of it is your own personal investment. What assets do you possess that can be used as *collateral* for the loan?

Based on your experience and reputation, a determination will be made regarding your *capability* and *character.* The type and amount of insurance *coverage* you plan to obtain is another important factor. The general *circumstances* of your business (competition, level of consumer demand, current economic environment) will also be taken into consideration.

Your ability to sell your banker on your strengths in each of these areas will directly affect the outcome of your loan application. Be prepared to provide such backup information as financial statements, references, market research data, and a detailed plan for achieving your company's objectives. Establishing your creditworthiness in this way makes it much easier to get a yes answer.

### Credit Unions

Credit unions generally offer lower interest rates than banks. To qualify for a loan, however, you must be a member. If you don't belong to a credit union, you might want to explore the possibility of joining one. Established for the purpose of providing members with low-interest loans, credit unions are usually formed around an employer, professional organization, church, or fraternal group.

The most common types of loans credit unions make are short-term consumer loans for automobiles, furniture, boats, and so on. However, you might be able to stretch these bounds to encompass furnishings for your business, equipment, or a company car. Most credit unions will lend up to $5,000 to purchase a computer. Also, if your credit rating is good, you could qualify for a personal signature loan up to $10,000.

### Savings and Loan Associations

Savings and loans (S&Ls) have traditionally focused their attention on making long-term loans to home buyers and have played only a small role in business financing. Over the years, though, more and more savings and loans have shown an increased interest in making business loans. The reason for this shift is simple. Business loans are normally repaid over a shorter time than home loans; this enables the S&Ls to recoup their money faster. Taking this into consideration, you might want to investigate your local savings and loans to find out which ones are probusiness.

If you own your own home, there's also the possibility that a savings and loan association will give you a loan based on your equity in your home. This route should be pursued with caution, though. Mortgaging your home to obtain business capital can be risky because a business loss could put your home in jeopardy.

**Small Business Administration**

The Small Business Administration (SBA) is a federal agency created in 1953 to provide businesses with both advice and financial aid. In this regard, it can make either direct or indirect loans to businesses. A *direct loan* is one made by the SBA itself. An *indirect loan* is a loan made by another lending institution, but guaranteed up to 90 percent by the SBA. Both kinds have lower interest rates and longer maturities than those associated with conventional loans, but the SBA is not in competition with the financial community. Calling itself the "lender of last resort," the SBA usually works in partnership with lending institutions, making or guaranteeing loans only when other financing isn't available.

In granting loans, the SBA is influenced favorably by the following conditions:

1. The business to be financed is the primary source of income for the family.
2. Financial assistance is not otherwise available on reasonable terms from private sources.
3. A reasonable amount is at stake in the venture. Generally, SBA will want at least 20 percent at stake in a start-up operation.
4. There is reasonable assurance of repayment.
5. The new venture is feasible and sound.
6. The applicant has ability and experience in the area of the business.
7. The applicant is of good character.
8. The borrower agrees not to discriminate in the business on grounds of race, creed, color, or national origin.

Before you attempt to put together a loan application package by yourself, the SBA suggests that you prepare and collect the following information (see the forms and questionnaire at the end of this chapter):

1. Business plan
2. Personal financial statement
3. Statement of personal history

4. Start-up costs
5. Forecast of profit or loss

Once you have gathered this information, you should contact your local SBA field office to discuss your business plans further. At that point you will receive advice regarding your proposal and the preparation of a loan package.

In addition to the SBA's main loan program–the 7(a) Loan Guaranty Program–the SBA also offers these programs for businesses that need smaller amounts of cash or that must raise funds quickly:

- *Low Doc Program.* For entrepreneurs who need $100,000 or less, the SBA has designed this program to rapidly process loans using a one-page application form that focuses on the credit and character of the applicant. In many instances, loans have been approved in as little as three to five business days.
- *Microloan Program.* This SBA program was created for entrepreneurs in need of short-term loans of $25,000 or less for start-up or expansion purposes, typically to purchase inventory, equipment, and furniture and fixtures or to provide working capital. These loans are made through selected nonprofit organizations and have a maximum repayment time of six years.

## Certified Development Companies

Certified Development Companies (CDCs) are public–private-sector organizations created by local governments to promote economic development within their regions. Funded by both the SBA and private financial institutions, CDCs provide long-term financing to local businesses so that they can create and retain jobs within their communities. Two of the main programs administered by CDCs are the

1. 502 Loan Program, which provides long-term, fixed-asset financing to small businesses in rural areas
2. 504 Loan Program, which provides long-term, fixed-asset financing to local businesses that add to the community's job base

## Small Business Investment Companies

Small Business Investment Companies (SBICs) are privately owned and operated companies that have been licensed and in some cases financed by the SBA to provide small businesses with long-term debt and equity financing. The intent of the 1958 Small Business Investment Act, authorizing the formation of SBICs, was to increase the number of private companies willing to invest in small businesses.

Though all SBICs must conform to SBA regulations and are subject to SBA control, they are not all the same. SBICs range from those specializing in the entertainment industry to those in the aerospace field. The preferred method of investment (debt versus equity) and the amount of that investment can also vary. If you are considering SBIC financing, you will therefore want to compare SBICs. To get additional information on SBICs and a list of those near you, contact your local SBA field office.

### Supplier Credit

Depending on your credit rating, some suppliers may be persuaded to provide such items as inventory, furniture, fixtures, and equipment on a delayed-payment basis. In the case of inventories, full payment would normally be due within 30 days. Furniture, fixtures, and equipment could be paid off over a longer period, perhaps as much as several years.

Supplier credit has two advantages. It allows you to stretch your available cash, and the related interest charges can be deducted from your taxes as a business expense. However, because many suppliers offer discounts for early payment, the corresponding disadvantage is that you will be paying higher prices.

### Finance Companies

Finance companies make loans that banks and other lenders regard as too risky. Known for their liberal credit policies and speedy loan processing, finance companies make both secured and unsecured loans for virtually any purpose. As such, they provide another business funding alternative–but an expensive one. Proof that convenience comes at a price is the significantly higher interest rates they charge. So, before relying on this source of capital, you should carefully consider your other options and what such a loan will cost.

### Venture-Capital Firms

One of the least known, but nonetheless important, sources of funds for businesses is venture-capital firms. These are privately owned investment companies that provide capital to new and growing businesses in exchange for an ownership stake in them. Keenly focused on just one factor–the business's profit potential–venture capitalists generally look for a 25 to 50 percent annual return on investment over a five-year period. Their ultimate goal is for the business to "go public," thus enabling them to recoup three to five times their investment by selling shares of stock in the business in a public stock offering.

Venture-capital firms are primarily interested in businesses that require an investment between $250,000 and $4 million. However, if an especially promising project requires more than that, a venture-capital firm will sometimes increase its investment or join forces with other firms to provide the necessary funds.

If your business has strong growth and profit potential, then venture capital is certainly a financing option to consider. Bear in mind, though, that you must be willing to give up part of your equity in the business and to permit investors to have a say in management decisions. By giving up a little, though, you could end up with a lot. It was venture capital that helped two young entrepreneurs–Stephen Wozniak and Steven Jobs–turn their business dream into Apple Computer.

You can find out more about venture-capital firms by checking such sources as bankers, accountants, venture-capital directories, and business/finance magazines (*Inc., Money, Fortune, Forbes*). Then get your business plan in order. The best way to get a venture capitalist's attention is with a winning business plan.

### Wealthy Investors

Wealthy investors, or "angels," are another little-known, but increasingly utilized source of business financing. Especially partial to start-up businesses, angels look for the same things that venture capitalists do, but they tend to pick businesses that are in keeping with their personal goals or philosophies. Whether operating alone or as part of an investment group, angels include doctors, lawyers, accountants, successful entrepreneurs, entertainers, athletes, and others with money. The best way to find them is by getting a referral from a mutual friend, relative, or business associate or through your accountant or stockbroker. Another alternative is to place an ad in the "Business Opportunities" section of a newspaper or magazine.

## SBA Business Plan Questionnaire

The SBA will ask you the following questions as part of their financing procedure:

1. What is your business experience and education?
2. What kind of business do you plan to start (construction, manufacturing, service, etc.)? What is your product? Describe the product or service you plan to make or sell.
3. Why did you choose this kind of business?
4. Will your business be a sole proprietorship, partnership, or corporation?
5. How large a loan is required, and how do you anticipate using the funds?
6. Where will the business be located? Why was this location selected?
7. How much capital do you have, and what will be invested in the business (briefly)?
8. Have you attended an SBA prebusiness workshop?
9. Do you have an accountant or bookkeeping service in mind to set up financial records?
10. What kinds of licensing will you require?
11. How many employees will you need?
12. What kind of insurance will you carry?

**SBA Start-up Costs Form**

Whether you are starting a new business, moving to a new location, opening a new branch, or expanding your business, you will have some "start-up" or one-time expenses. In all applications for such purposes, the following information will be required:

1. Furniture, fixtures, machinery, equipment:
   a. Purchase price (if paid in full with cash) $______
   b. Cash down payment (if purchased on contract) $______
   c. Transportation and installation costs $______
2. Starting inventory and supplies $______
3. Decorating/remodeling/leasehold improvements $______
4. Deposits
   a. Utilities $______
   b. Rents/leases $______
   c. Other (identify) $______
5. Fees
   a. Legal, accounting, other $______
   b. Licenses, permits, etc. $______
   c. Other (identify) $______
6. Other (working capital, etc.) $______

Total $______

Less equity injection $______

Amount of loan request $______

OMB Approval No. 3245-0188

U. S. SMALL BUSINESS ADMINISTRATION

## PERSONAL FINANCIAL STATEMENT

As of ________________, 19____

Complete this form for: (1) each proprietor, or (2) each limited partner who owns 20% or more interest and each general partner, or (3) each stockholder owning 20% or more of voting stock and each corporate officer and director, or (4) any other person or entity providing a guaranty on the loan.

| | |
|---|---|
| Name | Business Phone ( ) |
| Residence Address | Residence Phone ( ) |
| City, State, & Zip Code | |
| Business Name of Applicant/Borrower | |

| ASSETS (Omit Cents) | | LIABILITIES (Omit Cents) | |
|---|---|---|---|
| Cash on hands & in Banks | $ | Accounts Payable | $ |
| Savings Accounts | $ | Notes Payable to Banks and Others (Describe in Section 2) | $ |
| IRA or Other Retirement Account | $ | Installment Account (Auto) Mo. Payments $ | $ |
| Accounts & Notes Receivable | $ | Installment Account (other) Mo. Payments $ | $ |
| Life Insurance-Cash Surrender Value Only (Complete Section 8) | $ | Loan on Life Insurance | $ |
| Stocks and Bonds (Describe in Section 3) | $ | Mortgages on Real Estate (Describe in Section 4) | $ |
| Real Estate (Describe in Section 4) | $ | Unpaid Taxes (Describe in Section 6) | $ |
| Automobile-Present Value | $ | Other Liabilities (Describe in Section 7) | $ |
| Other Personal Property (Describe in Section 5) | $ | Total Liabilities | $ |
| Other Assets (Describe in Section 5) | $ | Net Worth | $ |
| Total | $ | Total | $ |

| Section 1. Source of Income | | Contingent Liabilities | |
|---|---|---|---|
| Salary | $ | As Endorser or Co-Maker | $ |
| Net Investment Income | $ | Legal Claims & Judgments | $ |
| Real Estate Income | $ | Provision for Federal Income Tax | $ |
| Other Income (Decribe below)* | $ | Other Special Debt | $ |

Description of Other Income in Section 1.

*Alimony or child support payments need not be disclosed in "Other Income" unless it is desired to have such payments counted toward total income.

**Section 2. Notes Payable to Bank and Others.** (Use attachments if necessary. Each attachment must be identified as a part of this statement and signed.).

| Name and Address of Noteholder(s) | Original Balance | Current Balance | Payment Amount | Frequency (monthly,etc.) | How Secured or Endorsed Type of Collateral |
|---|---|---|---|---|---|
| | | | | | |
| | | | | | |
| | | | | | |
| | | | | | |
| | | | | | |

SBA Form 413 (5-91) Previous Editions Obsolete. Ref: SOP 50-10 and 50-30 (tumble)

Personal Financial Statement (Front)

**Section 3. Stocks and Bonds.** (Use attachments if necessary. Each attachment must be identified as a part of this statement and signed).

| Number of Shares | Name of Securities | Cost | Market Value Quotation/Exchange | Date of Quotation/Exchange | Total Value |
|---|---|---|---|---|---|
| | | | | | |
| | | | | | |
| | | | | | |
| | | | | | |

**Section 4. Real Estate Owned.** (List each parcel separately. Use attachments if necessary. Each attachment must be identified as a part of this statement and signed).

| | Property A | Property B | Property C |
|---|---|---|---|
| Type of Property | | | |
| Name & Address of Title Holder | | | |
| Date Purchased | | | |
| Original Cost | | | |
| Present Market Value | | | |
| Name & Address of Mortgage Holder | | | |
| Mortgage Account Number | | | |
| Mortgage Balance | | | |
| Amount of Payment per Month/Year | | | |
| Status of Mortgage | | | |

**Section 5. Other Personal Property and Other Assets.** (Describe, and if any is pledged as security, state name and address of lien holder, amount of lien, terms of payment, and if delinquent, describe delinquency).

**Section 6. Unpaid Taxes.** (Describe in detail, as to type, to whom payable, when due, amount, and to what property, if any, a tax lien attaches).

**Section 7. Other Liabilities.** (Describe in detail).

**Section 8. Life Insurance Held.** (Give face amount and cash surrender value of policies - name of insurance company and beneficiaries).

I authorize SBA/Lender to make inquiries as necessary to verify the accuracy of the statements made and to determine my creditworthiness. I certify the above and the statements contained in the attachments are true and accurate as of the stated date(s). These statements are made for the purpose of either obtaining a loan or guaranteeing a loan. I understand FALSE statements may result in forfeiture of benefits and possible prosecution by the U.S. Attorney General (Reference 18 U.S.C. 1001).

Signature: Date: Social Security Number:

Signature: Date: Social Security Number:

PLEASE NOTE: The estimated average burden hours for the completion of this form is 1.5 hours per response. If you have questions or comments concerning this estimate or any other aspect of this information, please contact Chief, Administrative Branch, U.S. Small Business Administration, Washington, D.C. 20416, and Clearance Office, Paper Reduction Project (3245-0188), Office of Management and Budget, Washington, D.C. 20503.

*U.S. Government Printing Office: 1991 — 282-429/45503

Personal Financial Statement (Back)

Return Executed Copies 1, 2 and 3 to SBA

OMB APPROVAL NO 3245-0178
Expiration Date 5-31-90

SMALL BUSINESS ADMINISTRATION 1953

United States of America

SMALL BUSINESS ADMINISTRATION

STATEMENT OF PERSONAL HISTORY

**Please Read Carefully - Print or Type**

Each member of the small business concern requesting assistance or the development company must submit this form in TRIPLICATE for filing with the SBA application. This form must be filled out and submitted by

1 If a sole proprietorship by the proprietor
2 If a partnership by each partner
3 If a corporation or a development company, by each officer, director, and additionally by each holder of 20% or more of the voting stock.
4 Any other person including a hired manager, who has authority to speak for and commit the borrower in the management of the business

Name and Address of Applicant (Firm Name) (Street, City, State and ZIP Code)

SBA District Office and City

Amount Applied for

1 Personal Statement of (State name in full, if no middle name, state (NMN), or if initial only, indicate initial) List all former names used, and dates each name was used. Use separate sheet if necessary

First Middle Last

2 Date of Birth (Month, day and year)

3 Place of Birth (City & State or Foreign Country)

U.S. Citizen? ☐ YES ☐ NO
If no, give alien registration number
#

4 Give the percentage of ownership or stock owned or to be owned in the small business concern or the Development Company

Social Security No

5 Present residence address

From To Address

City State

Home Telephone No (Include A/C)

Business Telephone No (Include A/C)

Immediate past residence addres

From To Address

**BE SURE TO ANSWER THE NEXT 3 QUESTIONS CORRECTLY BECAUSE THEY ARE IMPORTANT.**

**THE FACT THAT YOU HAVE AN ARREST OR CONVICTION RECORD WILL NOT NECESSARILY DISQUALIFY YOU. BUT AN INCORRECT ANSWER WILL PROBABLY CAUSE YOUR APPLICATION TO BE TURNED DOWN.**

6 Are you presently under indictment, on parole or probation?

☐ Yes ☐ No If yes, furnish details in a separate exhibit. List name(s) under which held, if applicable

7 Have you ever been charged with or arrested for any criminal offense other than a minor motor vehicle violation?

☐ Yes ☐ No If Yes, furnish details in a separate exhibit. List name(s) under which charged, if applicable

8 Have you ever been convicted of any criminal offense other than a minor vehicle violation?

☐ Yes ☐ No If Yes, furnish details in a separate exhibit. List name(s) under which convicted, if applicable

9 Name and address of participating bank

The information on this form will be used in connection with an investigation of your character. Any information you wish to submit, that you feel will expedite this investigation should be set forth

Whoever makes any statement knowing it to be false, for the purpose of obtaining for himself or for any applicant, any loan, or loan extension by renewal, deferment or otherwise, or for the purpose of obtaining, or influencing SBA toward, anything of value under the Small Business Act, as amended, shall be punished under Section 16(a) of that Act, by a fine of not more than $5000, or by imprisonment for not more than 2 years, or both.

| Signature | Title | Date |
| --- | --- | --- |
| | | |

It is against SBAs policy to provide assistance to persons not of good character and therefore consideration is given to the qualities and personality traits of a person, favorable and unfavorable relating thereto, including behavior, integrity, candor and disposition toward criminal actions. It is also against SBAs policy to provide assistance not in the best interests of the United States, for example, if there is reason to believe that the effect of such assistance will be to encourage or support, directly or indirectly, activities inimical to the Security of the United States. Anyone concerned with the collection of this information, as to its voluntariness, disclosure of routine uses may contact the FOIA Office, 1441 L Street N W and a copy of §9 Agency Collection of Information from SOP 40 04 will be provided

SBA FORM 912 (5-87) SOP 9020 USE 6-85 EDITION UNTIL EXHAUSTED

**1. SBA FILE COPY**

Please Note The estimated burden hours for completion of this form is 15 minutes per response. If you have any questions or comments concerning this estimate or any other aspect of this information collection please contact Chief Administrative Information Branch, U.S. Small Business Administration 409 Third Street S.W. Washington D.C. 20416 or Gary Waxman Clearance Officer Paperwork Reduction Project (3245-0178) Office of Management and Budget Washington D.C. 20503

Statement of Personal History

**PROJECTED PROFIT/LOSS**

| | % | J | F | M | A | M | J | J | A | S | O | N | D | Total |
|---|---|---|---|---|---|---|---|---|---|---|---|---|---|---|
| Total net sales | | | | | | | | | | | | | | |
| Cost, goods sold | | | | | | | | | | | | | | |
| Gross | | | | | | | | | | | | | | |
| | | | | | | | | | | | | | | |
| Controllable expense | | | | | | | | | | | | | | |
| Salaries/wages | | | | | | | | | | | | | | |
| Payroll taxes | | | | | | | | | | | | | | |
| Legal/Accounting | | | | | | | | | | | | | | |
| Advertising | | | | | | | | | | | | | | |
| Automobile | | | | | | | | | | | | | | |
| Office supplies | | | | | | | | | | | | | | |
| Dues/Subscriptions | | | | | | | | | | | | | | |
| Telephone | | | | | | | | | | | | | | |
| Utilities | | | | | | | | | | | | | | |
| Miscellaneous | | | | | | | | | | | | | | |
| Total Con. Exp. | | | | | | | | | | | | | | |
| | | | | | | | | | | | | | | |
| Fixed Expenses | | | | | | | | | | | | | | |
| Rent | | | | | | | | | | | | | | |
| Depreciation | | | | | | | | | | | | | | |
| Insurance | | | | | | | | | | | | | | |
| Licenses/Permits | | | | | | | | | | | | | | |
| Taxes | | | | | | | | | | | | | | |
| Loan Payments | | | | | | | | | | | | | | |
| Total Fixed Exp. | | | | | | | | | | | | | | |
| | | | | | | | | | | | | | | |
| Total Expenses | | | | | | | | | | | | | | |
| | | | | | | | | | | | | | | |
| Net profit/Loss (before tax) | | | | | | | | | | | | | | |

Projected Profit/Loss Statement

## Financing Checklist

To get a better idea of the amount of capital you need and to find out whether you have thoroughly researched the avenues of financing that are open to you, answer the questions in the following Financing Checklist.

| Financing Checklist | Answer Yes or No |
|---|---|
| 1. Have you determined the amount of initial investment required for your business? | ________ |
| 2. Did you include a financial cushion in your estimate? | ________ |
| 3. Have you decided how much of your own money to put into the business? | ________ |
| 4. Have you weighed the pros and cons of debt versus ownership financing? | ________ |
| 5. Have you investigated each of these sources of capital? | |
| Family and friends | ________ |
| Partners | ________ |
| Shareholders | ________ |
| Bondholders | ________ |
| Banks | ________ |
| Savings and loan associations | ________ |
| Credit unions | ________ |
| Small Business Administration | ________ |
| SBICs | ________ |
| CDCs | ________ |
| Suppliers | ________ |
| Venture capitalists | ________ |
| Angels | ________ |
| 6. Have you spoken to your banker about obtaining a loan? | ________ |

*(continued)*

| Financing Checklist *(continued)* | Answer Yes or No |
|---|---|
| 7. Would you give yourself a positive rating in each of the six Cs of credit? | |
| Capital | ________ |
| Collateral | ________ |
| Capability | ________ |
| Character | ________ |
| Coverage | ________ |
| Circumstances | ________ |
| 8. Are you aware of the SBA's criteria for granting loans? | |
| 9. Have you spoken to an accountant regarding the various financing options open to you? | ________ |

# 9

# Controlling Your Inventory

Every business, regardless of whether its primary function is retailing, wholesaling, services, or manufacturing, has one thing in common: inventory. In fact, the major portion of your investment dollars will probably go for inventory. Included in this portion are expenditures for merchandise, supplies, raw materials, and parts, all of which are expected to earn profits for your business. To do so, however, these expenditures must be kept in proper balance. This is the aim of inventory control.

A good inventory-control system does four things:

1. It keeps inventory at the optimum level.
2. It orders goods in the most economical quantities.
3. It speeds up merchandise turnover.
4. It reduces inventory shrinkage.

In other words, it enables you to get maximum value out of your inventory at minimum cost. If it can do all that, it must be complicated, right? Not really. Actually, it's pretty simple. Just as a thermostat is keyed to react to changes in temperature, an inventory-control system reacts to changes (or the lack of changes) in your level of inventory. Once you've set up the system, it's almost totally automatic.

## The Optimum Level of Inventory

Many businesses mistakenly abide by the philosophy that the more inventory you have on hand, the better, as a way of making sure that no sales are lost. What they don't realize is that the costs of carrying the extra inventory could more than equal the potential profits from the additional sales. Added to the cost of the inventory itself are the costs of shipping, storage, insurance, and taxes. Also, there's always the danger that the inventory will become obsolete before it can be used or sold. That's a high price to pay for the security of having your shelves full.

Adopting a let-them-eat-cake attitude isn't the solution either. Purposely letting your business run short on the inventory used for operations or sales is guaranteed to alienate customers and employees alike. Among the costs incurred as a result of inventory shortages are

- Special handling charges and sacrificed purchase discounts because of the need to place rush orders
- Underutilization of personnel, equipment, and facilities
- Lost sales

When sales are involved, your loss can be far-reaching. This is because dissatisfied customers have a tendency to take their future business elsewhere.

This brings us to your objective–the optimum level of inventory. What is it? It's the level of inventory that is the most profitable. Rather than eliminating the costs of stock shortages altogether, or reducing inventory carrying costs to the lowest possible figure, it results in the lowest *total* of the two.

For example:

| *Inventory Level* | *Costs of Stock Shortages* | *Costs of Extra Inventory* | *Total* |
|---|---|---|---|
| A | $1,000 | $8,750 | $9,750 |
| B | $2,500 | $6,500 | $9,000 |
| C | $3,750 | $4,000 | $7,750 |
| D | $5,500 | $3,000 | $8,500 |

The optimum level at which to maintain inventory is level C because this reduces the total cost by the greatest amount.

Once you've established, through trial and error, the optimum level of inventory for your business, it's up to your control system to keep it at that level. This is accomplished by (1) measuring the goods on hand, (2) indicating the amounts needed, and (3) calculating delivery times.

### Measuring the Goods on Hand

This is the way to find out what you have and what you don't have. Does that carton on the top shelf contain a dozen widgets, as marked, or is it empty? There are three ways to find out: Make an educated guess, open the carton and count what's inside, or check your records.

1. *Educated Guess.* This method relies on your memory and powers of observation to determine what's in stock. In the event that your business is small and you're able to keep close tabs on the day-to-day operations, it might be fairly accurate. But there's also a good chance it could be wrong. To be on the safe side, you should do a physical count at least once a year.

2. *Physical Count.* The most accurate, albeit time-consuming, way to monitor your inventory levels is to do a physical count. This means tallying your goods on hand at periodic intervals to make sure that your estimated inventory matches up with your actual inventory.

3. *Perpetual Inventory.* A perpetual inventory system records changes in stock as they occur. Using the information obtained from stock tags, receipts, and requisition forms, the appropriate stock number, size, color, and so on are entered into the inventory system at the time the goods are received, used, or sold. This can be done manually or by computer, using an inventory-management or bar-code scanning system that tracks the goods received upon delivery and the goods sold at the cash register.

### Indicating the Amounts Needed

Having determined the extent of your inventory, you've reached the crucial point in the control process–deciding what to order and how much. This is where the automatic feature of your inventory-control system comes into action. Based on your estimates of the minimum quantities of goods that are required to keep your inventory in balance, the system is programmed to react to specific *reorder points.* Each reorder point represents the level at which an inventory item needs to be replenished. The actual amount to be purchased is determined by such information updates as

- Changes in operations activities
- Changes in customer preferences
- Changes in seasons
- Changes in products (improved, discontinued, and so on)
- Changes in profit margins
- Changes in suppliers

For instance, if the customer demand for a particular item is starting to taper off, you might decide to let that item drop below its reorder point without purchasing additional stock.

## Calculating Delivery Times

The success of your inventory-control system hinges on your ability to calculate delivery times. How long will it take the supplier to fill your order–not just to verify it over the phone, but actually to process the paperwork, pack the goods, and deliver them to your place of business? Unless the goods are on your shelves when you need them, not merely somewhere in transit, your hope of maintaining a balanced inventory is slight.

The way to minimize foul-ups in deliveries is to maintain good supplier relations. This means familiarizing yourself with each supplier's delivery capabilities (lead time needed, special-order policy, dependability, and so on) so that you know what to expect. It also means keeping your requests within reason (not "I need it yesterday"). When suppliers find that you have an understanding of their business operations, they are more inclined to take an interest in yours. If this policy fails and you get poor service, don't be afraid to switch suppliers.

As shown in the Inventory Ordering Cycle chart, by replenishing your stock when it drops to the reorder points, you should have the inventory you need on hand by the time stock levels reach the safety margin.

## Purchase Discounts

In placing your orders, pay close attention to purchase discounts, and determine the most economical order quantity (EOQ) for each item. The

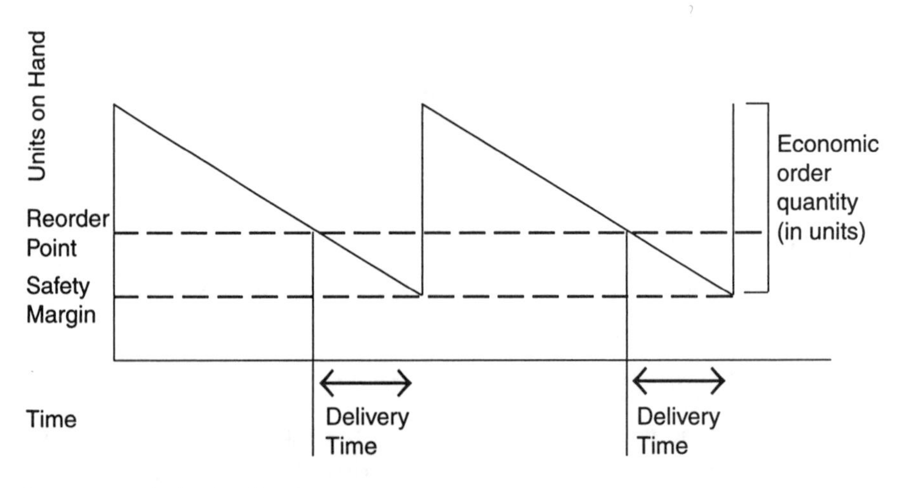


Inventory Ordering Cycle

EOQ is the number of units to order to achieve the lowest total cost when the order and delivery costs are balanced against the inventory carrying costs. For instance, with a large order, your inventory carrying costs are higher, but because of purchase discounts, your ordering and delivery costs are lower. Conversely, with a small order, your carrying costs drop, but your order processing and delivery costs go up.

Some of the purchase discounts that suppliers generally make available include ones linked to order size, total purchases per period, order season, and credit terms.

1. *Order Size.* A discount is given when a larger order is placed. This encourages customers to order in larger quantities, thus reducing the supplier's shipping and handling costs while increasing revenues.
2. *Total Purchases.* A discount is given as the total amount of your purchases per period increases. This is done to stimulate repeat buying.
3. *Order Season.* A discount is given when your order is placed prior to the peak ordering season. In this way, suppliers can even out demand levels and reduce storage requirements.
4. *Credit Terms.* A discount is given when prompt payment is made for goods that have been received. The most commonly offered discount is 2/10, net 30. This authorizes you to deduct 2 percent from your bill if payment is made within 10 days; otherwise you are expected to pay the full amount in 30 days.

By taking advantage of these discounts, you can further reduce your ordering costs. However, this doesn't mean that you should purchase more than you need or can afford in an effort to save money. Each inventory item purchased should be justified on its own merits, exclusive of any accompanying discounts.

## Merchandise Turnover

Your inventory-control system can help you speed up merchandise turnover in a variety of ways, such as by

- Improving purchasing methods
- Monitoring inventory levels
- Identifying hard-to-move items
- Adjusting for seasonal demand
- Recognizing trends

Rather than waiting until you're stuck with an oversupply of any one item, an effective system alerts you to the potential inventory problem before it happens. This enables you to stay on top of things by cutting back orders if necessary, modifying display and sales techniques, reducing markups, or increasing promotional efforts.

Much of the success of the Mrs. Fields Cookies empire can be readily attributed to the computerized inventory-control system in each cookie store. The system tracks cookie sales not just on a daily basis, but down to the hour, and it calculates the amount of cookie dough that's needed to meet the customer demand for fresh-baked cookies still hot from the oven. Monitoring the sales of each type of cookie, the inventory-control system even generates ideas for increasing sales if an item starts to drop below its normal sales volume.

## Universal Product Codes

If your inventory-control system is equipped to make use of bar-code data, so much the better. *Bar codes,* or *universal product codes* (UPCs), as they are officially called, are the vertical lines on packages and price tags that get scanned at electronic cash registers when a purchase is made. Along with telling you the price of an item sold, a bar code can help you to control your inventory by providing such information as the item's

- Stock number
- Size
- Color
- Category/department
- Season

When this data is scanned at the register and entered into your inventory-control system, you can get a good idea of what's moving and what's not.

Although retailers are the greatest users of bar-code data, manufacturers and others are making use of them, too. They may use them to process customers' orders, track inventory as it moves through the production process, and monitor workers' output. The only drawback to using UPC is the price of the electronic equipment. Just as with computers, however, this has been steadily dropping, so more and more small businesses are now utilizing UPC as an inventory-control/accounting tool. For more information on UPC, contact

Uniform Code Council
8163 Old Yankee Rd., Suite J
Dayton, OH 45458
(513) 435-3870

## Just-in-Time Management

Borrowing an idea from the Japanese, an increasing number of manufacturers and service providers, such as furniture manufacturers and film-processing labs, are using an inventory-control technique called *just-in-time* (JIT) management. Rather than optimizing inventory levels, this methods seeks to virtually eliminate them. This involves calculating inventory delivery times right down to the day, or even to the hour, when the supplies are needed. Then the shipment is ordered to be delivered at that precise time. Upon arrival, the inventory goes directly to the work station where it's needed and is immediately utilized. This method can be difficult to put into practice, but when it's successful, it reduces inventory storage and handling costs and gives businesses greater flexibility in adapting to customers' needs, resulting in increased productivity–and profits.

To make JIT work in your business, you'll have to know your inventory needs to the letter and hone your supplier relations to a fine edge. Cooperation is the key. It also helps to be located in close proximity to suppliers to facilitate deliveries. As an added precaution, it's a good idea to use more than one delivery carrier. Many businesses learned this lesson the hard way during the United Parcel Service strike in 1997.

## Inventory Shrinkage

*Inventory shrinkage* refers to unaccountable stock shortages. Inventory that should be in your stockroom or on your shelves may just disappear. This can be caused by employee or customer theft, misplaced stock, or simply poor recordkeeping. Whatever the reason, missing inventory can be a source of frustration and mystification to the business owner, who often feels powerless to stop it.

One way to combat shrinkage is to tighten security. The effectiveness of this method will be diluted, however, unless it is backed up by inventory control. To reduce shrinkage, try the following inventory controls:

- Log in inventory shipments when you receive them.

- Properly file purchase orders and invoices.
- Use requisition forms to keep track of the supplies, materials, and parts used in operating your business.
- Keep a record of all sales transactions.
- Take a physical inventory at least once each year.
- Match perpetual inventory figures against physical inventory results.

These tactics will help you to prevent most inventory shrinkage from occurring and to detect it quickly when it does occur.

## Inventory Checklist

To find out whether your inventory-control system is doing all the things it's supposed to do, answer the questions in the following Inventory Checklist.

| Inventory Checklist | Answer Yes or No |
|---|---|
| 1. Do you have an adequate system for monitoring your level of inventory? | ________ |
| 2. Is a physical count taken at least once a year? | ________ |
| 3. Have you determined the optimum level of inventory for your business? | ________ |
| 4. Have you established reorder points for replenishing inventory items? | ________ |
| 5. Do you make adjustments for changes in customer demand when placing orders? | ________ |
| 6. Are you familiar with suppliers' delivery capabilities? | ________ |
| 7. Do you order in the most economical quantities? | ________ |
| 8. Do you take advantage of purchase discounts? | ________ |
| 9. Do you keep track of slow-moving stock? | ________ |
| 10. Can you spot potential fast movers? | ________ |

| Inventory Checklist *(continued)* | Answer Yes or No |
|---|---|
| 11. Is your merchandise inventory balanced by price line, color, size, and type? | _______ |
| 12. Do you select merchandise items with your target customers in mind? | _______ |
| 13. Are you taking preventive action against inventory shrinkage? | _______ |
| 14. Is your inventory as profitable as it should be? | _______ |

# 10

# Setting the Price

In setting the prices for your products and services, among the facts to be considered are the reactions of your customers, the stiffness of the competition, and the state of the economy. Strange as it may seem, a price that's too low can be just as much of a turnoff to customers as a price that's too high. Low prices are often interpreted as signifying low value or inferior merchandise. As for the competition, because your business doesn't exist in a vacuum, you must recognize the role of the other businesses in influencing your prices. You may decide to go head-to-head with competitors on prices, matching them dollar for dollar, or to undercut them, or to charge higher prices. The strategy you choose is crucial to your pricing. Take care also not to overlook the state of the economy. Unemployment, inflation, interest rates, government policies, and levels of investment all have an effect on consumer spending and therefore on your prices.

You must also consider another factor: profit. If your prices are so low that they fail to cover your expenses, or so high that an insufficient number of people want to buy from you, the result is a loss of profits. Your goal is to meet the demands of customers, keep an eye on competitors and the economy, and assure yourself of satisfactory profits.

## Pricing and Customers

Part of knowing what prices to charge comes from knowing your customers. One customer's bargain may be another's extravagance. Affluent customers generally demand high-quality merchandise, personalized service, and an exclusive and attractive environment in which to shop. In exchange for these amenities, they are not only willing to pay more, but also *expect* to pay more. Low-income customers, on the other hand, are primarily concerned with stretching their dollars. They're willing to settle for less quality and service and a no-frills, discount-house environment in exchange for lower prices. In each case the price is what counts.

In the beginning, formulating a price strategy to please your customers may seem like trying to solve the riddle of the chicken and the egg. Which comes first? Should you set your prices and then wait for your target customers to find you, or should you wait to see what kind of customers you attract, and then develop an appropriate pricing strategy? The answer is both. To a great extent, your pricing strategy will be predetermined by your type of business, location, target customers, expenses, and so on. Even so, you also have to stay in touch with your customers to make sure that your prices, quality, and service continue to reflect their needs and wants.

## Pricing and Competition

Keeping tabs on competitors' prices helps you to assess your own pricing strategy. Are yours higher or lower than the competition? If your prices are higher, you're probably losing out on sales. If your prices are lower, you may be making more sales but passing up additional profits. In comparing your prices with the competition, don't forget to compare service as well. Services add to the value of a product and therefore to its price. Such services as a prestigious location, attractive facilities, personal attention, credit, gift wrapping, validated parking, warranties, and home deliveries benefit your customers. The more services you provide, the higher your prices are likely to be.

Here are some of the sources of information you can use to stay in touch with competitors' pricing strategies.

**Customers** Observe your customers' shopping habits, and listen to what they have to say, so that you can get a pretty good idea of how your prices stack up against the competition.

**Suppliers** Because *your* suppliers are also *their* suppliers, this is another source of competitive information. Don't forget that the information flows both ways. Your competitors can tap into the same source to find out about you.

**Advertising** By following competitors' promotional campaigns, you can keep track of pricing changes and obtain current information about the quality and service being provided.

**Competitors' Catalogs and Price Lists** When these are available, they are an excellent source of information, particularly because the prices are not only current but also conveniently arranged for easy reference.

**Price Checkers** These shoppers are employed by you to go out and gather information about competitors' prices. While pretending to shop, they actually record the prices of various key items.

## Pricing and the Economy

Customer shopping habits reflect the state of the economy. During a recession or depression, customers are at their most price conscious. Worried about the high cost of living, threats of unemployment, and cutbacks in credit, they want to make every dollar count. As the economy improves, customers become more optimistic about the future and are more willing to pay higher prices. When the economy is at its peak and business is booming, customers offer little resistance to rising prices. The general feeling is that there's more money where that came from, so why not spend it?

As a business owner, your ability to recognize these fluctuations in the economy and to adjust your prices accordingly adds to your competitiveness. To keep your prices in line with customers' expectations, you may add or drop services, raise or lower quality standards, change your markups, or put together some combination of these.

## Pricing and Profit

Your prices should be set at a level sufficient to reimburse you for the cost of the goods or services sold, cover your overhead costs, and provide a profit. The amount of profit you receive will be dependent on your gross margin, or *markup*. This is the difference between the cost and the selling price of the goods sold. The higher the markup, the greater your profit *per sale*. However, this doesn't necessarily mean that your overall profits will be higher. Why? Because higher markups usually result in reduced sales. This explains why discount stores are able to make healthy profits despite lower-than-average markups. Their sales volume is higher.

## Pricing Methods

There are a number of pricing methods to choose from, ranging from the simple to the complex. Here are three of the most commonly used methods.

1. *Competitive Pricing.* Prices are set at or below the competition's. Costs are made to conform to the prices that have been set.
2. *Standard Markup Pricing.* A standard markup is computed and then added to the cost of the goods or services sold. Some businesses apply a single markup across the board, while others have different markups for each sales category.
3. *Cost-Oriented Pricing.* Prices are set individually, based on the cost of the goods or services sold, the overhead, and the desired profit.

Of the three methods, cost-oriented pricing is the most accurate but also the most complex and time-consuming because each product or service is evaluated separately. A standard markup saves time by eliminating the need to do individual computations. For a store that carries hundreds or thousands of merchandise items, this can make a big difference. Competitive pricing is the simplest method of all. Prices are virtually preset, being based on what's acceptable for your industry.

Common sense and a little experimentation will soon tell you which method or combination of methods works best for you. If you're in a highly competitive industry where the key determinant of sales is the price, you'll have little choice but to use the competitive pricing method. For businesses with extensive inventories, time considerations alone will dictate that some sort of standardized markup be used. The cost-oriented pricing method is normally used by business offering one-of-a-kind products or specialized services.

## More about Markups

If you aren't careful in computing markups, you can easily shortchange yourself. A common mistake among new business owners is to forget to include all relevant expenses in the final figure. As a result, potential profits are eaten up and sometimes even converted into losses. Your markup needs to cover all administrative expenses, all selling expenses, and all losses stemming from merchandise discounts, theft, or damage. In addition, it has to provide a measure of profit.

This holds true regardless of which pricing method you use. In the standard markup method, these cost and profit considerations are all built into the markup figure itself. With cost-oriented pricing, they are added as you go. In competitive pricing, you work backward from the price to figure the markup.

### Markup to Price

You can determine what your selling price would be, given a particular markup, by using this formula:

$$\text{Selling price} = \frac{\text{Cost of goods or services}}{100 - \text{Markup}} \times 100$$

For instance, if a man's suit costs \$160 and your markup is 50 percent, you would calculate the selling price as follows:

$$\text{Selling price} = \frac{\$160}{100 - 50} \times 100$$

$$\text{Selling price} = \$320$$

### Price to Markup

If you're considering a particular price and want to know what the amount of your markup would be, you can figure that out, too:

$$\text{Markup} = \frac{\text{Selling price} - \text{Cost}}{\text{Selling price}}$$

Using the cost and selling price from the previous example, the markup would be calculated like this:

$$\text{Markup} = \frac{\$320 - \$160}{\$320}$$

$$\text{Markup} = \frac{\$160}{\$320} = 50\%$$

Many retailers use a method called the *keystone markup,* which avoids percentages altogether and entails simply doubling the cost of an item to obtain its selling price. Although quick and easy, this method obviously can't be used in all situations.

## Pricing Strategy

Now that you have the basics, it's time to consider strategy. If pricing were just a matter of plugging different numbers into a formula and coming up with the right figure, it wouldn't require any strategy at all—just a good head for numbers. This isn't the case. In addition to mathematical ability, you need marketing savvy.

### Market Response: Elasticity

The first thing you need to find out is how responsive your market is to a change in price. This responsiveness is called *elasticity*. Products such as eggs, baking soda, razor blades, and medicine are highly *inelastic*. Regardless of whether their prices are raised or lowered, customers continue to purchase them in approximately the same quantities. Customer demand for some products, on the other hand, fluctuates with the price. A small change in price–up or down–results in a decrease or increase in the number of units sold. This type of response is said to be *elastic*. For example, television sets, strawberries, clothing, and jewelry are highly elastic.

As a rule, items considered to be necessities are less elastic than those considered to be luxuries. This is because the customer's need, rather than the product's price, triggers the purchase of necessities. For instance, a person with a headache doesn't wait until aspirin is on sale before buying it. The need to get rid of the headache takes priority over the price.

How does all this affect your pricing strategy? For one thing, the more inelastic your product is, the easier it is to raise your prices without hurting your sales. That means greater profits on the same volume. To increase your profits on highly elastic products, rather than raising your prices, you might try lowering them. Although this reduces your profit on each unit sold, the resultant increase in sales volume should increase your overall profits.

### Other Determinants of Price

In addition to product elasticity, other pricing determinants include

- Volume
- Image
- Consumer psychology
- Product life span
- Profit objectives

**Volume** Are you selling to a mass market or just an elite few? High-volume businesses generally employ low markups. Conversely, the lower your volume is, the higher the markup you'll need to cover your overhead and provide a profit.

**Image** Do you want you business known for its quality or for having the best buys? If you're after a quality image, you may decide to use a *prestige* pricing strategy. This strategy calls for deliberately setting prices high in order to attract affluent customers. The opposite of prestige pricing is *leader* pricing. Used to draw large numbers of customers into a store, leader pricing emphasizes low-priced specials that have common appeal. Two-for-one sales and cents-off coupons are typical of this strategy.

**Customer Psychology** According to market researchers, consumers react more favorably to certain prices than others. An item selling for $9.95 or even $9.99 has a better chance of being purchased than the identical item at $10. Even though the difference is insignificant, psychologically it makes a difference.

**Product Life Span** What's the life span of your product? If you're selling fashion or *fad* items (string bikinis, pet rocks) that appeal to customers for only a brief time, you need to make your profits quickly. Otherwise, you could be left holding a bagful of expenses when the demand drops off. The longer your product's life span, the longer the period of time you have in which to earn your profits. This explains the numerous claims by advertisers that their products are new and improved. For the most part, such assertions are nothing more than attempts to stretch a product's life span and extend profits.

**Profit Objectives** In formulating a pricing strategy, the key is not to lose sight of your overall objective: maintaining profitability. This may mean taking a loss on one product to stimulate the sales of another (leader pricing). It can also call for changes in your method of operation (high volume versus low volume).

## Marketing Mix

Just as your business doesn't exist in a vacuum, neither do your pricing decisions. Price is only one of the four components that make up the *marketing mix.* The others–product, place, and promotion–must all be in harmony with the prices you set. The products and services you decide to sell, your distribution system, and the messages you communicate about your business directly influence your pricing strategy and profitability.

Based on your marketing-mix objectives, you may want to employ one or more of the following pricing strategies.

- Skimming
- Penetration
- Price lining
- Promotional pricing
- Price bundling
- Time-period pricing
- Value-added pricing
- Captive pricing

**Skimming** Used for new, innovative products that are just being introduced into the marketplace, a skimming strategy calls for you to set your price high in the beginning and then to lower it over time as a product becomes more widely accepted. The advantage of this approach is that it enables businesses to quickly recoup their research, development, and promotion costs. It is most often used for high-tech consumer electronics and computer products, or for high-fashion or fad products with short life spans.

**Penetration** This strategy involves pricing your products low and keeping the prices low in an effort to penetrate the market and gain wide distribution and consumer acceptance. Because it entails shrinking your profit margins, this strategy works only with low-cost products that can be mass produced and are capable of achieving high sales volumes. This strategy is usually employed for low-tech, frequently purchased items, such as soft drinks, soap, and candy bars.

**Price Lining** Businesses employing this strategy categorize their products within different price ranges, or *lines* (high, medium, low), and price them accordingly. A clothing retailer, for example, may carry men's ties that sell for under $12, $12.95–$24.95, and over $25. Depending on what customers are willing to spend, they can then choose from the preferred price range. This method makes it easier for businesses to price and display their products–and for customers to buy them.

**Promotional Pricing** As the name implies, this strategy offers lower, "limited time only" prices on specific products to stimulate sales. It can be utilized for special-purchase items that have been bought at a discount or are linked to customers' buying times (holidays, seasons, events, and so on). Lowering the price of hot dogs and buns during the World Series or having a special promotion on patio furniture during the summer are examples.

**Price Bundling** This strategy consists of "bundling" separate products or services together and selling them as a package. For example, a hotel might offer a "fun and sun" package that includes lodging, meals, and bicycle rentals. Other bundled-price packages include dinner combos (entrée, dessert, and beverage), beauty kits containing cosmetics products, and flashlights sold with batteries.

**Time-Period Pricing** This strategy raises or lowers prices based on consumer demand levels at various times, charging higher prices at peak times and lower prices during slow times. "Early bird" restaurant specials and off-season travel discounts are examples.

**Value-Added Pricing** A business using this strategy offers an additional service or gift when a customer makes a regularly priced purchase. Widely used in the cosmetics field, other examples of value-added pricing include offering a maintenance contract with a computer system, a T-shirt with a pair of running shoes, or a book with a magazine subscription.

**Captive Pricing** With this pricing strategy, you set your price low on one product, then make your profit by selling customers other products that go with it. Selling low-price razors to make money on the blades is a classic example. Utilizing this approach, a weight-loss clinic might offer low-price memberships in the clinic to make money selling food supplements and prepared meals to members (a captive market).

These are just some of the most frequently used pricing strategies. By taking a creative approach, you should be able to adapt them to your own needs or to come up with other pricing strategies that are uniquely suited to your business.

## Pricing Strategy Checklist

For help in developing your pricing strategy and keeping it on target, answer the questions in the following Pricing Strategy Checklist. Afterward, compare your answers to see whether there are any inconsistencies in your overall pricing strategy.

| Pricing Strategy Checklist | Answer Yes or No |
|---|---|
| 1. Do you try to evaluate the market forces affecting the demand for your products? | ________ |
| 2. Have you considered what price strategies would be compatible with your total marketing mix? | ________ |
| 3. Do you know which products are slow movers and which are fast? | ________ |
| 4. Do you know which products are elastic and which are inelastic? | ________ |
| 5. Do you know your competitors' pricing strategies? | ________ |
| 6. Are you influenced by competitors' price changes? | ________ |
| 7. Do you regularly review competitors' ads to update your information on their prices? | ________ |
| 8. Is your store large enough to employ a comparison shopper? | ________ |
| 9. Is there a specific time of year when your competitors have sales? | ________ |
| 10. Do your customers expect sales at certain times? | ________ |

*(continued)*

| Pricing Strategy Checklist *(continued)* | Answer Yes or No |
|---|---|
| 11. Would periodic special sales, combining reduced prices and heavier advertising, be consistent with the store image you are seeking? | ________ |
| 12. Should you use any leader offerings (selected products with quite low, less profitable prices)? | ________ |
| 13. Will you use cents-off coupons in newspaper ads or mailed to selected consumers on any occasion? | ________ |
| 14. Will odd-ending prices, such as $9.95 or $9.99, be more appealing to your customers than even-ending pricing? | ________ |
| 15. Have you determined whether to price below, at, or above the market? | ________ |
| 16. Do you determine specific markups for each product? | ________ |
| 17. Do you use standardized markups for product categories? | ________ |
| 18. Are your prices set so as to cover the full costs on every sale? | ________ |
| 19. Are additional markups called for because of cost increases or because an item's low price causes consumers to question its quality? | ________ |
| 20. Should employees be given purchase discounts? | ________ |
| 21. Should any group of customers, such as students or senior citizens, be given purchase discounts? | ________ |

# 11

# Staffing

The most valuable asset of any business is its people. Land, buildings, merchandise, and equipment may dominate a balance sheet, but they don't make a business successful; people do. The best businesses have the best people–capable, creative, energetic people. To attract these people, you need both ingenuity and initiative, but the payoff in productivity is worth it. Staffing your business with the best people available should be one of your highest priorities.

One way to get results is to place a sign in your window saying, "Help wanted, apply within"–but not necessarily the way to get the results you want. A sign in the window will probably bring in a stream of applicants. Unless they possess the skills to do the job, however, you may waste a great deal of time interviewing and still not find anyone you want to hire. Generally, the sign in the window works only when the position to be filled calls for little or no skill and entails minimal responsibility. How, then, should you go about hiring the people you need? First, it's important to realize that hiring is only one element in staffing. Staffing is an ongoing process that involves finding qualified people, hiring them, making the best use of their skills and abilities, and having them stay on the job instead of quitting and taking their talents elsewhere.

The steps you must take *before* you hire anyone are to (1) analyze each job, (2) prepare job descriptions, (3) check recruitment sources, (4) use application forms, (5) conduct interviews, and (6) verify information. *After* the hiring decision is made, you have to (1) provide job orientation, (2) provide training, (3) evaluate performance, (4) compensate employees, and (5) monitor employee turnover. By following these steps, instead of waiting for fate to send you perfect employees or complaining about your current employees, you can control and direct the staffing process.

## Analyze Each Job

This is the most important step in staffing because it forms the basis for any hiring decisions you make. Unfortunately, it's often skipped over by employers who, in a rush to get a position filled quickly, would rather hire now and ask questions later. Then, when confronted with poor performance, low morale, and high turnover, they wonder why it's so hard to find good workers any more. Taking a little more time in the beginning is the way to avoid a great many problems later.

During job analysis, ask yourself,

- What work has to be accomplished?
- Do I need additional help to do it?
- How many people do I need?
- Would part-time help be sufficient?
- What skills am I looking for?
- How much experience is required?
- Is the labor market favorable?
- How much am I able to pay?

You may find that you don't need to hire anyone after all. Perhaps, if you reschedule the work flow or juggle work assignments, your present staff can handle the work. Instead, you may find out that one additional person isn't enough. Maybe you need to hire two or more people to keep pace with the workload–perhaps a job you thought anyone can do may in fact require someone with specific skills. The answer to your questions can be surprising. That's the point of doing a job analysis. It's better to be surprised *before* you hire someone, rather than *after*. The choice is yours. You can be the one saying, "If only I'd known," or you can take the time to find out.

## Prepare Job Descriptions

A *job description* is a written record of the duties and responsibilities associated with a particular job. It serves a dual purpose, making it easier for you to match the right person to the right job and informing all employees of what their jobs entail.

In preparing a job description, include the following details:

- A general description of the job

- The duties to be performed
- The job responsibilities
- Specific skills needed
- Education and experience required

For instance, a receiving clerk in a store might have a job description that looks like the sample shown here. Once you've put everything down on paper, you're ready to start looking for the person who fits the description.

## Check Recruitment Sources

The method of recruitment that you decide to use depends on your business. Waiters and waitresses might easily be recruited from your local

*Job Title:* Receiving clerk

*Supervisor:* Store owner

*Summary:* Responsible for receiving shipments from suppliers. Removes goods from containers and places them on warehouse shelves. Prepares and processes paperwork and maintains receiving files.

*Duties and Responsibilities:*

- Removing stock from containers and placing merchandise on warehouse shelves
- Checking invoices against merchandise received
- Inspecting merchandise
- Entering data into computerized inventory system
- Maintaining inventory records
- Assisting in physical inventory
- Keeping warehouse clean and orderly

*Job Specifications:*

- Education: High school graduate
- Experience: Preferred, but not required
- Skills: Must be able to organize material; work with numbers; interact well with people; computer literate

Sample Job Description

high school. Finding qualified real-estate brokers or skilled carpenters calls for a different method. Some of the sources to choose from are

- Public employment agencies
- Private employment agencies
- Newspaper advertisements
- Local schools
- Unions
- Trade and professional associations

**Public Employment Agencies** Public employment agencies operate throughout each state, finding and placing both blue-collar and white-collar workers. They will recruit and screen job applicants, sending you only the ones who meet your specifications, at no charge.

**Private Employment Agencies** Private employment agencies operate much the same as public ones, except that there is a fee involved. Either you pay it or the person who is hired pays it.

**Newspaper Advertisements** A newspaper advertisement enables you to reach a large pool of interested job applicants quickly. However, it's important to design your ad in such a way as to attract those who are qualified while discouraging the unqualified. The way to do this is to (1) make it interesting, (2) give adequate details about the job, (3) indicate the skills needed, and (4) specify the education and experience. A general guideline is to stick to a straightforward approach because cute or exaggerated copy tends to generate a negative reaction.

**Local Schools** Contacting the placement centers at local high schools and colleges is a good way to find applicants who are long on potential, though usually short on experience. If you're looking for part-time help, definitely consider this source.

**Unions** For a number of jobs, ranging from plumbers to publicists, the way to recruit qualified personnel is to go through their respective unions. In some instances, this is your only alternative.

**Trade and Professional Associations** Most trade and professional associations are eager to help employers obtain the services of their members. Whether you need to find an accountant, sales manager, management trainee, computer specialist, or supervisor, the local association is a good place to check.

As your business grows, other recruitment sources such as employee referrals, previous job applications on file, and industry contacts will become increasingly useful. Another way to speed up the recruitment process is to have job applicants fax or e-mail their résumés to you. In time, you may want to set up a hiring website listing current job openings.

## Use Application Forms

Job-application forms simplify the hiring decision by helping you screen out unsuitable applicants and focus on qualified ones. The application can also serve as a starting point during an interview, suggesting questions or comments that make it easier to break the ice and establish rapport with the applicant.

Your application form needn't be long or complicated to be effective. In fact, the simpler you can keep it, the better. The important thing is to cover the information relevant to a prospective employee's job performance.

In developing the job application form you will be using, keep in mind that federal law prohibits discriminating against anyone on the basis of race, sex, religion, color, or national origin. Nor can you automatically rule out an applicant because of age or physical or mental handicap. To stay in compliance with the law, your best bet is to restrict your questions to those that focus on an applicant's ability to do the work.

## Conduct Interviews

Interviews of prospective employees give you the opportunity to find out more about each applicant's employment background, skills, and education, as well as to evaluate such factors as the applicant's enthusiasm, ability to communicate, poise, and personal appearance.

### Preparing for the Interview

In conducting interviews, select a private, comfortable location in which to talk. It is counterproductive to try to carry on a conversation over the sounds of machinery or ringing telephones. You want to put the appli-

Name ______________________________ Date ______________
(Last) (First) (Middle)

Address ______________________________ Telephone ______________

Social security number ______________ Are you over 18? ________

Job skills: ______________________________

Equipment you can operate: ______________________________

May we contact your present and previous employers? ______________

**Employment History (Last position first)**

From To Name & Address Position Reason for leaving

1. ______________________________
2. ______________________________
3. ______________________________
4. ______________________________

**Education**

Name & Address Major Degree

High School ______________________________

College ______________________________

Other ______________________________

**References**

Name & Address Telephone Relationship

1. ______________________________
2. ______________________________

I understand that if I am employed and any statement is then found to be not true, I may be released immediately.

Signature ______________________________ Date ______________

Application for Employment

cant at ease so that you can gather the information you need. The trick is to get the other person talking. Too many interviewers dominate the conversation themselves, and then when it's time to make an evaluation, they have little to go on.

The way to get the most out of interviews is to be ready for them. For a start, review the job application prior to each interview. This will give you some idea of the person you are about to meet. Keep the application with you during the interview as well, so that you can refer to it, as needed, or make notes on it. Many staffing experts also recommend that you write out a few questions in advance. Then, instead of worrying about what to ask next, you can really listen to what's being said. Immediately after the interview is over, jot down your evaluation of the applicant before you forget anything.

### Questions You Can and Cannot Ask

These guidelines should help you to avoid asking discriminatory questions. To make sure you are in compliance with the law, contact your state's Department of Fair Employment.

#### You Can Ask

- Have you ever used another name?
- What is your place of residence?
- If you are hired, can you show proof of age?
- Are you over 18 years old?
- If you are hired, can you provide verification of your right to work in the United States?
- What languages can you speak, read, or write?
- What is the name and address of a parent or guardian (if applicant is a minor)?
- Do you have any physical or mental condition that would keep you from performing your job?
- Have you ever been convicted of a felony?
- What skills have you acquired through military service?
- What professional organizations do you belong to?

**You Cannot Ask**

- What is your maiden name?
- Do you own or rent your home?
- How old are you? What is your birthdate?
- When did you attend school?
- Are you a U.S. citizen?
- Where were you born? Your parents?
- What is your native tongue?
- With whom do you live?
- Are you married, single, or divorced?
- What does your spouse do?
- How many children do you have? What are their ages?
- Have you made provisions for child care?
- What race are you? What color?
- What is your height and weight?
- Do you have any physical or mental disabilities?
- Have you ever applied for Workers' Compensation?
- What is your religion?
- Have you ever been arrested?
- When did you serve in the military? What type of discharge did you receive?
- What organizations or clubs do you belong to?

## Verify Information

Even if you're positive that you've found the best person for the job, don't hire anyone yet. Before you do, there's one more step: Verify the information you've been given. Regardless of how favorable a first impression may be, there's no substitute for checking the facts. It's not a matter of doubting your own judgment; it's just good business sense.

In verifying academic information, ask to see an official copy of the applicant's record from each school attended. Dates of attendance, courses taken, and grades received should all appear on the record. To check an applicant's work history, contact previous employers. This can be done by phone, by letter, or in person. In so doing, though, be prepared to take all comments with a grain of salt; former employers sometimes exaggerate a past employee's attributes, achievements, or failings. Your job is to try to separate the facts from the fiction.

## Make the Hiring Decision

Congratulations! Having gone through the previous steps, with any luck, you're now ready to select the person you want to hire. This is a time to celebrate–but not a time to rest on your laurels. The staffing process continues as you provide job orientation and training, evaluate performances, offer compensation, and monitor turnover.

### Provide Job Orientation

You need to help each employee feel comfortable in your business. Starting a new job is a cause for uncertainty, no matter how terrific the job is. Getting to know coworkers, keeping track of new duties and responsibilities, and attempting to figure out how the organization operates can easily overwhelm a new employee. It takes time to adjust to a new job. It also takes help from you.

The purpose of a job-orientation program is to answer as many questions as possible about your business and the new employee's position within it. Right off the bat, the employee should be filled in on the company's policies and regulations, as well as the employee's duties and responsibilities, compensation, and benefits.

Many businesses, small as well as large, provide new hires with an employee handbook that contains the information they need to know. While no substitute for personal communication exists, an employee handbook can help to put your business in the proper perspective and to simplify the employee's adjustment. In putting together a handbook, don't feel that it has to be a thick volume, complete with pictures and a fancy cover. A few typewritten pages of clearly presented information can generally do the job. Among the subjects you want to cover in detail are

- The company's history
- An explanation of the company's products or services
- Company policies and procedures
- Employee compensation and benefits

## Provide Training

The welfare of both your business and your employees rests on the quality of training that you provide. To carry out their current jobs and to obtain the skills necessary to advance into more challenging jobs, employees need guidance and training. Without it, skills and motivation begin to stagnate and decline, productivity drops off, and the business suffers–needlessly.

A training program helps employees to grow so that they can help your business grow. Some of the programs often used are on-the-job training, job rotation, specialized training, and management development.

*On-the-job training* endeavors to instruct an employee in how to carry out a particular job assignment. Equally useful in training new employees and employees who are changing jobs, it consists of four parts:

1. *Preparation.* The trainer finds out what the employee already knows about the job.
2. *Demonstration.* The trainer shows the employee how to do the job.
3. *Application.* The employee does the job alone.
4. *Inspection.* The trainer inspects the work and makes suggestions or comments on it.

*Job rotation* allows employees to learn new jobs and to broaden their skills by working at different assignments on a temporary basis. As a result, workers become more versatile, tedium is reduced, and scheduling is simplified because of worker flexibility.

*Specialized training* can enable an employee to hone old skills or to master new ones. Through courses offered by the company, or by outside sources such as local colleges or trade schools, employees can learn how to operate a new piece of machinery, type faster, improve sales presentations, read a blueprint, or do any number of things beneficial to both the employees and the company.

*Management development* is geared toward training people to enter management or to advance within the managerial ranks. By means of courses on such subjects as leadership, decision making, planning, and communication, employees can be groomed to accept more responsibility.

## Evaluate Performance

Employees need a yardstick by which to measure their performance and progress. This can be supplied in the form of performance evaluations.

Conducted at regular intervals, this evaluation should highlight an employee's strengths and pinpoint the areas that need improvement.

One method of evaluation that is popular with employees and employers alike is *management by objectives* (MBO). Its appeal stems from the fact that it contains no surprises or hidden clauses; everything expected of the employee is spelled out in advance as objectives. Furthermore, these objectives are determined jointly by the worker and the worker's boss. Together, as a team, they set down on paper the targets that the employee will strive to reach. Later, when it's time to evaluate the employee's performance, it's easy to see which objectives have been met and which ones need additional work. New objectives can then be set, and the evaluation process continues.

### Compensate Employees

To attract and retain high-caliber employees, it's necessary to compensate them at the going wage or better. Trying to get something for nothing just leads to employee dissatisfaction and high turnover. Also, if your employees feel that you're taking advantage of them, chances are that they'll find a way to take advantage of you. Work slowdowns and theft are just two of the many ways possible.

In addition to comparing favorably with the competition, your policy on wages should be equitable, rewarding employees on the basis of merit. This instills loyalty and motivates employees to work harder and to expand their skills, so that they can increase their earnings.

Another kind of compensation that employees have come to expect is a set of *fringe benefits.* These consist of such components as a health plan, pension plan, life insurance, bonuses, and profit sharing. These vary from company to company and may not be applicable or affordable for your business. They should certainly be considered, however.

### Monitor Employee Turnover

Once an employee quits, who cares what the employee thinks about your business? You do. It's just as important to pay heed to an employee's reason for leaving as it is to listen to a job applicant's reasons for wanting to work for you. This is your chance to find out something about your business that might help you to make it a better place in which to work. Hiring and training employees is costly and time-consuming. Any information associated with reducing turnover is worth listening to.

1. Name of employee ______________________________
2. Date ____________________
3. Department ____________________ 4. Shift ____________
5. Date hired ____________________
6. Address ______________________________
______________________________
7. Education ______________________________
8. Job title or position ______________________________
9. Name of supervisor ______________________________
10. Would you rehire? ____________
11. Previous training ______________________________
______________________________
12. Type of separation ______________________________
______________________________
13. Reasons for separation ______________________________
______________________________
14. Indirect causes for separation ______________________________
______________________________
15. Action taken ______________________________
______________________________

Exit Interview Report

Before the employee leaves, schedule an *exit interview.* During this interview, ask the employee the reasons for leaving (e.g., better salary, promotion, dissatisfaction with the job, return to school, spouse's job transfer). Also solicit the employee's opinions regarding the company, its policies, and its personnel. Your goal isn't to debate the issues or to convince a dissatisfied worker to stay, but to obtain information you can use in making future plans. A sample form to use for this interview is provided above.

## Staffing Checklist

In order to recruit, hire, and retain the best people available for your business, take a moment to answer the questions in the following Staffing Checklist.

| Staffing Checklist | Answer Yes or No |
|---|---|
| 1. Have you analyzed each job that you want filled? | __________ |
| 2. Have you prepared job descriptions? | __________ |
| 3. Do you know what sources to use in recruiting employees? | __________ |
| 4. Will you use an application form? | __________ |
| 5. Do you know the information that can and cannot be included on an application form? | __________ |
| 6. Do you know what questions to ask in an interview? | __________ |
| 7. Will you verify the information received from each applicant that you are seriously considering? | __________ |
| 8. Have you decided on the kind of job orientation to give your new employees? | __________ |
| 9. Have you prepared an employee handbook? | __________ |
| 10. Do you know which form(s) of job training to utilize? | __________ |
| 11. Have you determined how often to evaluate your employees? | __________ |
| 12. Do you intend to use an evaluation form when evaluating employees? | __________ |
| 13. Will your employees be adequately compensated for the work they perform? | __________ |
| 14. Are you planning to monitor employee turnover? | __________ |
| 15. Will you use an exit interview report? | __________ |
| 16. Do you intend to listen to the advice of employees who are leaving and take advantage of worthwhile suggestions? | __________ |

# 12

# Managing and Motivating

The key to entrepreneurial success is getting others to commit to your vision and to work at making it a reality. Few successful businesses are the result of one person's solo efforts. It isn't enough for an entrepreneur to be good at producing a product or performing a service. If your business is to grow and prosper, you must be a leader.

In addition to finding the best qualified people to work in your business, you need to come up with effective ways to manage and motivate them. Technical skills alone won't do it. Your technical skills can get your business started, but it's your human-relations skills that will keep it going.

## Developing Your Own Management Style

No one management style is best for everyone. You will have to find a style that you feel comfortable with and that works well in your particular situation. In the broadest sense, there are as many ways to manage as there are managers. When focusing on the most commonly used management styles, though, three become clear: autocratic, democratic, and free-rein.

### Autocratic Management

Business owners who use an *autocratic management style* keep most of the authority to themselves, making decisions without consulting others. More inclined to give orders than to seek advice, they generally adopt a take-charge approach to management. When the situation calls for fast, decisive action, they are ready to move.

The autocratic management style works best in fast-paced, volatile industries where there isn't time to confer with others and in situations where employees lack experience or motivation. The drawback to this style is that it can generate resentment and frustration among workers who feel that their input is being ignored. Furthermore, by making all the decisions alone, entrepreneurs can end up limiting their businesses' growth potential by failing to develop the employee management talent needed to run a larger operation.

### Democratic Management

As a name implies, a *democratic management style* gives employees a much greater say in decision making. Rather than making unilateral decisions and expecting employees to carry them out, the democratic entrepreneur encourages employees to get involved in the process. Business owners who take a *participative* approach to managing delegate authority whenever possible but retain the final right to approval.

The democratic management style works best with employees who have strong job skills and require only minimal supervision. Among its advantages are the feelings of belonging, pride, and commitment it can instill in workers and its ability to tap employees' ideas and ingenuity for the good of the business. The main disadvantages of this management style are the time it takes to get employees' input and the weakening or "watering down" of decisions that can occur in reaching consensus.

### Free-Rein Management

A *free-rein management style*–also called a *laissez-faire style,* from the French expression "leave it alone"–gives employees the most authority of all. Business owners who use this style hire the best workers they can find and let them make the majority of the decisions concerning their job functions and responsibilities. The entrepreneur, using a hands-off approach to managing, sets goals and objectives for the business but leaves employees relatively free to perform their duties as they see fit.

The free-rein management style works best with professionals (such as engineers, scientists, writers, and others) who are expected to function independently. It's often used with outside salespeople who operate in the field and must determine the best ways to manage their time and serve customers' needs. The main weakness of this style is that by letting employees set their own agendas, workers can end up pursuing their own interests rather than the ones most beneficial to the business.

## Choosing a Style

To find the right management style for you, you should look at three factors:

1. Yourself
2. Your employees
3. The work environment

**Looking at Yourself** Being a good manager isn't just knowing what makes people tick, but what makes *you* tick. The more you know about yourself, your management abilities, and your own temperament, the better you will be able to capitalize on your strengths and compensate for your weaknesses. How willing are you to share authority with others? Have you ever managed people before? How many? For how long? In what capacity? What's your approach to problem solving? Are you more comfortable working alone or as part of a team?

**Looking at Your Employees** Just as managers are different, so are the people they manage. Part of choosing a management style involves matching it to your workforce. Which of the following alternatives are your employees more likely to do?

1. Show initiative, work independently without supervision, accept responsibility, creatively solve problems, and take pride in doing their jobs well?
2. Avoid work when they can, goof off, wait for someone to tell them what to do, and cut corners when no one's looking?

In the first instance, less supervision is needed; a management style that gives employees more say in decision making should work well. In the second instance, though, a more autocratic management style is called for, which provides closer supervision and tighter controls.

**Looking at the Work Environment** The nature of the work being done also plays a big part in determining which management style is most effective. Are your employees performing creative, varied tasks that change from day to day or from one project to the next, or are they performing repetitive tasks that basically remain the same? Workers that perform varied tasks–scientists in a research lab or an ad agency's creative staff, for example–generally respond best to a management style that offers a high degree of freedom to carry out their respective tasks in the manner they think best. Workers who perform repetitive tasks–such as on an assembly line or processing forms–usually need a management style that is more direction-oriented, clearly stating what needs to be accomplished and when. This isn't to say that their inputs aren't equally valuable or shouldn't be sought out. They should be, but in a more structured way, possibly through *quality circles*–meetings where workers discuss ways to increase productivity and job satisfaction.

Once you've taken these factors into consideration, you should be able to arrive at the management style that provides the best fit for your specific business. If you don't hit on it immediately, though, don't feel upset or discouraged. Developing a management style takes time, and once you've found a method that works for you, you have to keep fine-tuning it. As people and circumstances change, so does the need for one management style or another.

## Knowing When to Delegate

Unlike corporate managers, who are used to getting things done through people, entrepreneurs often want to do everything themselves. Whichever management style you choose, you must become proficient at delegating authority. Whether you delegate the minimum amount possible (autocratic management) or the maximum amount (free-rein management), there will be times when you have to let someone else make the decision. It's not a question of whether to delegate, but *when*. One person simply can't do it all.

To make the delegation process go smoothly and get positive results, try following these suggestions:

1. *Go low.* One of the first rules of management is to delegate authority to the lowest *competent* level in an organization. How low can you go? To the person who has the knowledge, skills, and willingness needed to carry out the job. A clerk may be competent to order office supplies, but you wouldn't expect that person to choose a new site for your business. Pushing decisions down to the lowest competent level possible frees you and any higher-level workers in your business to focus your attention on more important matters.

2. *Give enough authority.* The most common mistake in delegating

is not giving workers enough authority to carry out their duties and responsibilities. Expecting salespersons to satisfy customers, but not giving them the authority to make exchanges or refunds, is an example.

3. *State what's expected.* Let employees know the scope of the work involved and what you want them to accomplish, such as buying merchandise, negotiating a contract, training a new employee.

4. *Be supportive.* Make it clear to employees that they can come to you for help if they need it. Just knowing that you're available to offer advice or information should help to relieve any job anxiety the employee may have.

5. *Keep communication channels open.* The easier it is for employees to communicate with each other and with you, the easier it will be for them to carry out their assignments. Making the information that workers need to have readily accessible not only speeds things up, but also helps to keep mistakes from happening.

6. *Establish controls.* Although the act of delegating involves giving up control, it also calls for you to establish controls. *Controls,* in this sense, are guidelines or limits within which the work must be performed. For example, telling a supervisor to increase the productivity in his or her department doesn't go far enough. How much should it be increased? Within what time frame?

7. *Create opportunities to succeed.* Rather than setting employees up for failure, set them up for success. By picking the right person for a job and providing the resources (people, time, money, information) needed to succeed, you can develop strong, confident managers capable of making your business thrive.

## Finding Ways to Motivate

One of the biggest challenges a business owner can face is finding ways to motivate employees. It would be simple if all people wanted the same thing from a job and were driven by the same needs. But they don't, and they aren't. People are different, and what motivates one person may not motivate another.

### Identifying Needs

Just as important as the ability to identify your customers' needs is the ability to identify your employees' needs. What's important to them?

What needs do they expect to be fulfilled by working for you? The need for money? Achievement? Recognition? Power? Creativity? Interaction with others? Security? Personal satisfaction?

One of the mistakes business owners make is thinking that money is the only motivator. Their common refrain is, "I pay a fair wage. I expect a fair day's work." Then when they don't get it, they wonder why employees are so lazy or don't care about doing a good job anymore.

The thing to realize is that money is just one of many motivators. In some situations, it may not even be a motivator. For example, a construction worker who's just put in two months of 60-hour workweeks may be less than thrilled by the prospect of earning additional overtime pay. Instead of being a motivator, the overtime is actually a *de*motivator. What the worker really wants is some time off to spend with family and friends.

You can use a number of motivators to increase workers' productivity. These include offering such incentives as

- Interesting work
- Opportunities for advancement
- Competitive salaries
- Bonuses
- Equity in the business
- Job training
- Recognition
- Responsibility
- New challenges
- Fair treatment
- Good fringe benefits
- Positive work environment
- Flexible hours
- Job security
- Praise
- Respect

The trick, of course, is knowing which incentives to use for which employees. Through careful observation and by taking the time to know your employees, you should be able to determine which incentives will work best with which people. For instance, an employee who is in debt or barely making ends meet is obviously going to be more motivated by financial incentives than by the opportunity to make friends on the job. The very opposite could be true, though, for someone who's new in the area or who worked in a business where the employees didn't get along. A person with low self-esteem is likely to respond to praise. A high achiever, who's already doing well, might do even better if given additional responsibilities or a stake in the business.

To be effective, the incentives you offer must meet both the needs of individual employees and the needs of your business. Few small businesses can match the salaries and benefits packages offered by major corporations, but they often have other incentives that many employees want even more: the chance to be part of a growing business, greater responsibility, enthusiastic coworkers, opportunities for creativity and recognition, or a piece of the pie (through partnerships, stock options, and so on). Rather than just being another cog in the wheel, following long-set policies and procedures, they can have a real impact on your business–if you'll let them.

To make sure that the incentives you use will motivate workers, rather than demotivating them, keep in mind that the incentive must be

- *Something that the employee wants.* In other words, it must meet some unfulfilled need.
- *Seen as something positive.* If you give an employee additional responsibilities, will that be viewed as a reward for good job performance or as a ploy to get more work done?
- *Known.* Employees must be aware of the incentive before it can motivate them. Praising an employee's work to a business associate, but not to the employee, for example, will not provide any incentive.
- *Fair.* If you show favoritism and reward some workers for their accomplishments, but not others, you demoralize employees and divide the workforce.
- *Attainable.* For instance, if you set a sales quota to qualify for a bonus beyond your employees' reach, you will obtain a reverse effect, causing them to cut back, rather than increase, their sales efforts.
- *Responsive to change as workers' needs change.* Once a need is fulfilled, it is no longer a motivator. An employee whose primary motivation was money is likely to want other things–recognition, personal satisfaction–once the need for financial security has been met.

### Sharing Your Vision

The best way of all to motivate employees is by sharing your vision for the business with them and showing how your success relates to their success. You need to make employees feel that they have a vested interest in the business; that it's theirs, too; and that the work they do is important.

To share your vision, you must be able to put it into words and communicate it to others. Every employee should know what your business stands for, what it hopes to accomplish, and the rewards to be earned by contributing to its success.

Only when employees can see that the business's future is interlocked with their own will they be willing to fully commit to your vision and to do the things necessary to enable you to achieve it.

## Developing a Corporate Culture

At the same time that you are building your business, you must also be developing its *corporate culture*–the combination of values, ethical standards, beliefs, and attitudes that the business strives to uphold. Despite the name, it isn't necessary to be a corporation to have a corporate culture. Every business has one whether the people in the business realize it or not. A good corporate culture inspires employees, guides their efforts, and unifies their actions. A bad corporate culture creates dissension and leads to employee apathy and poor customer service.

Your corporate culture is critical because it provides a framework showing employees which actions and behaviors will be rewarded and which ones won't. For instance, which employee attributes are most important to your business: independence or cooperation, technical skills or people skills, risk-taking or caution, innovation or implementation, attention to detail or seeing the big picture? Which business objectives are most important: being the biggest or being the best, filling a niche or selling to the masses? By answering these questions and more, your corporate culture also can serve as a recruitment and retention tool for attracting employees eager to be part of a business with a corporate culture in tune with their own feelings and work styles.

Though often difficult to define or describe, corporate cultures are easily recognized in the way that businesses conduct themselves, how they treat their employees and customers, their product offerings and promotions, and even such minute details as how the telephones are answered and the assignment of office and parking spaces. Anyone wanting the scoop on Ben & Jerry's corporate culture need look no further than its Rainforest Crunch ice cream, created in part for its taste and in part to draw attention to the need to save the Amazon rain forest. Obviously, this company places a high priority on human values, as well as on business values. Also, founders Ben and Jerry opt for T-shirts and Hawaiian prints over corporate pinstripes, thereby making it clear that work and fun go hand-in-hand.

To get started on developing the corporate culture for your business, begin by taking these steps:

1. *State your business philosophy and the underlying principles and values that you want to guide the enterprise.* For instance, Mrs. Fields Cookies sums up its emphasis on quality in its slogan: "Good enough never is." Nike, on the other hand, clearly is a place for action-oriented achievers, as evidenced by its command to "Just do it!"

2. *Establish a code of ethics detailing the types of conduct that are acceptable and unacceptable.* Take the areas of supplier relations and gift giving. At Wal-Mart, for example, no employees are permitted to accept money or gifts from anyone who does business with the retailer. This policy is explained to each employee in no uncertain terms. Other areas you might address include honesty, nondiscrimination policies, safety standards, legal responsibilities, conflicts of interest, marketing practices, and so on.

3. *Set a good example that shows you're not just giving lip service to high ideals but are actually living them yourself.* For example, telling your employees that you're all part of a team isn't going to do much to motivate them if you isolate yourself in a large corner office away from everyone else.

4. *Keep an open mind that allows for changes in your corporate culture as circumstances and situations change.* Just as your business grows and evolves over time, so must your corporate culture.

## Leadership Checklist

To evaluate your leadership skills and determine whether you are effectively managing and motivating your employees, answer the questions in the following Leadership Checklist.

| Leadership Checklist | Answer Yes or No |
|---|---|
| 1. Do you know the strengths and weaknesses of the three most common management styles? | |
| Autocratic | ________ |
| Democratic | ________ |
| Free-rein | ________ |
| 2. In evaluating each style, have you considered the major factors affecting your business? | |
| Your own abilities/preferences | ________ |
| Your employees | ________ |
| The work environment | ________ |
| 3. Have you chosen the management style that's best for you? | ________ |
| 4. Have you given thought to the responsibilities and authority that you're willing to delegate? | ________ |
| 5. Are you familiar with how the delegation process works? | ________ |
| 6. Have you identified the various needs of your employees? | ________ |
| 7. Have you determined the types of incentives that you want to use? | ________ |
| 8. Do you know which incentives will be the most effective at motivating which workers? | ________ |
| 9. Do you know how to keep incentives from having a reverse effect and becoming demotivators? | ________ |
| 10. Can you put your vision for your business into words? | ________ |
| 11. Are you ready to share your vision with others? | ________ |
| 12. Will helping you to achieve your goals enable employees to achieve their own goals as well? | ________ |
| 13. Are you taking steps to develop a corporate culture for your business? | ________ |

# 13

# Developing Your Promotional Strategy

If you build a better mousetrap, the world may indeed beat a path to your door–but not without a little help from you. In the first place, before people can buy your mousetrap, they have to know about it. In the second place, they have to know where to find your door. In the third place, it helps if the people you're trying to reach are having trouble with rodents.

The U.S. Patent Office has issued patents by the thousands for inventions that never made it in the marketplace. Putting aside the problems of unworkable designs or excessive production costs, many of the inventions failed simply because of poor or nonexistent promotional strategies. Having created their better mousetraps, the inventors didn't know what to do with them.

Forming a business is much the same as inventing a new product. To succeed, each needs to be promoted. Having answered the questions in Chapters 2 and 3 on planning and determining the best location, you've already evaluated the need for your particular product or service. You also have a pretty good idea who your potential customers are. Knowing this much is half the battle. Now, what's left is to convert those potential customers into satisfied customers. That's where your promotional strategy comes in.

A promotional strategy is a game plan for reaching your target market–those people most likely to use your product or service. At the simplest, most direct level, your promotional strategy might consist of relying on a sign in front of your door and the word-of-mouth comments of your present customers. In some instances–if you're in a very small town, or if you offer unique products or services, or if you have a long-standing reputation, for example–this tactic is sufficient. Normally, though, customers need more to go on before they are drawn to your business.

The goal of your promotional strategy should be to reach the greatest number of potential customers through the most economical use of your resources (money, personnel, and facilities). This entails using advertising and publicity to tune in to those channels of communication most widely used by your target customers. It also involves working within the limits of a budget to achieve the desired results. In this chapter, we first discuss the various media through which you can advertise your business and then the ways you can use publicity to promote your business.

## Advertising

*Advertising* involves the purchase of time or space in various communications media for the purpose of promoting your business. The two categories of advertising are institutional and product. *Institutional advertising* promotes your business in general, emphasizing its good name and any contributions that it has made to the well-being of the community. *Product advertising* promotes the specific products or services you sell, emphasizing the benefits associated with buying them from you. An oil company, for instance, can emphasize the time and money it spends in exploring for new sources of fuel (institutional advertising), or it can emphasize the special additives that make its gasoline better than the rest (product advertising). Your own objectives will determine whether to use one or both of these approaches.

The advertising media generally favored are newspapers, magazines, radio, television, direct mail, Yellow Pages, outdoor advertising, and the Internet. Other media include transit, specialty, movie theaters, flyers, e-mail messages, and faxes. Each medium has its own unique characteristics and is capable of reaching large numbers of people. Depending on your message, target customers, budget, and lead time, some will be better suited to your needs than others.

First of all, is your *message* simple and direct ("You'll save more money at Jones's"), or is it more complicated, involving a detailed explanation (a listing of the nutrients in your special health-food drink)? Does your message rely heavily on words, color, sound, or movement to make its point?

Second, is your *target customer* everyone (the mass market) or just a small segment of the market? The narrower your target, the greater the need to use selective media to reach it. Doctors, for instance, can be reached more effectively by means of a medical journal than a daytime soap opera.

Third, consider your *budget.* How much money can you spend? Despite the suitability of a particular medium, if you can't afford it, there's no sense in building your promotional strategy around it.

Finally, what is your *lead time*? Do you want the advertisement to start this week, next month, or next year? Lead times vary with the medium, and if you need a quick start, that limits your selection.

### Newspapers

Newspapers, which have traditionally been the favorite means of advertising for retailers, account for close to a fourth of all advertising dollars spent in the United States.

**Message** Newspapers are one of the best equipped of the media (along with magazines, direct mail, and the Internet) for explaining and describing a product. Not only is the space available, but also the only limitation on time is the reader's attention span. The effectiveness of your message can be quickly and easily measured through the use of redeemable coupons in your ads and subsequent customer demand for the featured items. If no one brings in a coupon or asks for the product, the ad isn't working.

**Target Customer** Because newspapers are local, they reach the people in your own community. Their readers are your potential customers. For greater selectivity, your ad can be placed in the sections most likely to appeal to your target customer (sports, business, world news, entertainment, food, real estate). An ad for a restaurant might run in either the entertainment or the food section.

**Budget** Newspaper rates are low compared to most other media. Even a business on a very limited budget can generally afford a small ad.

**Lead Time** Other than the Internet, newspapers have the shortest lead time of the media. Some ads can be placed given as little as two or three days' notice. This gives you a great deal of flexibility in deciding when and what to advertise.

**Limitations** Newspapers are short-lived; if your ad isn't read today, chances are that it won't ever be read. Reproduction quality is poor; products that require strong visual presentations are better served by other media. Most people don't read every page in a newspaper; unless you pay careful attention to your ad's placement, it could get lost in the shuffle.

**Rates** Advertising space is sold in column inches (14 lines to an inch). An ad that's 2 columns wide by 3 inches deep occupies 6 column inches. The rate per column inch is based on a paper's circulation: the larger the circulation, the higher the rates.

**Volume Rates** Bigger advertisers are entitled to discounts. This means that the more space you buy, the lower the rate per column inch.

**Preferred-Position Rates** If you specify a particular section, page, or position on the page, the rate is higher. If this gets people to see your ad, however, it's worth the money. Because of the way we read, ads at the upper right of the page generally have the most drawing power.

**Classified Rates** These rates are quoted by lines, rather than column inches. The ideal position is at the front of the classified section. The farther back that your ad appears, the larger the drop-off in readers.

**Comparing Costs** Depending on your location, there may be several newspapers to choose from. Based on each paper's rates and circulation, it's an easy matter to compare the costs and determine which is the best buy. You can do this by measuring each paper's cost per thousand people reached, or CPM.

$$\text{CPM} = \frac{\text{Cost of ad} \times 1{,}000}{\text{Total circulation}}$$

$$\text{CPM} = \frac{\$800 \times 1{,}000}{650{,}000} = \$1.23 \text{ per } 1{,}000 \text{ for newspaper A}$$

$$\text{CPM} = \frac{\$750 \times 1{,}000}{575{,}000} = \$1.30 \text{ per } 1{,}000 \text{ for newspaper B}$$

As you can see, although an ad in newspaper A is more expensive, its cost per thousand readers is actually less. This makes it the better buy.

### Magazines

Though used primarily by large advertisers, magazines are now starting to grow in popularity with smaller advertisers as well. This is because of the increase in special-interest magazines. Unlike general-interest magazines, these focus on a single topic (e.g., money, computers, travel, skiing, gardening) and enable advertisers to reach a specific audience.

**Message** Like newspapers, magazines are well suited to conveying in-depth information, and their effectiveness can be readily measured. Reproduction values are high, so products that need color or strong visuals to make an impact look their best. Furthermore, people tend to read magazines at a more leisurely pace than newspapers and are inclined to save them afterward. This lengthens the life span of your ad.

**Target Customer** Magazines enable you to be as selective as you want in pinpointing your target customer. Through careful placement of your ads in the right special-interest magazine, you're virtually guaranteed of reaching a receptive audience.

**Budget** Magazine ads can be expensive, particularly in national magazines with large circulations. If you're willing to do some research, however, there are bargains to be found. For information about rates, check the *Standard Rate and Data Service,* a monthly publication available at many libraries.

**Lead Time** Magazines have a much longer lead time than newspapers. Ads normally must be received two or three months prior to publication.

**Limitations** The long lead time reduces your flexibility; ads must be planned and space purchased well in advance. Magazine ads can get lost, too; position is important.

**Rates** Space is usually sold by the page or fraction of a page. Some magazines also have classified or mail-order sections in which space is sold by the line. These sections are generally at the back of the magazines. Rates are determined by circulation. However, a magazine that caters to a particularly affluent or hard-to-reach audience may still be able to charge high rates despite a small circulation. Other determinants of rates are

- *Color.* An ad that's in color is more expensive than a black-and-white ad.
- *Quantity Discounts.* These are based on the amount of space purchased in a 12-month period.
- *Frequency Discounts.* These are based on the number of times space is purchased in a 12-month period.
- *Positioning.* If a special position is requested, there is an additional charge.

**Comparing Costs** As with newspapers, magazines can be compared by the CPM technique to determine which is the most economical.

### Radio

Radio's main strength is its ability to reach people regardless of where they are or what they're doing. Whether at home, driving to work, or on vacation, people have their radios with them. In the United States today, there are almost two radios per person, with 99 percent of all households having at least one radio.

**Message** Radio uses words, music, and sound effects to communicate its message. It has strong emotional impact, derived from its ability to establish a rapport with the audience and move listeners to action. Jingles and slogans are common in radio commercials because listeners remember them later. This helps to reinforce brand identification.

**Target Customer** Radio stations, like special-interest magazines, gear themselves toward a particular audience. Through the program format you select (top-40 rock music, country music, classical music, middle of the road, easy listening, talk, news), it's possible to zero in on your target customer.

**Budget** The cost of purchasing air time depends on a program's popularity and the frequency of your commercials. To determine costs, check the *Standard Rate and Data Service.*

**Lead Time** Lead times vary. Certain programs may be booked as much as a year in advance, while others have immediate openings.

**Limitations** Many radio stations are competing for audiences; this may make it necessary to buy time on a number of stations to reach all your target customers. To be effective at all, your commercial needs to be broadcast more than once; this repetition increases your costs. The life span of your commercial is just seconds; unlike a print advertisement, it gets only one chance to communicate your message. Radio is a medium without visuals; if your product has to be seen to be believed, you're wasting your money.

**Rates** Time is sold in units of 60 seconds or less–that is, in 10-, 15-, 30-, and 60-second spots. Although 60-second commercials once dominated the airwaves, the trend is now toward shorter ones, with 30-second spots currently the most popular.

Rates are based on both a station's coverage and its circulation. *Coverage* is the geographical area covered by the station's signal. *Circulation* refers to the potential number of listeners in the area. Because the number of listeners can vary throughout the day, different rates are charged for different time periods.

**Drive Time** This is the most expensive time of day because it covers the intervals from 6 to 10 A.M. and from 4 to 7 P.M., when people are in their cars driving to and from work.

**Run-of-the-Station (ROS)** This is the cheapest time because it allows the station to put your commercial anywhere it pleases.

**Weekly Plan** A weekly plan offers a lower rate to advertisers purchasing a package of time. Each package contains a variety of time slots, ranging from drive time to ROS.

**Comparing Costs** Stations can be compared by means of the cost-per-thousand technique.

### Television

Though television trails newspapers as the most picked advertising medium, it is rapidly closing in on the top spot. The reason for television's growing popularity is simple: numbers. Currently, 98 percent of all American households have one or more television sets, and the average family watches for more than six hours per day. One of the newest of the media, television's impact on its audience is still being explored, but the fact that it can shape attitudes and change opinions is widely known.

**Message** Television is the most intimate of the media; combining sight, sound, color, and motion, it takes your presentation right into the viewer's home. Television lets you show off your product, rather than just tell about it. The viewer sees it in a natural setting that encourages acceptance. (If the people in the commercial are satisfied with the product, why shouldn't the viewer be, too?)

**Target Customer** More than any of the other media, television is a mass medium. At any one time, millions of viewers are watching. Programs such as the Super Bowl, the World Series, and the Academy Awards ceremony are tuned in by viewers worldwide. The question is, Are these your target customers? In selecting a program on which to advertise, it's as important to check the data describing the viewers (age, sex, income, interests) as it is to check the number of people who are watching.

**Budget** Unfortunately, advertising on television is expensive. Regardless of its appeal, the majority of small businesses will find it beyond their budgets. However, local and cable television stations offer considerably reduced rates, and these may be a viable alternative. Instead, if you have a unique product with wide appeal, you might contract with a company that produces infomercials and promote it through half-hour commercials designed to look like television programs. In the standard agreement, the infomercial producer covers the advertising costs and you receive a royalty for each unit sold.

**Lead Time** Top-rated television shows are likely to be booked a year in advance. Time slots on less popular shows and new shows are generally available on a few days' notice.

**Limitations** Television has less selectivity than the other media; using it to reach a small target audience could be an exercise in overkill. Viewers often leave the room during commercials; getting and holding their attention isn't easy. Television commercials, like radio commercials, become more effective with repetition; this adds to your cost.

**Rates** Time is sold in units of 60 seconds or less, with 30-second spots currently the most favored. Rates vary on the basis of the time period selected and the size of the audience for a given program–hence the importance of the Nielsen and Arbitron ratings, which rank programs in the order of their popularity.

**Prime Time** This is the most costly time. It covers the hours from 7 to 11 P.M., when the greatest number of viewers are watching television.

**Discounts** These are available on essentially the same terms as those offered by radio stations.

**Comparing Costs** The CPM technique applies.

### Direct Mail

*Direct mail* refers to any printed material of a promotional nature that is mailed directly to the intended customer–brochures, letters, price lists, catalogs, coupons. This technique is currently the third most popular choice with advertisers and is used by the majority of businesses, large and small.

**Message** Like newspapers and magazines, direct mail is one of the best formats for conveying in-depth information. It also offers the greatest flexibility because any message can be sent to anyone at any time. Direct mail is regularly used to

- Inform customers of sales
- Introduce new products
- Announce price changes
- Solicit mail-order business
- Solicit phone-order business
- Maintain customer contact
- Reach new customers
- Develop your image

**Target Customers** The success of a direct-mail campaign is primarily determined by the mailing list. Unless your mailing is going out to the people who are likely to buy your product, you're wasting both time and money. How can you obtain a mailing list that's right for you? You can either purchase it from someone else or build your own list. There are a number of companies in the business of compiling and selling mailing lists. These lists are available in literally thousands of categories (e.g., women between the ages of 18 and 49, teenagers, skiers, pet owners, recent graduates, cooking enthusiasts). Regardless of your target market, there is probably an applicable list. The cost may be as low as $15 per thousand names or as high as $500 per thousand.

If you prefer to build your own list, some of the sources you may be able to use are

- Your own customers
- Telephone directories
- Professional, trade, and industrial directories
- Credit bureaus
- Newspaper announcements (wedding, graduation, birth, new business, etc.)
- Construction permits on file in municipal and county offices

**Budget** Direct mail's flexibility makes it possible to structure a campaign to meet practically any budget. You should consider

- The cost of the mailing list
- The cost of the package (printed materials)
- The cost of postage
- The cost of labor (addressing, stuffing, and sealing envelopes)

The more extensive the mailing, the higher the cost.

**Lead Time** You control the lead time.

**Limitations** In terms of unit costs, direct mail is expensive; it has the highest cost per thousand of the media. There's only a fine line between direct mail and junk mail; make sure you are sending your mailing to the people who really want it.

**Rates** Because there is no space or time to be purchased, there are no set rates to consider.

### Yellow Pages

Adding to the appeal of Yellow Pages advertising is the growing number of specialty directories from which to choose: *The Neighborhood Directory, Silver Pages, Business to Business Directory*, and so on.

**Message** A Yellow Pages display ad is an attention-getting device. Because your ad is surrounded by those of your competition, it's important that you focus in on the best way to differentiate yourself from the rest–lowest prices, widest selection, friendliest service, latest technology, or whatever.

**Target Customer** The main advantage of Yellow Pages advertising is its ability to reach your target customer, at the time they want to buy. Thus, your audience is presold. Having already decided *what* to buy, customers are just looking for *where* to buy it.

**Budget** Yellow Pages ads are inexpensive in comparison to the other media.

**Lead Time** Your ad must be placed before the closing date for inclusion in the current directory.

**Limitations** You can't make changes in your ad; it runs as is until the next directory printing.

**Rates** Any business with a phone is entitled to a one-line listing, free of charge. To find out the rates for display ads, contact your local Yellow Pages sales representative.

### Outdoor Advertising

Outdoor advertising involves the use of signs, posters, and billboards to promote your business. In the simplest sense, it can serve as a marker identifying your location. In the broadest sense, it can create an image, getting people to think of your name whenever they think of a particular product.

**Message** Your message needs to be simple and direct. Concise copy, bold graphics, and a recognizable product are essential. The average passerby spends less than 10 seconds reading your ad.

**Target Customer** Although outdoor advertising is visible to anyone who cares to look, a fairly high degree of selectivity can be achieved through the geographic placement of your advertisement. For instance, ads for airlines, hotels, restaurants, shops, and tourist attractions are typically found on billboards near airports and along freeways where travelers can see them.

**Budget** The costs of outdoor advertising are among the lowest of the media.

**Lead Time** If you're just using signs at your place of business, the only lead time is the production and installation time. In the case of posters and billboards, space is rented on an availability basis, and there may be a waiting list for the locations you want.

**Limitations** Your advertisement is competing with numerous others; its effectiveness hinges on its ability to command attention. Some people regard outdoor advertising as a form of visual pollution; part of the response to your ads may thus be negative.

**Rates** The rates charged for posters and billboards are based on the size and location of the space being leased. Locations are classified by territories, which are priced according to traffic counts. The higher the count, the higher the cost.

**Comparing Costs** You can use the CPM technique to compare territories to determine the most economical purchase.

### Internet (the World Wide Web)

As mentioned in Chapter 3, the Internet is rapidly gaining acceptance as an effective marketing tool for reaching prospective customers. Originally created in the 1970s as a means of linking U.S. government scientists and researchers at various locations via computer, the Internet (or "information superhighway") has changed considerably since then. The most notable change was the creation of the World Wide Web–a portion of the Internet developed for commercial use, which became available to the public in 1993. By merging the visual characteristics and mass reach of television with the selectivity and interactive capabilities of a computer, the Web not only lets you reach out to customers, but also lets them reach back.

**Message** The more visually appealing and fast-paced you can make your site, the better. With visitors able to enter and exit websites at the click of a mouse, it's important to get their attention quickly and to hold onto it. Be sure to make use of the Web's interactive features, too. Rather than delivering a one-sided message, give your audience something to do.

**Target Customer** One of the main advantages of advertising over the Web is the ability to reach a very select audience. What's more, because visitors to your website have gone to the trouble to seek you out, they generally are already interested in your product offering and have some knowledge about it.

**Budget** The main expense is in developing the website and maintaining it once it's up and running. The cost varies, depending on how much you're able to do yourself, the sophistication of the graphics, and the number of visitors to the site. You can save money by designing the site yourself using website design software or by making use of the design services available through the Internet service provider (ISP) that hosts your site.

**Lead Time** You control the lead time. Depending on how complex the site is and who does the work, it can take anywhere from a day to a couple of weeks to get your site online. Once it's established, though, you can update it as often as you wish.

**Limitations** It takes time for browsers to scan your site, and they may not see everything you want them to see. Also, as the number of websites continues to increase, so does the competition for an audience.

**Rates** Depending on which ISP you choose, rates can vary widely, so it's important to shop around and compare prices and services. Typical fees include (1) setup costs, (2) monthly hosting fees, and (3) monthly transaction fees (which can be either fixed or a percentage of sales).

### Internet Marketing Tips: Ten Things to Avoid

1. Having poorly designed, boring Web pages
2. Having too little user interaction
3. Having slow pages (e.g., with complex graphics) that keep viewers waiting
4. Including dated or incorrect information on your site
5. Promising more than you can deliver
6. Listing your business on inappropriate sites
7. Failing to link your site to other sites
8. Failing to use key search words that make it easy to find your site
9. Failing to check the site regularly and respond to customers
10. Failing to relate the site to your overall marketing program

### Other Advertising Media

Some of the other forms of advertising you may wish to consider are

- *Transit Advertising.* Messages are displayed on the exteriors and interiors of trains, buses, and taxicabs.
- *Specialty Advertising.* Your company's name or logo imprinted on such items as calendars, memo pads, bookmarks, ashtrays, matchbooks, key chains, and T-shirts.
- *Flyers.* These can be handed out to passersby or placed on automobile windshields.
- *Theater-Screen Advertising.* Ads are shown during intermissions.
- *E-mail Messages and Faxes.* These are sent to your intended prospects. To avoid negative feedback, make sure to get the recipients' permission before sending your transmissions.

## Publicity

In addition to advertising, you can use publicity to promote your business. This involves getting information about your company's activities or products reported in the news media. Such coverage is provided when the information is thought to have news value or to be of interest to the public.

## Publicity versus Advertising

Although publicity and advertising are similar, they differ in three vital areas: *cost*, *control*, and *credibility*. Publicity is free. There is no cost to you for the media coverage you receive. Nor do you have any control over that coverage. Unlike advertising, publicity can be favorable or unfavorable—as likely to point out your business's flaws as its accomplishments. If a news broadcast chooses to focus on a lawsuit that's been brought against you, rather than on your volunteer service to the community, there's nothing you can do about it. This very lack of control is what gives publicity its greatest strength—credibility. The fact that it's the news media, rather than a sponsor, delivering your message makes it more believable than advertising.

While it's impossible to control the publicity you get, it *is* possible to influence it. The way to do this is by maintaining good press relations, providing timely and accurate information in the form of press releases, pointing out the angle that makes your story interesting or newsworthy, being available to answer questions, and not making unreasonable demands. By learning to work within the limitations of publicity, you can put yourself in a position to take full advantage of it.

## Press Releases

Far from being anything mysterious, a press release is simply a fact sheet. It states the details of the story you want the press to tell, explaining who, what, where, when, and how. It also makes the reporter's job easier by emphasizing *why* your story will be of interest to the public. Possible *whys* include

- Having a unique product or service
- Staging a special event
- Helping a charity
- Winning an award
- Giving a speech

This story angle—or *hook*, as it is called—is the most important infor-

**Business Name**
**Address**

Contact: Your name
Phone numbers
E-mail address

Release Date (For Immediate Release; For Release after October 20, etc.):

Start copy here and begin with your angle: Why

Provide all necessary details: Who

What

Where

When

How

Write in short, clear sentences and paragraphs.

Two pages should be the maximum length.

Double-space, using one-inch margins on all sides.

Put your name and phone number on each page.

Type "-30-" after the last line of copy, to indicate the end. This is a symbol commonly used by printers.

Press Release Format

mation of all, helping to justify your story to the media and to shape the coverage you receive.

To give your press releases a professional look, use the format shown here. In so doing, though, don't make the mistake of cramming too much information into one press release. If you find yourself writing a book or trying to tell two stories at once, the situation probably calls for more than one press release or for a *media kit.*

Although a media kit sounds elaborate and expensive, it needn't be. All it takes is a standard-size folder with two inside pockets. Then, depending on the information you want to send out, you can fill it with such materials as:

- The press release(s)
- A business fact sheet and history
- A list of suppliers or customers
- A brochure
- Photographs (5 × 7", black and white)

## Preparing an Advertising Budget

In preparing their advertising budgets, the majority of businesses base their allocations on a percentage of annual past sales, estimated sales, or a combination of these. For example, 4 percent of $300,000 in sales equals an advertising budget of $12,000. Some of the reasons for this method's general acceptance are that it gives you more to go on than guesswork, it emphasizes the relationship between advertising and sales, and it's easy to use.

In determining the percentage of sales you want to invest in advertising, you should consider your business's needs, the competition, and the economic environment. To find out what similar businesses are spending, it's a good idea to check such sources as trade journals and the reports published by Dun & Bradstreet, Robert Morris Associates, the Accounting Corporation of America, the U.S. Census Bureau, and the Internal Revenue Service. You can find some examples in the chart of typical ad budgets as a percentage of sales on the accompanying page.

Once you have calculated your budget, the next step is to allocate it over the coming year, indicating the amount to be spent each month and the media to receive it. Keep in mind that some months will require greater expenditures than others. Also, don't forget to plan for any sales or special events you wish to promote. See the sample advertising budget on the accompanying page to see how this works.

**Advertising for Small Businesses**

| *Category* | *Typical Ad Budget as Percentage of Sales* | *Primary Media Selected* |
|---|---|---|
| Auto supply stores | 1.0–2.0 | Direct mail, flyers, newspapers, Yellow Pages |
| Beauty salons | 2.5–4.0 | Direct mail, newspapers, Yellow Pages |
| Bookstores | 1.8–2.2 | Direct mail, Internet, newspapers, Yellow Pages |
| Catering services | 2.0–3.0 | Direct mail, flyers, Yellow Pages |
| Clothing stores | 2.5–3.5 | Direct mail, newspapers, radio |
| Computer/electronics stores | 1.5–2.5 | Internet, newspapers, radio, TV |
| Consultants | 1.0–8.0 | Direct mail, directories, Internet |
| Dry cleaners | 1.2–1.7 | Direct mail, flyers, newspapers, Yellow Pages |
| Flower shops | 1.0–2.0 | Newspapers, radio, Yellow Pages |
| Furniture stores | 5.5–6.5 | Newspapers, magazines, radio, TV, Yellow Pages |
| Gift shops | 2.0–2.5 | Magazines, newspapers, radio, Yellow Pages |
| Health clubs | 3.0–5.0 | Direct mail, newspapers, radio, TV, Yellow Pages |
| Ice cream/yogurt shops | 1.0–2.5 | Newspapers, radio, Yellow Pages |
| Insurance agencies | 1.0–1.5 | Direct mail, newspapers, Yellow Pages |
| Jewelry stores | 2.5–3.5 | Direct mail, magazines, radio, TV, Yellow Pages |
| Mail order | 18.0–30.0 | Direct mail, Internet, magazines, newspapers, TV |
| Office supplies | 2.0–3.0 | Catalogs, fax, Internet, newspapers, Yellow Pages |
| Photography stores | 2.5–4.0 | Direct mail, magazines, newspapers, radio, Yellow Pages |
| Restaurants | 2.0–3.0 | Direct mail, newspapers, radio, Yellow Pages |
| Sporting goods stores | 2.0–2.5 | Newspapers, radio, TV, Yellow Pages |
| TV and appliance stores | 1.5–2.5 | Newspapers, radio, TV, Yellow Pages |
| Toy/game stores | 1.0–1.5 | Direct mail, Internet, newspapers |
| Travel agencies | 1.5–2.5 | Direct mail, Internet, newspapers, Yellow Pages |
| Upholsterers | 0.2–0.8 | Shopping guides, Yellow Pages |
| Wedding planners | 1.5–2.5 | Direct mail, magazines, Yellow Pages |

**Sample Advertising Budget**

| *Camera Shop Budget* | | |
|---|---|---|
| Sales for 2000 | $300,000 | |
| Ad budget as percentage of sales | 4% | |
| Total ad budget | $12,000 | |
| Direct Mail | | $ 5,400 |
| Flyers | | 1,200 |
| Yellow Pages (one payment) | | 1,440 |
| Newspapers | | 3,960 |
| Total ad budget | | $12,000 |
| Best selling months | | |
| Christmas holiday (November, December) | | |
| Graduation/Weddings (May, June) | | |
| Summer vacation (June, July) | | |

*Breakdown by Month*

| *Month* | *Direct mail* | *Flyers* | *Yellow Pages* | *Newspapers* | *Total* |
|---|---|---|---|---|---|
| January | | | | $330 | $330 |
| February | | | | 330 | 330 |
| March | $ 650 | | | 330 | 980 |
| April | | | | 330 | 330 |
| May | 1,350 | | | 330 | 1,680 |
| June | | $ 600 | | 330 | 930 |
| July | 1,350 | | | 330 | 1,680 |
| August | | | | 330 | 330 |
| September | | | $1,440 | 330 | 1,770 |
| October | | | | 330 | 330 |
| November | 700 | | | 330 | 1,030 |
| December | 1,350 | 600 | | 330 | 2,280 |
| Total | $5,400 | $1,200 | $1,440 | $3,960 | $12,000 |

## Promotional Strategy Checklist

To help launch your promotional campaign and reach your target market in the most economical way possible, answer the questions in the following Promotional Strategy Checklist.

| Promotional Strategy Checklist | Answer Yes or No |
|---|---|
| 1. Do you know who your potential customers are? | ________ |
| 2. Have you established a game plan for reaching your target market? | ________ |
| 3. Do you know the difference between institutional and product advertising? | ________ |
| 4. Do you know the benefits and limitations of each of the following media? | |
| Newspaper | ________ |
| Magazines | ________ |
| Radio | ________ |
| Television | ________ |
| Direct mail | ________ |
| Yellow Pages | ________ |
| Outdoor advertising | ________ |
| Internet | ________ |
| 5. Can you compare costs between like forms of advertising (CPM)? | ________ |
| 6. Do you know the rates of the different media? | ________ |
| 7. Do you know the difference between advertising and publicity? | ________ |
| 8. Do you know how to maintain good press relations? | ________ |
| 9. Have you prepared an advertising budget? | ________ |
| 10. Have you determined which are the best advertising media for your business? | ________ |
| 11. Do you know what media are being used by your competition? | ________ |
| 12. Do you keep track of competitors' advertising campaigns? | ________ |
| 13. Do you know the best times to advertise during the year? | ________ |

# 14

# Selling and Servicing

Your first priority as a business owner should be to please the customer. Far more important than any single sale that you make is your ability to meet customers' needs and to establish long-term relationships that will keep customers coming back again and again.

Businesses that are more interested in "moving the goods" than in giving customers what they really need and want usually don't last very long. To go the distance, your personal selling and customer-service efforts must be directed at satisfying each customer.

## A Positive Approach to Selling

Personal selling involves more than just giving a sales presentation and writing up the order. Today's top salespeople–the kind you want to be or to have in your business–are problem solvers. Equally good at listening as talking, they are able to correctly identify customers' needs and match them to the products or services they sell. Rather than assuming what customers want or pushing the products they want to sell, the best salespeople find out what customers *do* want and then show them how they can have it.

### The Selling Process

Like any skill, personal selling entails a set of steps that leads to a successful outcome–in this case, a satisfied customer. As shown here, there are six steps in the selling process. What you and your salespeople do at each step will directly affect your ability to make individual sales, to get repeat sales and referrals, and to build a positive image.

### Prospecting

Many sales experts consider this to be the most important step of all: the search for potential customers, or "prospects," to whom you can sell your products or services. In developing a list of prospects (through customer referrals, contacts, market research, mailing lists, and so on), your goal is to focus your attention on those who can be considered *good prospects.* Beyond being able to use your product, a good prospect also (1) has a need for it, (2) can afford it, and (3) is authorized to buy it.

Whether you do prospecting alone or you involve salespeople as well, it must be done. Good prospects are the lifeblood of any business. To expand your customer base and raise sales revenues, you need to actively seek out new customers.

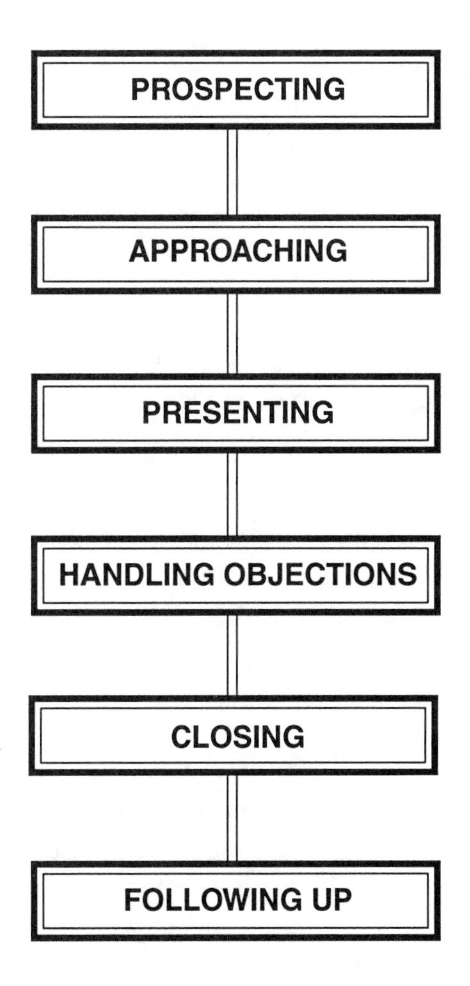


The Six Steps in the Selling Process

### Approaching

This step calls for you to make initial contact with the prospect. Your main concern at this point isn't to make an immediate sale, but rather to open up a dialogue with the prospect and to begin to assess his or her needs. During this step, what you say, how you dress, and how you act can work either for you or against you. Everything from your greeting, tone of voice, body language, demeanor, and attire should be directed at creating a positive image. As the saying goes, "You don't get a second chance to make a good first impression."

### Presenting

Successful sales presentations don't just happen; they are *planned.* Instead of "winging it" or relying on fast talking and fancy footwork to get through sales presentations, the best salespersons plan their presentations carefully. This doesn't mean that you should memorize each word–"canned" presentations tend to come off as stilted and one-sided–but rather that you should think about what the customer's needs are, what points you'd like to make, and what visual aids or demonstration techniques you want to use.

In planning your presentation, your goals should be to *inform* and *persuade* so that the customer understands what you have to offer and is inclined to buy. Here it helps to do the following:

- Outline the various points you want to make and the order in which to present them.
- Determine how much time you will need (keeping your presentation as concise and to the point as possible).
- Practice your presentation several times until it comes naturally.
- Prepare for different responses so that as you and the customer interact, you're able to "go with the flow."

**Two-Way Communication** During the presentation itself the most important thing to remember is that communication is a two-way street. In addition to telling the customer things, you must also tune in to what the customer is telling *you.* Is the prospect's response positive or negative? Rather than just steamrolling ahead, you must become adept at recognizing both the *verbal* and the *nonverbal* messages the prospect is sending you. Is the person asking questions? If so, that could either be a sign of interest or a defense mechanism to avoid having to make a purchase decision. Is the person leaning in to hear more (generally a good sign) or backing away?

**The Five Senses** Throughout the presentation you should also appeal to the prospect's five senses: the ability to hear, see, touch, smell, and taste. The more senses you can appeal to, the stronger your presentation will be. Rather than just telling how well a car handles, get the prospect to "test drive" it. In the case of a computer, for example, have the prospect sit down and actually use it. Food-related products and services especially lend themselves to this, as prospects find out firsthand how good something looks, smells, and tastes. With some ingenuity, even an intangible product such as insurance can be made to appeal to the senses. For example, you could show prospects photographs or a video of smiling policyholders whose insurance policies got them through their misfortunes.

**Benefits versus Features** Another way to strengthen your sales presentation is by emphasizing benefits rather than features. Whereas features merely describe a product or service, benefits are the *advantages* the prospect will derive from the purchase. As you can see from these examples, the essential difference is that benefits give the prospect a *reason to buy*:

| *Features* | *Benefits* |
|---|---|
| This computer program is "user-friendly." | You can start using the program immediately. |
| These skin products contain special moisturizers. | You'll look younger. |
| These toys are recommended by educators. | Your child will do better in school. |
| This ski parka is down-filled. | This parka will keep you warm on the ski slopes. |

Converting features into benefits in this way can significantly increase sales. By shifting your focus from what a product or service *is* to what it can *do* for customers, you enable prospects to more easily envision themselves using it.

## Handling Objections

Nice as it would be to conclude each sales presentation by having the customer say, "Yes, I'll take it," that isn't going to happen often. You must be prepared for objections. Instead of taking them personally or letting them upset you, just accept the fact that objections come with the territory. Everyone in sales encounters them at one time or another. Many sales professionals go so far as to insist that "the selling doesn't start until the customer says no."

What separates the successful sellers from those who aren't is how they handle the objections. To turn objections into orders, try following these suggestions:

1. *Don't get angry or defensive.* This will just turn the prospect against you and force an end to the sales dialogue.
2. *Deflect the objection in a positive way.* For example, if a prospect thinks your price is too high, you can either point out that it is comparable to your competitors', if that's the case, or explain why it's higher–because you offer better quality, have better service, provide a warranty, and so on.
3. *Ask the prospect to restate the objection.* Sometimes when you ask the prospect to restate or explain the objection, you get lucky and the prospect either deflects it for you or gives you the information to deflect it yourself. For example, "Well, I really wanted a car that's sportier than that." This gives you the opportunity to show the prospect the two-door version of the car or to show a different model.
4. *Question the objection.* As politely as you can, question the objection that has been raised. Your goal isn't to be confrontational, but rather to determine whether the stated objection is indeed the real objection. For example, instead of saying that something is too expensive, a prospect will often raise another objection to avoid making a purchase. If the price (or some other factor) is the real reason, then you can address it: "We have financing available," or, "You can use our installment plan, if you like."
5. *Shift the prospect's focus.* Ignore the objection, if you can, and shift the prospect's attention to some other aspect of your product or service that you think will be particularly appealing. For example, if a prospect comments that a house you're showing is small, you might answer, "Yes, it requires very little upkeep," or, "but look at that view!"

6. *Keep the prospect talking.* The most important thing of all is to keep your dialogue with the prospect going. This gives you the opportunity to do more *probing*–asking questions that enable you to learn more about the prospect's true needs and individual circumstances.

In handling objections, you must also keep in mind that you won't be able to overcome each and every objection. It may be that, for whatever reason (price, style, size, color, fit, purpose, timing, or something else), your product or service *isn't* right for the prospect. In that case, not only will it be difficult to make the sale, but also you *shouldn't* make it. Even if you could convince the prospect to buy, it wouldn't be in his or her best interest–or in yours. Rather than create a dissatisfied customer, you're better off foregoing the sale and trying for the next best thing: a referral.

## Closing

Once you've gotten past any objections, you must be able to do one more thing: close. This is the moment of truth, when you ask the prospect to buy. This step should be a natural extension of the dialogue you've been having with the prospect. Unfortunately, it's a step that many business owners are reluctant to take because they fear rejection. Instead, either they just let their sales presentation trail off into nothing, hoping the customer will *ask* to buy, or they end up saying something like, "Well, that's it. If you need any more information, just ask." That's very nice, and it may be a good fallback position to take later, but it *isn't* a close, and it's not likely to result in a sale.

You can close in a number of ways. The simplest and most direct method is to *ask for the order.* "Shall I go ahead and write that up for you now?" This method can get fast results. The main problem with it, though, is that, by asking what's known as a *yes/no* question, you may be setting yourself up for the no.

One way to avoid asking a yes/no question is to *assume the order.* Rather than asking the prospect to buy, you can simply assume the sale has been made and proceed accordingly: "If you'll just fill in this information, I'll finish writing up your order." This method works fine *if* the prospect goes along with you. If the prospect doesn't, then be prepared to ask more questions to keep the dialogue going and try for a second close.

Another popular (and effective) close is the *alternative close.* This avoids the problem of the yes/no question by asking the prospect to choose between two or more alternatives: "Would you prefer the blue or the green?" Or, "Which day would you like it delivered, Monday or Tuesday?" The beauty of this closing technique is that, if the prospect picks one of the choices, the sale is made.

Two other closes you might use are the *added-inducement close* and the *warning-to-buy close.* The first one offers a price reduction, free service, gift, or some other inducement if the prospect buys now: "If you place your order today, I'll pay the shipping charges." The second close warns the prospect to buy before it's too late: "These are the last ones I have in stock. To guarantee delivery, I need to receive your order today." Both closes, while effective, should be used sparingly. The added-inducement close cuts into your profit margins and the warning-to-buy close, if used too often, can be perceived as a high-pressure tactic.

These and other closing methods that you may decide to use can help you to make more sales. Again, it's important to remember, though, that you don't want to force customers into buying what they don't want. The purpose of a close is to make it easy for prospects to choose what's right for them.

### Following Up

The selling process doesn't stop when the sale is made. To keep the customer happy and to assure yourself of repeat sales and referrals, you must do everything possible to see that the customer is satisfied with the purchase. In a sense this last step is the *first,* offering you the opportunity to reestablish contact with the customer and to begin the selling process again.

## Maintaining Good Customer Relations

Considering the time and money that go into finding prospects and convincing them to buy, it makes sense to maintain good customer relations. After all, it's easier to sell to a customer who's already sold on your business than it is to sell to someone who doesn't know anything about you. This explains why so many businesses claim that, "After the sale we don't forget the service."

To make sure that your customers are getting the service they deserve, it's important for you to do the following:

- Expedite each purchase.
- Provide personal service.

- Answer questions.
- Handle complaints.
- Solve problems.
- Stay in touch.

### Expedite the Purchase

Nothing is more frustrating to a customer than deciding to buy something and then having to wait longer than necessary to receive it. As the seller, you want to make certain that there are no delays in getting your product or service to the customer. Once the sale is made, you should do everything possible to expedite the purchase by (1) reassuring the customer that the purchase is the right one, (2) speeding delivery of the goods, and (3) overseeing any installation or implementation that may be required.

### Provide Personal Service

In an age of "cookie-cutter" service that treats all customers the same, or that offers no service at all, providing personal service can be a powerful customer-relations tool for winning customer loyalty. Everyone likes to be thought of as special or to get something extra. You can meet these needs by addressing each customer by name, paying attention to individual preferences, and doing more than is expected.

Contrary to what you might think, providing a personal touch doesn't have to increase your costs. What it requires more than expenditures of money is thoughtfulness. Examples include

- A restaurant owner remembering a customer's favorite table
- A toy store that has the batteries a customer needs (especially on Christmas Eve) to go with the toys purchased
- A pet-sitting service that also collects the client's mail and waters the plants while caring for the family pet
- A computer store that includes "user-friendly" instructions with the computers it sells.

Because these little things often mean a lot to customers, paying attention to them can give you a distinct advantage over businesses that don't.

## Answer Questions

Another way to serve your customers is to let them know that you're available to answer any questions that come up after the purchase is made. You might also want to set up a telephone/fax hot line or a website that customers can use when they need to get information in a hurry. This not only provides customers with a sense of security, but also can keep minor problems from becoming major ones. What's more, by keeping the lines of communication open, you stand a better chance of making more sales in the future.

## Handle Complaints

In addition to answering questions, you must also be prepared to handle complaints. Complaints are a fact of business life. Even the most service-oriented businesses can expect to receive them. The issue isn't who's right or who's wrong, but what needs to be done to satisfy the customer. If there is something wrong with your products or services, you want to determine what you can do to improve them. If a customer is unhappy with a purchase, you must decide how you can remedy the situation.

To handle complaints more efficiently and to let your customers know that you're on their side, it helps to follow these guidelines:

1. Listen to what the customer is telling you without interruption.
2. Don't become defensive or angry.
3. Ask questions to get additional details, if necessary.
4. Show the customer that you care.
5. Take steps to resolve the problem as quickly as possible.
6. Thank the customer for bringing the problem to your attention.

Even if you think that the complaint is unjustified or that the customer is wasting your time, remember that there's something worse than having to deal with a dissatisfied customer who complains. That's having a dissatisfied customer who *doesn't* complain and just takes his or her business someplace else.

## Solve Problems

The most successful sellers are problem solvers, not just when it comes to making the sale, but at helping customers put the products or services they've bought to best use. Instead of leaving customers to fend for themselves or saying, "That's your problem," they work with customers to find solutions to their problems. This joint approach to problem solving benefits not only the customer, but you as well. Customers who might not otherwise have come back will buy again and recommend you to the people they know.

### Stay in Touch

Instead of waiting for customers to contact you, take the initiative yourself. Staying in touch with customers on a regular basis shows that you care and puts you in a better position to anticipate customers' needs and to provide a high level of customer service.

Some of the ways that you can stay in touch include

- Telephoning from time to time to see how customers are doing
- Sending a card or a small gift at Christmas
- Sending out mailings with up-to-date information on your products, services, and prices
- Making periodic sales calls

And, of course, whenever you make a new sale, it never hurts to send the customer a thank-you note.

### Manage Expectations

When it comes to satisfying customers, it's not just what customers get from you that counts, but what they expect to get. Is your service as good as or better than customers expect it to be? Do they get as much for their money as they think they should get–or even more? A restaurant that includes a complimentary dessert with the meal at no extra charge exceeds customers' expectations and adds to their satisfaction. On the other hand, a restaurant that offers good food but in small portions may not live up to customers' expectations and be viewed as overpriced.

The key to satisfying your customers is to understand what they want and to manage their expectations. As shown in this formula, customer satisfaction is made up of two components:

$$\text{Customer satisfaction} = \frac{\text{Delivered performance}}{\text{Expected performance}}$$

"Expected performance" is what customers assume they will get when they buy a product or service. "Delivered performance" is what they actually get. The higher the expected performance is (for instance, everyone's saying how exciting a new movie is), the higher the delivered performance (lots of action and special effects) must be to avoid disappointment.

Thus, to keep customers satisfied, you can either (1) lower their expectations or (2) raise your delivery capabilities. Better still, you can do both, following the advice of customer-service experts to "underpromise and overdeliver."

Some of the things you can do to manage customers' expectations include

- *Keeping hype to a minimum.* Promising "the experience of a lifetime" or that a cosmetic product "will take off 20 years" creates expectations that will be difficult or impossible to meet.
- *Providing specifics.* Make it clear what's included in the product offering and what's extra, how much it will cost and how long it will take to receive it. In this way, customers won't have any unpleasant surprises later.
- *Letting customers know what's happening.* If there's a problem or a delay, it's important to keep customers up to date on the situation and the steps you are taking to set the matter straight.
- *Providing a little bit extra.* Is there something else you can offer customers or do for them? It doesn't have to be a lot, but it shows that you care–the "baker's dozen" of 13 doughnuts for the price of 12, free gift wrapping, a ride to work while a car is being repaired, or alterations included with clothing purchases.

## Empower Employees to Give Good Service

As your business expands, you must still do everything possible to empower your employees to provide good customer service. This means trusting them to make the right decisions and giving them the authority to head off problems before they occur or to resolve little problems before they become big ones. You'll need to work out some guidelines, of course, and to establish parameters within which employees may act on their own. Generally speaking, however, by empowering the employees who have direct contact with customers to take action themselves, the better your service will be. For example, this might include allowing front-line employees to

- Handle merchandise exchanges and returns
- Provide upgrades from one level of service to another
- Run credit checks and approve purchases
- Make minor adjustments on accounts when disputes occur
- Give customers refunds or complimentary goods or services to compensate them for poor service

## Customer Service Checklist

To determine whether you're doing everything you can to build a positive relationship with each customer, answer the questions in the following Customer Service Checklist.

| Customer Service Checklist | Answer Yes or No |
|---|---|
| 1. Is your selling strategy oriented toward satisfying each customer? | ________ |
| 2. Do you try to establish long-term relationships rather than just make a sale? | ________ |
| 3. During the selling process, do you find out what the customer's needs are? | ________ |
| 4. Are you a good listener? | ________ |
| 5. Do you know how to interpret the verbal and nonverbal messages that customers send? | ________ |
| 6. Do you show customers the benefits of buying your products or services? | ________ |
| 7. Will you forgo making a sale if the purchase isn't right for the customer? | ________ |
| 8. After a sale is made, do you follow up on it later to see that the customer is pleased with the purchase? | ________ |

*(continued)*

| Customer Service Checklist *(continued)* | Answer Yes or No |
|---|---|
| 9. Do you provide personal service? | ________ |
| 10. Are you available to answer any questions that customers may have? | ________ |
| 11. Do you handle complaints quickly and courteously? | ________ |
| 12. Are you a problem solver? | ________ |
| 13. Do you make it a point to stay in touch with customers? | ________ |
| 14. Do you try to give customers something extra for their money? | ________ |
| 15. Do you genuinely care about your customers? | ________ |
| 16. Do you know how to manage customers' expectations? | ________ |
| 17. Have you empowered your employees to provide good customer service? | ________ |
| 18. Do you believe that the customer is always right? | ________ |

# 15

# Safeguarding Your Business

The very act of forming your own business entails risk. The rewards of prosperity and self-fulfillment must be balanced against the risks of financial loss and personal dissatisfaction. There are no sure things in business. Still, such factors as planning, experience, adequate financing, managerial expertise, creativity, and a willingness to work hard can swing the odds in your favor. For these to be effective, though, you need an ongoing program of risk management.

Suppose any of the following should happen:

- Your building is damaged by fire.
- A customer is hurt in your store.
- An employee steals your merchandise.
- A car drives through your store window.
- Your accountant embezzles a large sum of money.
- One of your employees is injured on the job.
- Your store is burglarized.
- Your business is suffering because of shoplifting.
- Your partner dies.

What would you do? A likely answer is, "Call my insurance agent." Relying on insurance is only one of the ways to deal with these hazards, however.

## Risk Management

An effective program of risk management enables you to cope with risks by eliminating them, reducing them, accepting them, or transferring them. These methods can be used singly or in combination, depending on the risk, as well as on your own circumstances.

### Eliminating the Risk

Certain risks can be entirely eliminated. Among these are the risk of employee injury because of substandard materials or unsafe equipment, the risk of customer injury because of a hazardous store layout, and the risk of fire because of faulty wiring. There's no excuse for allowing risks that are solely the result of negligence or indifference. One who persists in doing so could wind up not only financially liable but criminally liable as well. And it's not enough merely to carry insurance. Gross negligence, or the flagrant violation of health and safety standards, is sufficient ground for an insurance carrier to void your policy.

### Reducing the Risks

It would be impossible for you to eliminate every business risk, even if you were aware of every one. Your best bet, then, is to reduce the risks. Close evaluation of your workplace, workers, and customers will enable you to take precautionary actions to reduce most of your business risks.

The risk of falling off a ladder can't be eliminated, but the use of safety ladders, with guardrails on either side, can reduce this risk. Keeping all merchandise boxes, cleaning supplies, tools, and electrical cords clear of customer walkways reduces the risk of having customers trip and injure themselves. The risks of breakage and theft can be reduced by displaying merchandise in locked cases. Electronic tags on merchandise, alert salespeople, closed-circuit cameras, burglar alarms, and security guards can also help you to combat theft.

### Accepting the Risk

Self-insurance, a method whereby you create your own contingency fund to pay for whatever business losses might arise, is another way of coping with risk. This enables a business to protect itself while avoiding payment of insurance premiums. Unfortunately, the protection this method provides is usually inadequate. Given current high replacement costs for buildings, equipment, furniture, and fixtures, as well as the staggering amounts of some judgment claims in liability cases, a small business that relies solely on self-insurance could easily be wiped out.

A policy of accepting the risk might be applied, however, when the risk cannot be eliminated and buying outside insurance is not profitable. For instance, if your losses from shoplifting are less than the insurance premiums to protect yourself against it, accepting the losses makes more sense. Furthermore, even when you do carry insurance against a particular type of risk, part of the risk usually must be accepted because of the policy's deductible provision.

### Transferring the Risk

The purchase of coverage from an insurance company enables businesses to transfer their risks. In exchange for a fee, the insurance company accepts the risks that the business wishes to be protected against. In effect, when you buy insurance you arrange to absorb small periodic losses (premiums) rather than a large uncertain loss. To adequately protect your property and avoid large damage claims that result from public liability or employee injury suits, you need insurance.

## Types of Insurance Coverage

### Fire Insurance

In a standard fire-insurance policy, your building, the property contained within it, and property temporarily removed from it because of fire are protected against damage inflicted by fire or lightning. This coverage does not extend to accounting records, bills, deeds, money, securities, or manuscripts. Nor are you protected against such hazards as windstorms, hail, smoke, explosions, vandalism, automatic sprinkler leakage, and malicious mischief. To guard excluded valuables and protect yourself against loss from these hazards, you must obtain additional coverage. Neither fire resulting from war nor actions taken under the orders of a civil authority are covered by insurance.

Depending on the terms of your policy, compensation may be made in any of three ways: (1) the insurance carrier may pay you the current cash value of the damaged property, (2) the property may be repaired or replaced, or (3) the property may be taken over by the insurer, who then reimburses you at its appraised value.

Most fire-insurance policies are written for a three-year period, and both you and the insurer have the right to cancel. You may cancel your policy at any time. The insurer, however, must give you five days' notice before canceling. In either event, you will be reimbursed for any premiums that have been paid in advance. If you are the one to cancel, however, a penalty as set forth in your policy may be assessed against your refund.

To keep your fire-insurance policy valid, it's your responsibility to use all reasonable means to protect the insured property both before and after a fire. If you knowingly increase the fire hazard–by renting part of your building to a fireworks manufacturer, for example–this could void your policy. Hiding pertinent information from the insurer, or leaving your building unoccupied for more than 60 days, is also cause for voiding your policy.

Should it become necessary for you to file an insurance claim, you will be required to provide the insurance company with a complete inventory list, detailing the types, quantities, and values of the damaged property. Unless an extension is granted, you generally have 60 days in which to do this.

### Liability Insurance

As the operator of your own business, you are responsible for the safety of your employees and customers. If a customer slips on a wet floor, you may be liable for damages. You're also responsible for the products or services you sell. For instance, the owner of a garage could be held liable for using a car wax that strips the paint off a customer's car, or for employing a mechanic who forgets to set the hand brake on a car that rolls into the street and causes an accident. In the first case, the garage owner might have to cover the cost of a new paint job. In the second, there's no telling how much the cost might be. Was the car damaged? Were other cars damaged? Was anyone injured in the accident? These are just the physical damages for which the garage owner may be liable. What about the mental anguish of the parties involved in the accident? By the time all the costs have been added in, the entire assets of the garage could be wiped out.

Most liability policies cover losses stemming from bodily injury or property-damage claims, expenses for medical services required at the time of the accident, investigation, and court costs. The actual amount that your policy will pay depends on both the limit per accident and the limit per person provided for in it. For example, if your policy has a per-accident limit of $1 million and a per-person limit of $300,000, and if one person receives a $500,000 judgment against you, the insurance company will pay only $300,000. This means you are responsible for paying the remaining $200,000 even though it is within your per-accident limit. The guide word here is *caution.* Make sure you understand and agree with any limitations in your policy. If the limit is $300,000 per person, is that adequate coverage?

If an accident does occur, even if it seems minor, contact your insurance agent immediately. This enables the insurance company to begin its investigation while the relevant information is readily available. Failure to notify the company can void your policy.

The most common types of liability insurance are

- *General liability insurance.* The most far-reaching type of liability insurance available, it provides basic coverage against all liabilities not specifically excluded from the policy.
- *Product liability insurance.* This insurance protects you against financial loss in the event that someone is injured by a product you manufacture or distribute.
- *Professional liability insurance.* For doctors, lawyers, consultants, and others who provide advice or information or perform a service, this insurance protects you against damage claims brought by dissatisfied clients.

**Marine Insurance**

To protect yourself against damage to your property while it is being transported from one place to another, you should obtain marine insurance. Originally issued to protect ship cargoes against the perils of the high seas, this type of insurance now covers property losses on both water and land. *Ocean marine insurance* protects property carried on board a ship at sea or in port. *Inland marine insurance* protects property being transported by ship, rail, truck, or plane.

**Automobile Insurance**

If you plan to use one or more cars or trucks in your business, automobile insurance is a must. Coverage can be provided to protect you against

- Bodily injury claims
- Property damage claims
- Medical payments
- Uninsured motorist damages

- Damage to your vehicle
- Towing costs

The amount of coverage you need and the costs of an automobile insurance policy depend on

- The number of cars or trucks being insured
- Their value
- The kinds of driving that will be done (making deliveries, hauling equipment, driving clients around)
- Your location

When five or more motor vehicles are used in your business, you can generally insure them under a low-cost fleet policy. As far as deductibles go, the higher they are, the lower your premiums.

You may find that automobile insurance is a good buy even if you don't plan to use any motor vehicles in your business. This is because you could be held liable for employees or subcontractors who operate their own vehicles, or those of customers, while on company business.

### Workers' Compensation Insurance

Common law requires that an employer (1) provide employees with a safe place to work, (2) hire competent coworkers, (3) provide safe tools, and (4) warn employees of existing danger. An employer who fails to do so is liable for damages, including claims for on-the-job injury and occupational diseases. Sometimes payment can be required for the remainder of the disabled worker's life.

Under workers' compensation insurance, the insurance pays all sums you are legally required to pay a claimant. One way to save money on this insurance is to make sure your employees are properly classified. Because rates vary with the degree of hazard associated with each occupational category, improperly classifying an employee in a high-risk occupation unduly raises your rates. Another way to save money is to use safety measures that will lower your accident rate and thereby reduce premiums.

### Business-Interruption Insurance

Many business owners fail to purchase business-interruption insurance because they don't think they need it. If a building burns down, they think a standard fire insurance policy will suffice. But what about the loss of business income during the months it takes to rebuild? What about the expenses that continue to mount up even though your doors are closed– taxes, interest on loans, salaries, rent, utilities? Yet not until it is too late does many a business owner realize that fire insurance alone isn't enough.

Only business-interruption insurance covers your fixed expenses and expected profits during the time your business is closed down. Also, make sure that the policy is written to provide coverage in the event that your business isn't totally shut down but is seriously disrupted. Some policies pay off only in the event of a total shutdown. You should also remember that an indirect peril could force you to suspend operations as well. What if an important supplier's or customer's plant burned down, temporarily interrupting your business? What if your power, water, or phone service were disrupted for a spell? Protection against these hazards can be written into your business-interruption policy, but you have to ask for it.

### Glass Insurance

Although glass insurance may seem insignificant, most businesses should have it. The costs of replacing broken plate-glass windows, panels, doors, signs, and display cases are so high that you can't afford to be without it. Furthermore, delays in making the replacement can result in vandalism or theft, which in turn results in additional property loss.

A glass insurance policy covers the cost not only of replacing the glass itself, but also of redoing any lettering or ornamentation on the glass, installing the glass (including temporary glass or boards, if needed), and repairing any frame damage. The only exclusions in the standard all-risk glass insurance policy are for glass damage from fire or war. In the case of fire, your fire-insurance policy provides coverage.

### Fidelity Bonds

Most new business owners are unaware that, on average, thefts by employees far surpass business losses from burglary, robbery, and shoplifting. The accountant who embezzles thousands of dollars and then goes to Acapulco and the salesclerk who dips into the cash drawer come readily to mind. Less obvious examples include

- Putting fictitious employees on the payroll and pocketing their paychecks
- Ringing up lower prices on merchandise sold to friends or accomplices

- Stealing merchandise, equipment, or supplies
- Misappropriating company property for personal use
- Lying on expense vouchers
- Falsifying time cards

Unless you or members of your immediate family handle all phases of your business operation, you should obtain fidelity bond protection. This is available in three formats: individual bonds, schedule bonds, and blanket bonds. *Individual bonds* cover theft by a specific named individual. *Schedule bonds* list every name or position to be covered. *Blanket bonds*, the most encompassing of the three, cover all employees without reference to individual names or positions.

Before an employee is bonded, the insurance company issuing the bond conducts a character investigation to determine whether anything is known of past acts of dishonesty. Then, if the employee is deemed bondable, coverage is provided. If a prospective employee refuses to be bonded, this could be a tip-off that the applicant has something to hide.

### Crime Insurance

Crime insurance covers you against business losses resulting from the criminal activities of people who aren't associated with your business. The three categories of crime insurance are burglary insurance, robbery insurance, and comprehensive insurance.

1. *Burglary insurance* protects your safes and inventory against thefts in which there is evidence of forcible entry. This means that if a thief enters through an unlocked door or window without disturbing the premises, your burglary policy does not cover any losses. Nor does the standard burglary policy protect accounting records, manuscripts, or certain valuables, such as furs, that are kept in display windows. To cover these, additional insurance is necessary. Besides protecting you against losses from stolen property, burglary insurance provides coverage for damage sustained during the burglary.
2. *Robbery* differs from burglary, in that it involves a face-to-face confrontation. The robber actually uses force, or the threat of violence, to take property from the person guarding it. A *robbery insurance* policy covers the money, property, or securities taken, as well as property damage that occurs during the robbery. Another feature of this policy

is that it isn't limited to robberies that take place inside your building. Thus, if you are robbed while making a delivery, you are covered.

3. *Comprehensive insurance* is popular because, in addition to protecting you against burglary and robbery, it also protects against a variety of other hazards, including counterfeit money and forged checks. For instance, deception does not constitute robbery. If a con artist tricks you or an employee into parting with property, no force or threat of violence is involved. Therefore, it isn't a robbery, and unless you have a comprehensive policy, you aren't covered. Coverage is also provided against the thief who gains entry to your business without any apparent use of force.

### Personal Insurance

Just as there's a need to insure your property against loss, there's an equal need to insure both yourself and your employees. Group health and life insurance, a retirement plan, and key personnel insurance all help to do this. The need for these may seem a long way off, but more and more small businesses are offering an employee benefits package that includes health and life insurance as a way of retaining valued personnel. If you decide to incorporate a retirement plan, too, there's another advantage. Contributions made to the plan for yourself and your employees are deductible from your federal income tax.

*Key personnel insurance*, long a staple in the insurance portfolio of major corporations, can be just as necessary for the small business owner. Could your business survive the death or disability of a partner or a key employee? If not, key personnel insurance can at least ease the loss. The proceeds from the insurance are exempt from income tax and payable directly to the business. The policy itself has a cash value and may be used as loan collateral.

## Recognizing Warning Signals

The old adage that an ounce of prevention is worth a pound of cure readily pertains to risk management. Before you can take precautionary measures to head off an impending danger, however, you have to recognize the danger. The way to do this is to be alert to the warning signals around you. The following examples indicate a fire, accident, or theft waiting to happen–if it hasn't happened already:

**Fire**

1. Overloaded circuits
2. Fuse blowouts
3. Frayed electrical cords
4. Overheating of equipment
5. Inoperative or inaccessible fire extinguishers
6. Trash piled up
7. Smoking permitted in high-risk areas
8. Improper procedures in use, storage, or disposal of flammable materials
9. Power plant, heating, ventilation, and air-conditioning equipment not checked out at regular intervals

**Accident**

1. Workers inadequately trained for their jobs
2. Lack of safety rules or failure to enforce them
3. Use of substandard materials or equipment
4. Poor quality control
5. A hazardous layout
6. Admitting customers to the work area
7. Letting customers use equipment themselves
8. Lack of knowledge about products you sell

**Employee Theft**

1. Inadequate reference checks on employees
2. An employee who refuses to take an annual vacation
3. An employee who never leaves the work area during lunch
4. An employee who always arrives at work early and stays late
5. One employee handling all bookkeeping procedures
6. Expenses that are higher than predicted
7. Inventory shortages

8. Finding merchandise or equipment in trash bins
9. Checks and money orders left sitting on desktops
10. Unfamiliar names on the payroll
11. An increase in sales returns
12. Slow collections

On the surface, none of these examples is proof of embezzlement, but their occurrence does indicate the need for additional investigation or tightened management controls.

**Crime**

1. Accepting checks without asking to see proper identification
2. Accepting checks that have been endorsed twice
3. Accepting blank checks that don't have computer-coded characteristics
4. Keeping large amounts of money in cash registers
5. Inattention to customers when they
   a. Wear loose clothing
   b. Carry a large purse or open shopping bag
   c. Seem nervous or anxious
   d. Wander into a restricted area
   e. Are left unsupervised in dressing rooms
6. Easily removable tickets on merchandise
7. Failure of the cash register operator to open and inspect items that might conceal stolen goods
8. Messy displays that make it difficult to spot what's there and what's missing
9. Employee unfamiliarity with the merchandise your store carries
10. Poor lighting
11. Unsuitable locks on doors and windows
12. Loose handling of keys

## Insurance Checklist

To make sure that you've adequately insured your business, use the following Insurance Checklist to indicate the coverage you need.

| Type of Insurance | Purchase | Do Not Purchase |
|---|---|---|
| **Property insurance** | | |
| Fire | ______ | ______ |
| Windstorm | ______ | ______ |
| Hail | ______ | ______ |
| Smoke | ______ | ______ |
| Explosion | ______ | ______ |
| Vandalism | ______ | ______ |
| Water damage | ______ | ______ |
| Glass | ______ | ______ |
| **Liability insurance** | ______ | ______ |
| **Workers' Compensation** | ______ | ______ |
| **Business interruption** | ______ | ______ |
| Fidelity | ______ | ______ |
| Robbery | ______ | ______ |
| Burglary | ______ | ______ |
| Comprehensive | ______ | ______ |
| **Personal** | | |
| Health | ______ | ______ |
| Life | ______ | ______ |
| Key personnel | ______ | ______ |

# 16

# International Marketing

As geographic distances continue to shrink with each new advance in technology and transportation, international marketing is becoming an increasingly attractive source of revenues for businesses large and small. In the past, businesses generally needed a large sales force and considerable financing and connections to make their way in the global marketplace, but this is no longer the case. Aided by the Internet and improved telecommunications equipment, entrepreneurs are finding that once hard-to-reach foreign customers are often just a keystroke or fax away.

## Why Go Global?

It is not only easier to get a foothold in foreign markets these days, but also sensible and smart to do so for several reasons:

1. *Changing consumer needs.* As consumers undergo demographic and lifestyle changes, moving from one age, income level, and family or work stage to the next, these changes can raise or lower their demand for specific goods and services, providing increased domestic opportunities for some marketers while forcing others to look abroad. For example, as American birth rates drop and the population ages, Johnson & Johnson, Gerber's, and other companies in the baby-products field have expanded their overseas operations.
2. *Saturated domestic markets.* Even "hot" must-have products eventually reach their peak, and sales start to decline as everyone who wants the product already has it, or a "new and improved" product comes along to take its place. Introducing the product into new countries is a way to reach untapped markets and to extend the product life cycle.
3. *Competitive advantages.* Operating in more than one country can give businesses a competitive edge when it comes to spotting new trends, building name recognition, and guarding against economic downturns in any one market.

4. *Cost factors.* Often it's less expensive to do business overseas, so your profit margins go up. Also, increasing your market size through foreign expansion can provide *economies of scale* (lower unit costs) due to larger production runs, as well as an outlet for excess inventory.
5. *Tax incentives.* In an effort to encourage international trade, the United States government and many foreign governments provide a variety of business-tax incentives in such areas as the handling of corporate and personal income tax, value-added tax (VAT), duty-free import tax, depreciation allowance on plant and machinery, research-and-development expenditures, and interest on loans.
6. *Government regulations.* Depending on the laws and regulations in place, some countries can be more probusiness than others, making it easier to conduct business there than elsewhere. As an added inducement to do business in their countries, some foreign governments are willing to cut through red tape, expediting licenses and permits, for example, or to waive certain restrictions, such as those pertaining to hours of operation or product content requirements.

## Evaluating Foreign Markets

For all its appeal, though, international marketing isn't something to enter into casually. Finding the right markets for your goods and services takes time and research. Also, because consumer needs and preferences often vary from one culture to another, expanding globally may entail modifying your product offering–changing its name, characteristics, appearance, packaging, pricing, advertising, or distribution methods–to satisfy local trends.

High-tech products can run into compatibility problems with existing products or systems in place in a country, or they can end up being too advanced for some markets, while technologically inadequate for others. Even simple products can present difficulties in entering new markets. Take canned soup, for instance, a staple in most American homes. In Mexico, the cans need to be larger than in the United States because the average family is larger. In South America, where cooking from scratch is the norm, it wasn't just the serving size that needed to be modified, but the soup itself–from a canned concentrate to a dry ingredient mix that consumers could use as a seasoning, rather than a substitute, for their own homemade soups.

Even when a product is fine as it is, marketers may discover that the brand name or advertising message identifying it is wrong in some parts of the world. General Motors learned this lesson the hard way when its popular Chevrolet Nova got a negative response in Latin America. Why? Because the automobile's name "Nova" sounded like the Spanish phrase "*no va*"–doesn't go! Along with names, slogans can be especially difficult to translate into foreign languages successfully. Pepsi Cola's famous "Come Alive! You're in the Pepsi generation!" slogan was interpreted in some countries to mean that Pepsi could raise the dead. And a major airline's campaign asking customers to enjoy the comfort of flying in its leather seats actually invited them to enjoy the comfort of flying naked.

As you can see, when it comes to entering foreign markets, overcoming the barriers of time and distance is just the beginning. To adequately evaluate each new market, you must consider its cultural, economic, political, legal, and competitive environment to gauge the demand for your products and services and the profit potential of doing business there.

In evaluating each country, among the questions you should ask are these:

- Is there a need for my products or services?
- How would they be used?
- Who would buy them? Where? Why? How often? In what quantities?
- How big is the market? Is it growing or shrinking?
- What kinds of modifications would I have to make?
- What are my projected revenues and expenses?
- What competition would I face? How strong is it?
- What laws or regulations would have an impact on my business?
- What is the local government doing to help or hinder those who do business there?
- Are there any tax incentives or other inducements?
- Would I have ready access to suppliers and distributors? What about skilled labor?
- Are the local media adequate and affordable for promoting my business?
- How good is the country's infrastructure (roads, water, electricity, transportation, communications)?
- Are the political and economic systems stable?
- Is the country safe?

At the same time you're looking at the various trade opportunities in foreign countries, you should also look at your own business in terms of its current situation and its overall objectives. For instance,

- What are your short-term and long-term plans?
- What are your strengths and weaknesses?
- What resources (land, labor, capital, technology) are available to you?
- What level of personal commitment are you able to give to expanding your business internationally?
- What level of support can you count on from others–partners, employees, investors, lenders, suppliers, government, and so on?
- What impact would foreign trade have on your domestic operations?
- What are the costs and benefits of entering foreign markets?
- What changes would you have to make in your product offering or methods of operation to successfully adapt to the global marketing environment?

In shifting your attention back and forth between the global environment and your domestic business, keep in mind that a foreign market that's desirable for one business may not be for another with different objectives, products, or resources. It's important to make sure that the opportunities you pursue are in sync with what's best for your business and will take it in the direction you want.

## Utilizing Marketing Research Data: Secondary versus Primary Data

The more you know about the foreign markets in which you do business or are thinking about entering, the greater your ability to make the right decisions. To accurately assess where and how to invest your resources for the best return, there's no substitute for good market research data.

As you'll quickly find, there's an abundance of marketing research data available on international trade. To make the most of the time and money you put into gathering it, though, it's important to know the difference between secondary and primary data. *Secondary data* is information that has been gathered by someone else and that you can readily find in books, newspaper and magazine articles, government and industry reports, the Internet, computer databases and programs, and other print or electronic sources. Because this data can be quickly obtained, often at a low cost or even free of charge, you should use it *first*. *Primary data*, on the other hand, is information you gather yourself or hire someone to obtain for you. You or your researcher will probably specially tailor the research to meet your needs, using interviews, surveys, observations, and other investigative techniques to gather the required data. Inasmuch as it's more costly and time-consuming to obtain, you should use primary data *after* you've exhausted your sources of secondary data.

## Sources of Information

To get the information you need and to make an accurate evaluation of the foreign demand for your goods and services, you will find these public and private sources of marketing research data particularly helpful:

- United States government
- Foreign governments
- International organizations
- Trade and professional associations
- Commercial banks and investment houses
- Marketing research firms
- Advertising agencies
- Export management companies
- Publications, software, and websites

### United States Government

The U.S. government offers more information on international trade than any other source. Through its agencies, programs, services, publications, and databases, there's virtually no end to the marketing research data you can obtain from it. The following government agencies are the key ones to contact for information or to get help in such areas as obtaining financing, locating foreign buyers or sellers, and dealing with regulations.

**Department of Commerce** In addition to the major role it plays in supporting and promoting business activities in the United States, the Department of Commerce (DOC) is deeply involved in helping to generate foreign trade. To accomplish this, it maintains an extensive database of global marketing information and oversees the working of these agencies specializing in foreign trade: the International Trade Administration, U.S. and Foreign Commercial Service, Bureau of Export Administration, Center for International Research, and the U.S. Travel and Tourism Administration.

***International Trade Administration*** Through its headquarters in Washington, DC, and district offices throughout the United States and Puerto Rico, the International Trade Administration (ITA) provides marketing research data and counseling to businesses involved in foreign trade. The ITA can provide current information on thousands of products in more than 200 markets or prepare customized research reports specifically designed for your business. One of the ITA's greatest strengths is its *country desk* operation–a network of specialists that monitors worldwide economic and political activity on a country-by-country basis. These specialists (known as "country desk officers") can assist individual businesses seeking to know more about a country and the types of market conditions that exist there.

The ITA also has a *trade development* unit made up of experts in various industries whose job is to help promote American business interests in seven industry sectors: (1) aerospace; (2) automotive affairs and consumer goods; (3) basic industries; (4) capital goods and international construction; (5) science and electronics; (6) services, textiles, and apparel; and (7) trade information and analysis–a cross-sectional unit providing general information on export promotion.

***U.S. & Foreign Commercial Service*** With trade specialists located in major cities throughout the United States and abroad, this agency works closely with American businesses seeking to find trading partners and set up foreign channels of distribution for their products or services. Providing ongoing, one-on-one counseling, US&FCS specialists can assist you in several ways, including compiling background information on foreign businesses; putting you in touch with sales representatives, agents, and buyers; and setting up meetings with government officials.

***Bureau of Export Administration*** This is the agency to contact for information on export licensing and export controls on the goods and services that can be traded with foreign countries. The BXA operates the Export License Application and Information Network (ELAIN)–an electronic system for evaluating and processing export license applications that you can access via computer.

***Center for International Research*** A division of the U.S. Census Bureau, the Center for International Research (CIR) gathers worldwide statistical data on population growth, demographics, health and life spans, education and literacy rates, employment, and other economic and social trends. The information the CIR compiles can be especially helpful in providing insight into how people live in various countries and the types of goods and services they are most likely to purchase.

***U.S. Travel and Tourism Administration*** This agency is charged with promoting the American travel and tourism industry. By working with industry members to develop foreign interest in the United States as a destination for business and leisure travel, the USTTA is active in helping American businesses to expand into other countries and to create alliances with foreign companies in the travel field. In addition to providing data on international travel and foreign market characteristics, it assists businesses in overcoming trade barriers and contacting potential overseas partners.

**Department of State** The Department of State (DOS) maintains embassies and consulates throughout the world, which can be excellent sources of foreign marketing information. Drawing on these resources, the DOS, like the ITA, also has a *country desk* operation of specialists who can provide businesses with the latest research data on a country-by-country basis. Headquartered in Washington, DC, country-desk officers communicate regularly with DOS members stationed overseas and are in a good position to keep American businesses informed of foreign developments that might have an impact on them.

**Small Business Administration** In addition to providing small businesses with management assistance and access to financing, the Small Business Administration (SBA) offers export counseling and other services to help small businesses enter foreign markets. SBA trade specialists in Washington, DC, and at local offices conduct trade seminars, compile information on foreign markets, advise on trade regulations and laws, and identify potential overseas buyers, distributors, licensees, and joint-venture partners. Much of this activity is carried out in partnership with Small Business Development Centers (SBDCs) run by colleges and universities. For more information on SBDCs and the services they offer, see Chapter 18.

**U.S. Customs Service** Operating under the Treasury Department, the U.S. Customs Service enforces the laws pertaining to goods imported into the United States or exported to other countries. Possessing broad authority, the Customs Service has the power to inspect cargo, seize goods, detain shipments, or have them returned to their countries of origin. Thus, to ensure that any goods you will be sending or receiving comply with U.S. laws regarding the goods themselves, their points of origin or destination, and so on, it's a good idea to check with the Customs Service before making any arrangements. Personnel at the Customs Service headquarters in Washington, DC, or a local office in your area can answer your questions.

**Foreign Agriculture Service** The Foreign Agriculture Service (FAS), a division of the Department of Agriculture, is a good source of marketing information and assistance for businesses involved in farming or food processing and distribution. With trade specialists at U.S. embassies in numerous countries and FAS offices in key foreign markets, agency representatives often serve as facilitators, helping American businesses to reach prospective buyers and promote their agricultural and food products. The FAS also works closely with agricultural and food industry trade associations and participates in international expositions and food shows that provide opportunities to showcase U.S. exports.

### Foreign Governments

Most foreign governments are eager to assist American businesses in finding out about the trade opportunities in their countries. You can reach foreign government officials in their countries or by contacting them in the United States through their embassies and consulates, foreign trade offices, and travel and tourism offices. The *commercial attachés* at embassies and consulates are especially good information sources to use because they know about current business developments in their countries and often can help you to reach the right people and cut through bureaucratic red tape.

### International Organizations

Many international organizations gather country-specific data that can be useful to businesses in exploring overseas markets. In terms of the quality and quantity of the data they collect, these organizations are among the best.

**United Nations** The United Nations is unsurpassed in the breadth and depth of the global information it compiles on everything from global health matters and quality of life to telecommunications and technology. It produces numerous reports throughout the year, which are available in printed or electronic form, including its *Statistical Yearbook, International Trade Statistics Yearbook,* and *Demographic Yearbook.*

**Organization of Economic Cooperation and Development** Made up of the world's leading industrialized nations, the OECD's goal is to promote goodwill and trade among its member countries. Toward this end, it produces economic surveys on each of the countries in the group, trade reports by country and commodity, and special reports on issues such as the environment, technology, consumer policy, and social problems.

**World Bank** Formed at the end of World War II to assist countries in their rebuilding efforts, the World Bank now focuses its attention on helping developing nations to achieve economic independence by providing them with financial advice and access to investment capital. In this capacity, it has put together an extensive database on the socioeconomic conditions in these countries, as well as opportunities for American businesses to obtain contracts on current development projects.

**World Trade Center Association** Comprising more than 160 World Trade Centers in cities around the globe, this organization enables the centers to share information and combine their resources in order to stimulate international trade and business activity. The WTCA maintains an online international data link of business opportunities and market information on prospective buyers and sellers. In addition to this, individual centers provide meeting and exhibit facilities, education and training, seminars, counseling, and research data on foreign markets. To reach the organization's headquarters or locate specific centers, contact the World Trade Center Association, One World Trade Center, New York, NY 10048, telephone (212) 313-4600.

## Trade and Professional Associations

Trade and professional associations representing specific industries or professions, such as the telecommunications, travel, food service, and engineering fields, can be valuable research tools–both for their information on foreign markets and their networking opportunities. To find out about the full range of services these associations have to offer and about how to contact the ones relevant to your business, see Chapter 18.

## Commercial Banks and Investment Houses

Commercial banks and investment houses often have international departments that collect foreign market data and financial information that can be of use to their business customers. In addition to helping you to evaluate local market conditions and to find foreign lenders or investors, they can also help with day-to-day matters such as determining exchange rates, running credit checks, and arranging for letter-of-credit payments (guarantees) on sales or purchases.

## Marketing Research Firms

Marketing research firms with expertise in studying foreign markets can assist you in obtaining both secondary and primary data. This might include such typically requested secondary data as reports and statistics on economic conditions and consumer spending. Or, if you need specific information directly related to your products or services–say, how a product tastes or consumers' reactions to its name or image–a marketing research firm can determine what primary research techniques to use (surveys, focus groups, and so on) and can gather and interpret these data.

## Advertising Agencies

International advertising agencies or foreign-based local agencies can sometimes provide useful marketing research data, as well. In order to create effective advertising campaigns and promotional materials, it's important for them to know about the cultural characteristics of the markets in which their work is used. As a result, agencies often end up doing their own marketing research or using outside firms to get a better handle on these markets. This information is then used on behalf of clients or made available to them to use in formulating their international marketing strategies.

### Export Management Companies

Export management companies (EMCs)–companies that represent manufacturers overseas, soliciting and handling sales transactions–can be another source of marketing information. What makes them so useful is their firsthand knowledge of foreign competitive environments and local distribution channels. Of all the information sources available, EMCs tend to be closest to the customer–to the product users themselves.

### Publications, Software, and Websites

In researching international marketing opportunities, there's no shortage of information readily available in print or via computer programs and online databases. As noted, many government agencies and private organizations continually generate data, which you can access for nominal fees. Also, with the continued growth of the Internet, more information is available every day. It's just a matter of knowing where to look. The information sources that follow are all good places to start.

### Publications

- *Breaking into the Trade Game,* U.S. Small Business Administration, Washington, DC.
- *Business America,* U.S. Government Printing Office, Washington, DC. Published biweekly, the purpose of this publication is to help U.S. businesses compete more effectively overseas by providing them with information and analysis on foreign developments.
- *Developing Your International Business Plan.* Lake Michigan College, International Business Center, Benton Harbor, MI.
- *International Business.* American International Publishing Corporation, New York. This monthly publication focuses on current development in international trade and the global marketing environment.

### Software/Databases

- International Business Network, American International Publishing Company, New York; online network for international business research.
- National Trade Data Bank, U.S. Department of Commerce, Washington, DC; CD-ROM disc released monthly that provides updated in-

formation on international trade activity and country-specific developments.

- PC GLOBE, Michigan Small Business Development Center, Wayne State University, Detroit; software program on world demographics and geographic information.

**Websites**

- www.embpage.org Embassy home page connects you to embassies and consulates around the world.
- www.exporthotline.com Includes thousands of market research reports, a trade library, market intelligence on 80 countries, and numerous links to other sites.
- www.exim.gov Provides access to the Export–Import Bank of the United States.
- www.ita.doc.gov The ITA of the DOC provides trade information and statistics, addresses and phone numbers of export-assistance centers throughout the United States, and country data and analysis on foreign markets.
- www.sba.gov The U.S. SBA offers a wealth of information and resources on international marketing and on the SBA's various export-support programs.
- www.tradecompass.com Trade Compass provides export information, access to international business Web links, and a variety of online resources.
- www.tradeport.org This site has a great deal of information on exporting.

## Choosing Your Entry Strategy

After doing your research, if you decide to go ahead and make your move into the international marketplace, the next step is to choose your entry strategy. As you can see from the following chart, there are a number of strategies you can use, each one requiring a different level of investment and risk.

**Exporting/Importing**

The quickest way to enter the international marketplace with the smallest investment of capital and the least risk is through exporting and import-

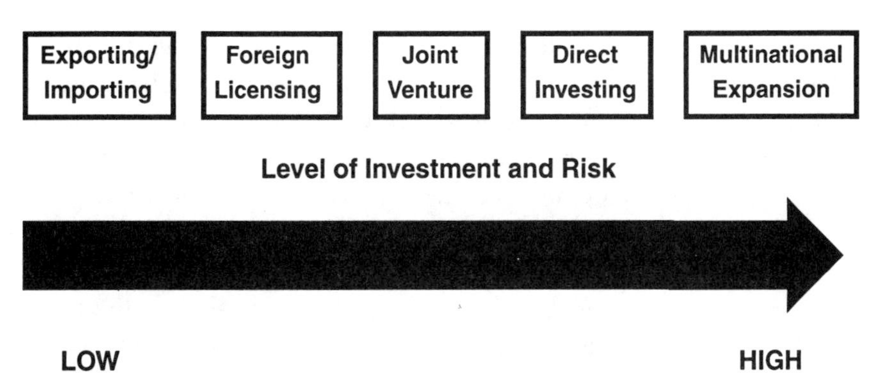

International Marketing Entry Strategies

ing–selling your goods and services to buyers overseas or bringing foreign-made products into the United States. The most common entry strategy, this move is often prompted when a business starts to receive requests for product information from foreign buyers or discovers a product overseas that its U.S. customers might like. Whether handled on a limited basis by your business itself or on a wider scale through foreign agents and distributors, this method is easy to employ. Also, because any losses are limited to the value of the goods themselves, the level of risk is minimal.

## Foreign Licensing

A business that uses this entry strategy authorizes another business to use its name, technology, processes, or patents to manufacture and sell goods or services in foreign markets, in exchange for a fee and/or royalty payments. The advantage of this method is that it generates income for your business without requiring any cash outlay on your part. It's also a good way to test the demand for your products in other countries and to build your name recognition. However, if the quality of the products or services that your licensees sell overseas isn't on a par with your own, this strategy can damage your reputation. Also, if you decide to enter the same markets yourself later on, you could end up competing with your own licensees. These factors add to the risk.

## Joint Venture

This entry method, which has been used successfully by both small businesses and large ones, such as McDonald's and Disney, involves teaming up with a foreign partner to jointly start and run an overseas business. Rather than going it alone, you and your partner pool your resources and agree to share in the rewards and risks associated with the venture. This approach not only reduces the amount of investment capital you need, but also gives you the advantage of having a partner who is familiar with the tastes and culture of the country where the business is located. Even with these advantages, though, this method requires more commitment from you and entails a higher level of risk than the earlier ones. As noted in Chapter 5, the key to making a joint venture work is to choose your partners well. For help in locating potential international joint-venture partners, the SBA offers an electronic database called Reach Strategic Venture Partners (RSVP). RSVP is available through SBA online (www.sbaonline.sba.gov).

### Direct Investment

If a suitable partner isn't available or you prefer to retain sole control of a foreign business operation, then a possible strategy is to make a direct investment in the country, setting up the business by yourself. This lets you run the business the way you want to and gives you the full benefits of ownership. At the same time, though, it puts the entire burden of costs and risks on you, as well as the responsibility to make the business succeed.

### Multinational Expansion

The most far-reaching of the entry strategies, this one offers the greatest potential rewards but also has the highest degree of risk. Rather than sending your products *to* foreign markets, your business becomes a *part* of those markets, with facilities and personnel within the countries. Taking the direct-investment strategy one step further, it calls for your business to see itself not only as an American business, but also as a business of the world, as a "multinational company," or MNC, with customers (and possibly investors) around the globe. Obviously requiring a high level of commitment and resources, this entry strategy takes time to develop over the life of a business and generally doesn't come into play until the business has gained experience in using some of the earlier market-entry methods.

## International Marketing Checklist

To compete successfully in today's global marketplace and make the most of any foreign trade opportunities you pursue, answer the questions in this International Marketing Checklist.

| International Marketing Checklist | Answer Yes or No |
|---|---|
| 1. Have you identified a demand for your products or services in foreign markets? | ________ |
| 2. Do you know who your foreign customers would be? | ________ |
| 3. Have you researched your intended customers' needs, wants, preferences, and purchasing habits? | ________ |
| 4. Would you be able to compete effectively in the markets you wish to enter? | ________ |
| 5. Are your products or services compatible with the local technology? | ________ |
| 6. Would entering foreign markets enable you to achieve economies of scale? | ________ |
| 7. Would you be able to keep any produc-modification costs low enough to make your desired profit? | ________ |
| 8. Have you considered which channels of distribution to use? | ________ |
| 9. Are you familiar with the local government regulations that would apply to your business? | ________ |
| 10. Have you evaluated the tax implications of entering foreign markets? | ________ |
| 11. Do the countries you would operate in have strong enough infrastructures to support your business activities? | ________ |
| 12. Do you have the necessary resources to carry out your foreign expansion plans? | ________ |
| 13. Would entering foreign markets strengthen your overall business operations? | ________ |

# 17

# Franchising

An alternative to forming your own business from scratch is to purchase a franchise. According to Department of Commerce statistics, franchising has grown to such proportions that franchised operations now account for annual sales of more than 40 percent of all U.S. retail sales. Although commonly associated with fast-food outlets, franchising applies to more than the food-service industry. Franchises have become particularly visible in a variety of areas, including hotels and motels, print shops, automobile dealerships, service stations, beauty salons, travel agencies, convenience stores, employment agencies, accounting services, and real-estate brokerages. In fact, there seem to be few, if indeed any, businesses that don't lend themselves to franchising. The most recent entrants have been the legal and medical professions.

The boom in franchising began shortly after World War II and has continued ever since, despite fluctuations in the economy and added government regulations. The boosters of franchising predict that the future will be even better because franchising offers investors a tested business concept and support system. The critics of franchising, on the other hand, are quick to point out that many who enter into franchising agreements end up working harder and earning less than they expected.

## The Definition of Franchising

*Franchising* is a method of doing business whereby a company (the franchisor) grants to others (the franchisees) the rights to produce, sell, distribute, or market the company's products or services. In so doing, franchisees are permitted to use the franchisor's name, trademarks, reputation, procedures, and selling techniques. To obtain these rights, each franchisee agrees to pay the franchisor a sum of money (the franchise fee), a percentage of annual gross sales, or both. Many franchisees agree to purchase equipment or supplies from the franchisor as well.

Franchisors view franchising as a way to expand their businesses without having to rely on loans or stock issues to raise capital. In addition to providing expansion capital, franchisees generally can be counted on to bring high levels of energy and commitment to the company–a real plus, particularly if the going gets rough. Franchisees, for their part, view franchising as a way to tap into a good thing–a hitch-your-wagon-to-a-going-concern strategy.

## The Price

How much does it cost to purchase a franchise? That depends. Your initial investment can vary from a few thousand dollars to upward of a million. On top of that is the annual percentage of gross sales, or royalty fee, required by most franchisors. This can be as high as 18 percent. Other charges may also be stipulated in the franchise agreement. Franchising, albeit an alternative to forming your own business from scratch, is not necessarily a cheap alternative.

## The Advantages and Disadvantages of Franchising

To determine whether the franchising route is right for you, take a look at both the advantages and disadvantages of buying a franchise.

### The Advantages

***Only limited experience is needed*** As a franchisee, you have access to the franchisor's experience. Instead of spending years learning the ropes in your intended business, you can be running it.

***Training and continued assistance are provided*** Rather than being left to sink or swim on your own, you have the franchisor there to provide additional support. This includes training programs and the ongoing services of consultants.

***Financing is often available*** The franchisor may permit you to make partial payment of your start-up costs (construction, equipment, inventory, promotion, and so on) and defer the balance over a period of years. This reduces the amount of capital immediately needed for your initial investment.

***Purchasing power can be increased*** It's often possible to purchase the products, supplies, equipment, and services used in your business directly from the franchisor at reduced rates. This enables you to stretch your dollars further.

***Promotion is generally strong*** Franchisors put a great deal of effort into making their companies' names recognizable to the public. As a result of the franchisor's promotional campaign, your business benefits.

***Customer acceptance is high*** Because the goods and services of the franchisor are proven and well known, your business has virtually instant pulling power. Whereas a new business might spend years developing its reputation, yours is already established.

## The Disadvantages

***Guidelines must be followed*** The franchisor sets the rules; your freedom to make decisions is limited by the necessity to follow standardized procedures and offer specific products or services.

***Contracts tend to favor the franchisor*** Because the franchise agreement is prepared by the franchisor, your bargaining power may be less than equal. Should a dispute arise, the franchisor generally has the edge.

***Profits are shared with the franchisor*** Normally franchisees are required to pay the franchisor a percentage of gross annual sales, thus reducing their own profits. In the event that your business fails to make a profit, this percentage must still be paid.

***Transfer of ownership is limited*** Your right to dispose of your franchise is restricted by the provisions of the franchise agreement. This means you may not be permitted to sell it to the highest bidder, bequeath it to a relative or friend in your will, or even give it away without the franchisor's approval.

***Purchasing power can be reduced*** Some franchisees have been required to purchase the products, supplies, equipment, and services used in their businesses only from the franchisor, even when other sources could provide them for less. The courts now consider such tie-in practices to be illegal, and you should be wary of any agreement that imposes them.

***Other franchisees' actions reflect on you*** A consumer who receives poor service in another one of the franchisor's outlets is likely to assume your franchise offers poor service, too. Your business suffers as a result, regardless of its merits.

***Paperwork is time-consuming*** The franchisor requires that you fill out a variety of reports, which takes time. Unless you're organized, you could end up buried under an avalanche of paperwork.

## The Franchise Agreement

The franchise agreement forms the basis for your relationship with the franchisor. Therefore, it must state clearly and in adequate detail the rights and responsibilities of both parties to the agreement. Anything that's ambiguous should be clarified at the outset. Waiting until later to straighten it out can have unfortunate consequences. Make sure that you are willing to accept *all* of the provisions contained in the contract. Once you've signed the agreement, you will be bound by it. If you find a clause unreasonable, try to have it deleted from the contract or modified. Barring these possibilities, you may decide not to enter into an agreement with the franchisor. The best way to protect yourself is to obtain the advice of your own attorney before signing any papers.

In evaluating the merits of a particular franchise agreement, you should give careful attention to the following provisions in the agreement:

**Total Franchise Cost** How much money does it really take to own and operate the franchise? Not just for the franchise fee, but for everything. It's surprising how many people fail to take into consideration all the charges that may be assessed. Among these are

- *Franchise Fee.* Grants you the right to engage in business as a franchised operation
- *Physical Facilities Fees.* Cover the cost of establishing you in an appropriate location (market research, construction, lease, and so on)
- *Equipment and Fixtures Costs.* Cover the costs of outfitting your building
- *Inventory and Supplies Costs.* Cover the costs of stocking your business with the necessary inventory and supplies.
- *Royalty Payments.* Represent a percentage of annual gross sales (one of the requirements for operating the franchise)
- *Promotion Costs.* Cover your share of the advertising costs (these may be included in the royalty payments)

- *Finance Charges.* Include all interest due on loans made to the franchisee.

Only when you have added up all these charges (and any others that may be levied) can you determine the total franchise cost.

**Contract Life** What is the life of the contract? Does your right to operate the franchise extend indefinitely, or is it limited to a specific number of years? What are the renewal provisions? The average contract life, excluding renewal provisions, is 15 years.

**Termination Clause** Go over the termination clause, often referred to as the "franchisor's exit clause," with great care. Essentially, what it represents is the franchisor's right to terminate your relationship by canceling your contract or failing to renew it. This right is retained by the franchisor on the grounds that it is the only way to maintain standards and protect the company's image. Unfortunately, it can also be used to punish franchisees who allegedly fall out of line, even though there may be no good cause for doing so.

For your protection, make note of these four points:

1. The actions on your part that constitute grounds for termination by the franchisor
2. The method that will be used to determine the value of the franchise in the event of termination (original cost or fair-market value)
3. Whether you have the right to terminate the agreement yourself and at what cost
4. Whether you have the right, upon termination, to enter into direct competition with the franchisor in the franchise area

**Transfer of Ownership** Do you have the right to sell or otherwise transfer ownership of the franchise to another party? In the majority of agreements, the franchisor reserves the right to buy back the franchise when the contact is terminated–often at the original price. Thus after investing several years' worth of time and money in your franchise, you could end up getting back only what you paid for it.

**Franchise Territory** The franchise territory is the selling area in which you are licensed to operate your franchise. In evaluating a prospective territory, you should determine the following:

1. Its sales potential (given local consumer demand and competition)
2. The characteristics (demographics and psychographics) of the neighborhood
3. The territory's projected market growth
4. Whether the franchisor is licensing others in the same territory
5. Your right to open additional franchises in your territory or in other territories. (Under existing antitrust laws, the franchisor has almost no legal power to stop you from branching out into other areas. However, bucking the franchise system is sure to strain your relationship.)

**Procedures** The procedures by which your franchise is expected to operate are included in the franchise agreement or the company's procedures manual. These can cover anything from the way to greet a customer to the way to keep the books. To safeguard your sanity later, take the time to familiarize yourself with them before you purchase the franchise. Remember that your way of doing business has to be compatible with the franchisor's way of doing business; otherwise, you're in for trouble.

**Management Training and Assistance** What kind of management training and support can you count on the franchisor to provide? Some training programs are quite extensive, including one or more weeks at the franchisor's training headquarters, on-the-job training in an established franchise outlet, and continuing guidance once you're set up in your own franchise. Other training programs consist of little more than a few stapled-together pages of information, bolstered by an imaginary support system. Make sure the full details of the franchisor's training and assistance programs are spelled out in advance–and included in your contract. Also, don't forget to find out who foots the bill for the costs.

**Promotional Activities** What activities is the franchisor engaging in to promote the company's name and develop goodwill? Is advertising primarily at the local and regional level, or does it extend nationwide and beyond? Because one of the major selling points of a franchise is that it has a recognizable name, backed up by solid promotion, you need to know in advance the nature and extent of the company's promotional activities. Also, once again, the matter of who pays for these costs comes up. Is your contribution included in the royalty fee, or is it an additional percentage of gross sales on top of that?

The franchise agreement merely sets down on paper the terms and conditions of the franchise relationship. As such, it isn't to be regarded with awe but is to be explored as fully as possible. Don't let a lot of pages or legal jargon keep you from gaining a complete understanding of the agreement's contents. The best way to avoid getting burned is to enter into the relationship with your eyes open.

## How to Find Franchise Opportunities

You can refer to numerous sources of information for help in finding franchise opportunities. The major sources are

- Newspapers
- Internet
- Franchisors
- Trade publications
- Franchise associations
- Franchise specialists
- Your banker
- The government

**Newspapers** Chances are that you've already seen a variety of franchise offerings listed in the financial or classified section of your local newspaper.

**Internet** Go online to check out the opportunities available. Through company websites, industry groups, and associations, you can get a good overview.

**Franchisors** If you already have a particular industry in mind, write directly to the franchisors in that field for details about the requirements for obtaining a franchise. By writing to more than one company, you can compare opportunities.

**Trade Publications** Read the trade publications for the industries that appeal to you. Franchisors seeking to expand their businesses will normally advertise in these publications.

**Franchise Associations** Franchise associations publish magazines and reports on franchising, and they sponsor exhibitions where you can meet with franchisor representatives.

**Franchise Specialists** For a fee, specialists in the area of franchising will help you find and research franchise opportunities. Their services include both obtaining financial and marketing data on the companies being considered and providing recommendations.

**Your Banker** Your banker is tuned into the business community and probably can provide you with information on current franchise offerings or the names of people to contact.

**The Government** Government sources ranging from the DOC to the Federal Trade Commission can provide you with information on franchising. Probably the best ones to start with are the SBA and your local SBDC.

## Evaluating a Franchise

To determine whether a particular franchise opportunity is right for you, it's important to investigate it thoroughly, rating it on such factors as

- The quality of its products or services
- The level of customer demand for them
- The strength of the company and its management
- The resources the franchisor can provide you–financing, training, promotion, purchasing power, and so on
- The terms of the franchise agreement and what you would be getting for your money
- The amount of enjoyment you would get from running the business
- The cost of buying the franchise
- The profit potential of the business

The Federal Trade Commission requires franchisors to provide prospective franchisees with a Franchise Offering Circular, which includes detailed information on the company and a copy of the franchise agreement. This must be given to you on or before your first personal meeting with a representative from the company. In addition to carefully going over the material with an attorney and an accountant, there are a number of other things you can do to get an accurate view of the franchise opportunity. These include

- Trying the products or services yourself
- Examining the company's promotional and training materials
- Visiting franchises to see how the individual units operate
- Talking to current and past franchise owners
- Researching the company in newspaper and magazine articles and online databases
- Contacting government and consumer organizations for information

Given the amount of time and money you would be putting into a franchise, your evaluation needs to be as comprehensive as possible, taking into consideration your own needs, as well as those of family members who will be affected by the decision. For more information on evaluating a franchise, visit these websites:

- International Franchise Association: http://www.franchise.org/
- American Association of Franchisees and Dealers: http://www.aafd.org/

## Franchising Checklist

Evaluating a franchise requires a clear head. Keeping track of all the information, weighing the pros and cons, and listening to your own feelings isn't easy. The following Franchising Checklist should help you bring order out of the chaos.

| Franchising Checklist | Answer Yes or No |
| --- | --- |
| 1. Has the franchisor been in business long enough to have established a good reputation? | ________ |
| 2. Have you checked the Better Business Bureau, the Chamber of Commerce, Dun & Bradstreet, or your banker to find out about the franchisor's business reputation and credit rating? | ________ |

| Franchising Checklist *(continued)* | Answer Yes or No |
|---|---|
| 3. Has the franchisor shown you certified figures on the net profits of one or more going operations? Have you checked them yourself? | ________ |
| 4. Has the franchisor given you a specimen contract to study with the advice of counsel? | ________ |
| 5. Has the product or service been on the market long enough to have gained good consumer acceptance? | ________ |
| 6. Would you buy the product or service on its merits? | ________ |
| 7. Is the product or service protected by a patent? | ________ |
| 8. Does product-liability insurance protect both you and the franchisor? | ________ |
| 9. Does the contract give you an exclusive territory for the life of the franchise? | ________ |
| 10. Does the territory provide adequate sales potential? | ________ |
| 11. Have you made any study to determine whether the product or service you propose to sell has a market in your territory at the price you will have to charge? | ________ |
| 12. Will you be compelled to sell any new products or services introduced by the franchisor after you have opened the business? | ________ |
| 13. If there is an annual sales quota, can you retain your franchise if it is not met? | ________ |
| 14. Does the franchise fee seem reasonable? | ________ |
| 15. Do continuing royalties or payments of percentages of gross sales appear reasonable? | ________ |
| 16. Does the cash investment include payment for fixtures and equipment? | ________ |

*(continued)*

| Franchising Checklist *(continued)* | Answer Yes or No |
|---|---|
| 17. Can you purchase supplies from another source when available at a lower price? | _________ |
| 18. If you will be required to participate in company promotion and publicity by contributing to an advertising fund, will you have the right to veto any increase to the fund? | _________ |
| 19. Will your training include an opportunity to observe and work with a successful franchise for a time? | _________ |
| 20. Does the franchisor provide continuing assistance through supervisors who visit regularly? | _________ |
| 21. Is the franchise agreement renewable? | _________ |
| 22. Can you terminate the agreement if, for some reason, you are not happy about it? | _________ |
| 23. May you sell the business to anyone you please? | _________ |
| 24. Does your attorney approve of the contract? | _________ |

# 18

# Getting Help

The major cause of most business failures is management that lacks the knowledge, skills, experience, or simply time needed to run a business efficiently. Because new businesses can rarely afford to hire specialists who enable big business to carry out its objectives, they are at a distinct disadvantage. The way to compensate for this, however, and still keep payroll expenses to a minimum, is to utilize outside services.

Many outside services are willing and eager to help your business succeed. Whether you need help in obtaining financing, keeping your books in order, coming up with new concepts for products and ways to promote your business, training and motivating personnel, or solving a variety of business problems, there are services available to you. Some of these services cost money, but surprisingly many of them are provided free of charge.

## Sources of Outside Help

Here are some of the individuals and institutions that can assist you in operating your business, listed in alphabetical order:

- Accountants
- Advertising agencies
- Attorneys
- Bankers
- Chambers of commerce
- Colleges and universities
- Government agencies, including the Department of Commerce, economic development offices, Federal Trade Commission, Government Printing Office, Internal Revenue Service, International Trade Administration, Small Business Administration, and Small Business Development Centers

- Insurance agents
- Libraries
- Management and marketing consultants
- Temporary help services
- Trade associations

Each source can provide you with specific useful information that otherwise might not be readily accessible to your business. In addition, various publications, SBA offices, SBDCs, and small-business resource websites may offer you help.

## Accountants

An accountant can be instrumental in helping you to keep your business operating on a sound financial basis. Even if you are already familiar with recordkeeping procedures, or you employ a bookkeeper to maintain your records, the services of an outside accountant may still be required. In addition to designing an accounting system that's suitable for your specific needs, an accountant can also assist in the following areas:

- Determining cash requirements
- Budgeting
- Forecasting
- Controlling costs
- Preparing financial statements
- Interpreting financial data
- Obtaining loans
- Preparing tax returns

You can find public accountants listed in the Yellow Pages of the telephone directory, but for best results, try to locate one through a personal recommendation. Ask your banker or attorney to suggest an accountant. Because the work of bankers and attorneys causes them to communicate with accountants regularly, both should be able to provide the names of accountants who can meet your requirements. Another approach is to contact one of the national or state accounting associations. One of the larger associations is

American Institute of Certified Public Accountants
1211 Avenue of the Americas
New York, NY 10036

## Advertising Agencies

An advertising agency can help you to plan, produce, and place your business's advertising. Advertising agencies perform the following activities:

- Develop promotional strategies
- Create advertising pieces (writing copy, designing graphics and layout, producing the finished product)
- Choose the appropriate media
- Make sure that ads are run according to schedule

Whether you need to use an advertising agency depends on the amount of advertising you intend to do.

To find out which advertising agencies offer which services and how to contact them, check the *Standard Directory of Advertising Agencies*, available at many public libraries. Another source of agency information is to talk to media sales representatives and to get their opinions about the various advertising agencies. The advertising agencies in your area should also be listed in the Yellow Pages.

## Attorneys

An attorney can be useful to your business from the very start, helping you to determine which legal form of business is right for you, drawing up agreements, filing government paperwork, and/or negotiating the lease or purchase of your building. Later on, your attorney can continue to help by

- Representing you in court
- Providing legal advice
- Interpreting legal documents
- Assisting in tax planning
- Helping you to comply with employment laws

- Working out arrangements with creditors
- Reorganizing the business, if needed

Your accountant or banker should be able to recommend an attorney. If not, your state's bar association can provide you with the names of attorneys in your area. Other sources of information include business acquaintances, friends, and the Yellow Pages.

## Bankers

Your banker can be a valuable ally to your business if you take the time to establish good rapport–preferably before you ask for a loan. The advice or information your banker can provide includes

- How to open a checking account
- How to obtain a line of credit
- How to apply for a loan
- How to prepare financial reports
- How to bill customers
- How to set up your payroll

Furthermore, because bankers are constantly interacting with various segments of the community, your banker is likely to hear news that affects your business before you do.

## Chambers of Commerce

Chambers of commerce are traditionally the information agencies of a community. Each chamber's goal is to represent and promote its area's economy, to encourage business and industrial investment, and to provide employment. As a new business owner, you should get in touch with your local chamber to find out what it has to offer (moral support, research data, general information about the community, or whatever). You might also decide to become a member. Chambers of commerce offer these benefits:

- They promote local businesses.
- They protect business interests.
- They act as the political voice of the business community.
- They are businesses united together.

## Colleges and Universities

The colleges and universities in your area are a vast resource of information, skills, and training. They offer access to

- The school's library for books, periodicals, government reports, reference works, maps, charts, and audiovisual aids
- Professional consultants in a variety of business-related areas
- Labor in the form of students who are receiving training in your field
- Additional education in the form of classes in management theory, business operations, advertising, and so on
- Seminars, especially for small business owners (often tied to the Small Business Administration)

## Government Agencies

Agencies of government at the local, state, and federal levels can provide you with an abundance of useful information at little or no cost.

### Department of Commerce

One government agency that specializes in businesses' concerns, the DOC, oversees the research and distribution of information of direct interest to the economic community. These data are collected and made available to the public in the form of publications and reports, including

- *Survey of Current Business*, a monthly periodical that provides updates on changes in the nation's economy and the levels of business production and distribution
- *Census Bureau Reports*, covering such areas as population statistics (age, income, level of education, family status, and other demographic data) and manufacturing, business, and agricultural trends

In addition to these reports, DOC specialists can advise you in such specific areas as domestic and foreign market opportunities, contacting foreign representatives, and deciphering tariff and trade regulations. DOC publications are available at many public libraries or at the various department offices located throughout the United States. For more information, or to reach a DOC specialist, contact the Department of Commerce, Washington, DC 20230, or visit the DOC website: www.doc.gov.

### Economic Development Offices

Many communities maintain their own economic development offices. These differ from chambers of commerce in that they are maintained by local governments rather than local businesses. They can provide you with current statistical information regarding the economy, building activity, housing units, sales trends, population demographics, zoning, transportation, utilities, labor force, wages and salaries, community services, banks and savings and loan associations, traffic flows, and important telephone numbers.

### Federal Trade Commission

The Federal Trade Commission regulates trade practices to protect the public against unfair methods of competition. It is empowered to collect information pertaining to business conduct and activities and to distribute this to both government and the public. The information available includes guidelines on what constitutes deceptive pricing, deceptive guarantees, bait advertising, and other illegal practices. For more information, write to the Federal Trade Commission, Washington, DC 20580.

### Government Printing Office

The U.S. Government Printing Office oversees the publication and distribution of government documents, pamphlets, reports, and books on a variety of subjects, many of which directly relate to business. These are for sale, usually at nominal prices, at local Government Printing Office bookstores, which are generally located in federal buildings. If one isn't near you, or it doesn't stock a publication you want, write directly to the U.S. Government Printing Office, Superintendent of Documents, Washington, DC 20402. You will be sent a catalog of the publications available and any publications that you request.

### Internal Revenue Service

The Internal Revenue Service can answer any questions you have concerning your federal income taxes. Tax specialists in local IRS offices can handle specific questions, or you can refer to any of the numerous IRS guides and publications. One particularly valuable guide is the *Tax Guide for Small Businesses*, which is updated annually. It contains approximately 200 pages of information covering such subjects as books and records, accounting periods, determining gross profit, deductible expenses, depreciation, tax credits, and ways to report income. This is available free of charge at your local IRS office. Some of the other IRS publications are listed later in this chapter.

### International Trade Administration

The International Trade Administration, operating under the auspices of the DOC, can provide you with a wealth of information concerning trade and investment opportunities abroad, foreign markets, financing for exporters, export documentation and licensing requirements, and so on. ITA district offices are located throughout the United States and Puerto Rico.

In addition to its counseling services and publications, the ITA also has country desk officers headquartered in Washington, DC, who track world economic trends. Desk officers maintain up-to-date information on the commercial conditions in their assigned countries and can provide you with the data you need about countries in which you are planning to sell your goods or services. For more information on the ITA or its country desk organization, contact the DOC or the ITA's website: www.ita.gov/.

### Small Business Administration

The SBA is designed to aid small businesses in the following ways:

- Helping to obtain financing
- Providing management and technical assistance
- Conducing business seminars and workshops
- Assisting in procuring government contracts

These forms of help are provided through the operation of more than 100 district offices, the distribution of publications, and the activities of the Service Corps of Retired Executives (SCORE) and the Active Corps of Executives (ACE), volunteer groups of professionals who assist the SBA in advising small businesses.

*Financing* by the SBA takes the form of direct and indirect loans to businesses. Loan proceeds can be used for working capital; for purchase of inventory, equipment, and supplies; or for building construction or expansion. The SBA also makes loans to help small businesses comply with federal air- and water-pollution regulations and meet occupational health and safety standards. In addition, economic-opportunity loans are available to help persons who are socially or economically disadvantaged. Although money for venture or high-risk investments is difficult to obtain from the SBA, it licenses Small Business Investment Companies (SBICs), which *do* make such loans. For more information about SBA or SBIC lending practices, check Chapter 8.

The SBA offers *management and technical assistance* in many forms. There are numerous titles to choose from in its list of business publications. SBA form 115A lists publications that are for sale for a nominal fee. A sampling of the titles is shown later in this chapter.

In-depth counseling is also provided by SBA management-assistance staff, augmented by SCORE and ACE volunteers. Among the subject areas in which you can receive guidance are opening a business, marketing, advertising, profit goals, borrowing, accounting, bookkeeping, personnel, inventory controls, customer analysis, forecasting, and insurance. Meetings with these business counselors can be arranged through your local SBA field office. There is no charge for their services.

To help small entrepreneurs protect their investments, the SBA offers a variety of *seminars and workshops.* One that is of particular interest to prospective business owners is the prebusiness workshop. This is a one-day session in which participants are helped to determine their readiness to go into business and advised of the steps involved in getting started. Once the decision is made to go ahead, the SBA assists participants in developing workable business plans. Other topics covered in workshops or seminars include

- Sales promotion and advertising
- Basic business operations
- Business planning
- Women in business
- Foreign trade
- Retail-store security

The SBA's procurement assistance officers can guide you in the process of selling to the government and obtaining *government contracts.* They can help you to win subcontracting assignments, too. The SBA works closely with large government contractors to make sure that they use qualified small businesses as subcontractors on their projects.

### Small Business Development Centers

Entrepreneurs seeking one-on-one business consulting services, technical assistance, and training can find this and more at small business development centers (SBDCs) throughout the United States. Generally operated by colleges and universities, SBDCs draw on a combination of government, education, and private-sector resources to provide business owners with such services as

- Individualized counseling
- Assistance in planning
- Workshops and seminars
- On-site employee training
- Information about government programs
- Referrals and networking opportunities
- Access to economic and business data–books, reports, pamphlets, software, video- and audiocassette programs, and online databases

The goal of the SBDCs is to stimulate the economy by helping small and medium-size businesses to function more effectively. Toward this end, SBDC counselors and outside experts in such areas as accounting, law, computers, marketing, and finance work closely with entrepreneurs to achieve their goals. Serving the needs of both prospective and current entrepreneurs, SBDCs assist small businesses at all stages of their development.

To find out whether there's an SBDC near you, check the list later in this chapter, or contact your local college's business department for information.

## Insurance Agents

An insurance agent can analyze your business's specific needs and help you to obtain adequate coverage. Aspects of risk management that you should discuss with your agent include how to protect your assets, workers, and earnings and how to stay in compliance with the law. Because the welfare of your business depends on the safeguards you provide, you should give a high priority to finding a good insurance agent.

The best ways to find an insurance agent are through personal recommendations (your accountant, attorney, or banker may be able to suggest someone) and comparison shopping. Talking to different agents not only lets you evaluate the levels of coverage and compare the costs of different insurance plans but also gives you an idea of which agent is the most knowledgeable about your type of business. You can find the names of insurance agents and companies in the Yellow Pages.

## Libraries

Much of the information you need in order to operate your business can be obtained free of charge from libraries. The answers to many of your everyday business questions can be found not only in the books but also in the magazines, newspapers, reference works, government publications, maps, charts, and audiovisual aids available in the library itself and by accessing the Internet on library terminals. Management and marketing approaches, technical explanations, statistical data, industry information, trends, and economic forecasts are just some of the subject areas on which you can find information.

In addition to public libraries, there are also libraries sponsored by colleges and universities, private industry, trade and professional associations, labor unions, and research centers. The most useful of these generally have separate business reference sections.

## Management and Marketing Consultants

Management and marketing consultants can detect weaknesses in your methods of operation or your marketing strategy and can recommend corrective measures. They can also be of help *before* problems arise, providing advice on new product development, market research, business expansion, administration, employee motivation, cost control, security, and so on.

Many businesses make a practice of calling in a management or marketing consultant whenever a major decision in these areas needs to be made. This enables the business owner to benefit not only from the consultant's knowledge and experience, but also from something equally valuable: the consultant's objectivity. Unlike employees, consultants have nothing to gain or lose from the outcome of a decision. Furthermore, the variety of their contacts in the business community usually gives them a broader perspective.

The best way to locate a management or marketing consultant is through recommendations, preferably from the consultant's satisfied clients. Contacting the business departments at the colleges in your area is another good idea, or you can check the listings in one of the several directories of consultants available at public libraries.

## Temporary Help Services

There are temporary help service firms throughout the United States, providing experienced and well-qualified temporary help at a moment's notice. You may contract for a typist, receptionist, bookkeeper, salesperson, engineer, machinist, or other office, professional, and industrial workers. The temporary help service firm takes care of all screening, interviewing, and testing of applicants, as well as the checking of references. Temporary help service firms can be located through personal recommendations, local chambers of commerce, or the Yellow Pages.

## Trade Associations

Trade associations are organizations with members in a particular business or industry (garment industry, banking and finance, restaurants, automotive repair). The concerns and services of trade associations are directed at helping members to improve their operating efficiency and cope with business problems. This help is in the form of

- *Accounting Services.* Provides accounting forms and manuals, ratio data, cost studies, and consultations
- *Advertising and Marketing Services.* Provides advertising materials and forecasts of future demand levels and trends
- *Publicity and Public Relations Activities.* Provides members and the mass media with information about industry activities
- *Educational Programs.* Provides a variety of training courses and aids to assist business owners and employees in developing their skills
- *Research Activities.* Provides members and government agencies with statistics about the industry–method of operation, product standards, certifying and grading, and so on
- *Employee Relations Programs.* Provides members with information about industry wages, work schedules, and fringe benefits, as well as assisting in the negotiation of labor contracts
- *Government Relations Programs.* Provides members with a collective voice to use in communicating with the government; informing members of government actions pertaining to their businesses

In addition, trade associations are active in public service, consumerism, and environmental safety. Of course, not all associations provide all these services. To find out which ones are provided, contact the association in your field of business.

To obtain information on trade associations or to find out which ones represent your industry, check these publications, available at most public libraries:

- *National Trade and Professional Associations of the United States*, Columbia Books, Inc., Publishers, Washington, DC, www.d-net.com/columbia
- *Encyclopedia of Associations*, Gale Research Inc., Detroit, MI, www.gale.com

## Publications

The following is a sampling of IRS and SBA publications.

### IRS Tax Publications

The following publications can provide you with additional information about business taxation. These publications should be available at your local IRS office; if not, you can obtain them by writing to the Internal Revenue Service, Washington, DC 20224.

| *Title* | *No.* |
|---|---|
| *Your Rights As a Taxpayer* | 1 |
| *Employer's Tax Guide (Circular E)* | 15 |
| *Your Federal Income Tax* | 17 |
| *Tax Guide for Small Business* | 334 |
| *Fuel Tax Credits and Refunds* | 378 |
| *Travel, Entertainment, and Gift Expenses* | 463 |
| *Tax Withholding and Estimated Tax* | 505 |
| *Excise Taxes* | 510 |
| *Moving Expenses* | 521 |
| *Tax Information on Selling Your Home* | 523 |
| *Taxable and Nontaxable Income* | 525 |
| *Charitable Contributions* | 526 |
| *Residential Rental Property* | 527 |

| *Title (continued)* | *No.* |
|---|---|
| *Miscellaneous Deductions* | 529 |
| *Tax Information for Homeowners* | 530 |
| *Self-employment Tax* | 533 |
| *Depreciation* | 534 |
| *Business Expenses* | 535 |
| *Net Operating Losses* | 536 |
| *Accounting Periods and Methods* | 538 |
| *Tax Information on Partnerships* | 541 |
| *Tax Information on Corporations* | 542 |
| *Sales and Other Dispositions of Assets* | 544 |
| *Nonbusiness Disasters, Casualties, and Thefts* | 547 |
| *Investment Income and Expenses* | 550 |
| *Basis of Assets* | 551 |
| *Recordkeeping for Individuals* | 552 |
| *Federal Tax Information on Community Property* | 555 |
| *Examinations of Returns, Appeal Rights, and Claims for Refund* | 556 |
| *Retirement Plans for the Self-employed* | 560 |
| *Taxpayers Starting a Business* | 583 |
| *Business Use of Your Home* | 587 |
| *Tax Information on S Corporations* | 589 |
| *Individual Retirement Arrangements (IRAs)* | 590 |
| *The Collection Process (Employment Tax Accounts)* | 594 |
| *Guide to Free Tax Services* | 910 |
| *Tax Information for Direct Sellers* | 911 |
| *Business Use of a Car* | 917 |
| *Employment Taxes for Household Employers* | 926 |
| *How to Begin Depreciating Your Property* | 946 |
| *Per Diem Rates* | 1542 |

## Small Business Administration Publications

The following publications can provide you with additional information about small business operations. To purchase these nominally priced publications, write to the Small Business Administration, Washington, DC 20417 to obtain an order form.

| *Title* | *No.* |
|---|---|
| **Products/Ideas/Inventions** | |
| *Ideas into Dollars* | PI1 |
| *Avoiding Patent, Trademark and Copyright Problems* | PI2 |
| *Trademarks and Business Goodwill* | PI3 |
| **Financial Management** | |
| *ABC's of Borrowing* | FM1 |
| *Profit Costing and Pricing for Manufacturers* | FM2 |
| *Basic Budgets for Profit Planning* | FM3 |
| *Understanding Cash Flow* | FM4 |
| *A Venture Capital Primer for Small Business* | FM5 |
| *Accounting Services for Small Service Firms* | FM6 |
| *Analyze Your Records to Reduce Costs* | FM7 |
| *Budgeting in a Small Service Firm* | FM8 |
| *Sound Cash Management and Borrowing* | FM9 |
| *Record Keeping in a Small Business* | FM10 |
| *Simple Break-Even Analysis for Small Stores* | FM11 |
| *A Pricing Checklist for Small Retailers* | FM12 |
| *Pricing Your Products and Services Profitably* | FM13 |
| **Management and Planning** | |
| *Effective Business Communications* | MP1 |
| *Locating or Relocating Your Business* | MP2 |
| *Problems in Managing a Family-Owned Business* | MP3 |
| *Business Plan for Small Manufacturers* | MP4 |
| *Business Plan for Small Construction Firms* | MP5 |
| *Planning and Goal Setting for Small Business* | MP6 |
| *Should You Lease or Buy Equipment?* | MP8 |
| *Business Plan for Retailers* | MP9 |
| *Choosing a Retail Location* | MP10 |
| *Business Plan For Small Service Firms* | MP11 |
| *Checklist for Going into Business* | MP12 |

| *Title (continued)* | *No.* |
|---|---|
| *How to Get Started with a Small Business Computer* | MP14 |
| *The Business Plan for Home-Based Business* | MP15 |
| *How to Buy or Sell a Business* | MP16 |
| *Purchasing for Owners of Small Plants* | MP17 |
| *Buying for Retail Stores* | MP18 |
| *Small Business Decision Making* | MP19 |
| *Business Continuation Planning* | MP20 |
| *Developing a Strategic Business Plan* | MP21 |
| *Inventory Management* | MP22 |
| *Techniques for Problem Solving* | MP23 |
| *Techniques for Productivity Improvement* | MP24 |
| *Selecting the Legal Structure for Your Business* | MP25 |
| *Evaluating Franchise Opportunities* | MP26 |
| *Small Business Risk Management Guide* | MP28 |
| *Quality Child Care Makes Good Business Sense* | MP29 |
| **Marketing** | |
| *Creative Selling: The Competitive Edge* | MT1 |
| *Marketing for Small Business: An Overview* | MT2 |
| *Is the Independent Sales Agent for You?* | MT3 |
| *Marketing Checklist for Small Retailers* | MT4 |
| *Researching Your Market* | MT8 |
| *Selling by Mail Order* | MT9 |
| *Market Overseas with U.S. Government Help* | MT10 |
| *Advertising* | MT11 |
| **Crime Prevention** | |
| *Curtailing Crime–Inside and Out* | CP2 |
| *A Small Business Guide to Computer Security* | CP3 |
| **Personnel Management** | |
| *Checklist for Developing a Training Program* | PM1 |
| *Employees: How to Find and Pay Them* | PM2 |
| *Managing Employee Benefits* | PM3 |

# SBA Field Offices

Following are various SBA field offices.

## Regional Offices

**Region I**
10 Causeway St.
Boston, MA 02222-1093
617/565-8415

**Region II**
26 Federal Plaza Room 31-08
New York, NY 10278
212/264-1450

**Region III**
Allendale Square, Suite 201
475 Allendale Road
King of Prussia, PA 19406
215/962-3700

**Region IV**
1720 Peachtree Road, NW
Atlanta, GA 30309-2482
404/347-4995

**Region V**
500 W. Madison St.
Chicago, IL 60661-2511
312/353-5000

**Region VI**
4300 Amon Carter Blvd.
Ft. Worth, TX 76155
817/885-6581

**Region VII**
323 W. 8th St., Suite 307
Kansas City, MO 64105-1500
816/374-6380

**Region VIII**
721 19th St.
Denver, CO 80201
303/844-0500

**Region IX**
455 Market St., Suite 2200
San Francisco, CA 94105-2445
415/744-2118

**Region X**
1200 6th Ave., Suite 1805
Seattle, WA 98101-1128
206/553-7310

## Disaster Area Offices

**Area 1: Regions I–II**
360 Rainbow Boulevard S., 3rd Floor
Niagara Falls, NY 14303
716/282-4612
In NY: 1-800-221-2091
Outside NY: 1-800-221-2093

**Area 2: Regions III–IV**
One Baltimore Place, Suite 300
Atlanta, GA 30308
404/347-3771

**Area 3: Regions V–VII**
4400 Amon Carter Boulevard, Suite 102
Ft. Worth, TX 76155
817/885-7600

**Area 4: Regions VIII–X**
P.O. Box 13795
Sacramento, CA 95853-4795
916/566-7240

## District, Branch, and Post-of-Duty Offices

**Alabama**
2121 8th Avenue North, Suite 200
Birmingham, AL 35203-2398
205/731-1344

**Alaska**
222 W. 8th Avenue, Room A36
Anchorage, AK 99513-7559
907/271-4022

**Arizona**
2828 N. Central Avenue
Phoenix, AZ 85004-1025
602/640-2316

**Arkansas**
320 W. Capital Avenue, Room 601
Little Rock, AR 72201
501/378-5277

**California**
211 Main Street, 4th Floor
San Francisco, CA 94105-1988
415/744-6801

2719 N. Air Fresno Drive, Suite 107
Fresno, CA 93727-1547
209/487-5189

660 J Street, Room 215
Sacramento, CA 95814-2413
916/498-6410

550 W. C Street, Suite 550
San Diego, CA 92101
619/557-5440

330 N. Brand Boulevard
Glendale, CA 91203
818/552-3210

200 W. Santa Ana Blvd., Suite 700
Santa Ana, CA 92701
714/550-7420

**Colorado**
721 19th Street, Suite 426
Denver, CO 80202-2599
303/844-3984

**Connecticut**
330 Main Street, 2nd Floor
Hartford, CT 06106
203/240-4700

**Delaware**
824 N. Market St., Suite 610
Wilmington, DE 19801-3011
302/573-6294

**District of Columbia**
1110 Vermont Avenue, NW
Suite 900
Washington, DC 20043-4500
202/606-4000

**Florida**
7825 Baymeadows Way, Suite 100-B
Jacksonville, FL 32256-7504
904/443-1900

1320 S. Dixie Highway
Suite 501
Coral Gables, FL 33146
305/536-5521

**Georgia**
1720 Peachtree Road, NW, 6th Floor
Atlanta, GA 30309
404/347-4745

**Guam**
400 Route 8, Suite 302
Mongmong, Guam 96910
671/472-7277

**Hawaii**
300 Ala Moana Boulevard
Room 2213
Box 50207
Honolulu, HI 96850-4981
808/541-2990

**Idaho**
1020 Main Street, Suite 290
Boise, ID 83702-5745
208/334-1696

**Illinois**
500 W. Madison, Room 1250
Chicago, IL 60606
312/353-4528

511 W. Capitol Street, Suite 302
Springfield, IL 62704
217/492-4416

**Indiana**
429 N. Pennsylvania Street, Suite 100
Indianapolis, IN 46204-1873
317/226-7272

**Iowa**
210 Walnut Street, Room 749
Des Moines, IA 50309-2105
515/284-4422

215 Fourth Ave., SE, Suite 200
Cedar Rapids, IA 52401-1806
319/362-6405

**Kansas**
100 E. English Street
Wichita, KS 67202
316/269-6616

**Kentucky**
600 Dr. Martin Luther King, Jr. Place
Room 188
Louisville, KY 40602
502/582-5971

**Louisiana**
365 Canal Street
New Orleans, LA 70130
504/589-6685

**Maine**
Federal Building
40 Western Avenue, Room 512
Augusta, ME 04330
207/622-8378

**Maryland**
10 S. Howard St., Room 6220
Baltimore, MD 21202
410/962-4392

**Massachusetts**
10 Causeway Street, Room 265
Boston, MA 02222-1093
617/565-5590

Federal Building & Courthouse
1550 Main Street, Room 212
Springfield, MA 01103
413/785-0268

**Michigan**
515 McNamara Building
477 Michigan Avenue
Detroit, MI 48226
313/226-6075

228 W. Washington, Suite 11
Marquette, MI 49855
906/225-1108

**Minnesota**
610-C Butler Square
100 North 6th Street
Minneapolis, MN 55403-1563
612/370-2324

**Mississippi**
One Hancock Plaza, Suite 1001
Gulfport, MS 39501-7758
601/863-4449

First Jackson Centre
101 W. Capitol Street, Suite 400
Jackson, MS 39201
601/965-4378

**Missouri**
Lucas Place
323 West 8th St. S. 501
Kansas City, MO 64105
816/374-6708

815 Olive Street, Room 242
St. Louis, MO 63101
314/539-6600

620 S. Glenstone Street, Suite 110
Springfield, MO 65802-3200
417/864-7670

**Montana**
301 South Park
Drawer 10054, Room 334
Helena, MT 59626
406/441-1081

**Nebraska**
11145 Mill Valley Road
Omaha, NE 68154
402/221-3622

**Nevada**
301 East Stewart Street, Room 301
Box 7527 Downtown Station
Las Vegas, NV 89125-2527
702/388-6611

**New Hampshire**
143 N. Main St., Suite 202
Concord, NH 03302-1258
603/225-1400

**New Jersey**
Two Gateway Ctr., 4th Floor
Newark, NJ 07102
201/645-2434

**New Mexico**
625 Silver Avenue, SW, Suite 320
Albuquerque, NM 87102
505/766-1870

**New York**
26 Federal Plaza
New York, NY 10278
212/264-2454

111 W. Huron Street, Room 1311
Buffalo, NY 14202
716/551-4301

333 East Water Street, 4th Floor
Elmira, NY 14901
607/734-8130

35 Pinelawn Road, Room 102E
Melville, NY 11747
516/454-0750

Federal Building, Room 410
100 State Street
Rochester, NY 14614
716/263-6700

401 S. Salina St., 5th Floor
Syracuse, NY 13202
315/471-9393

**North Carolina**
200 N. College St., Suite A2015
Charlotte, NC 28202-2137
704/344-6563

**North Dakota**
Federal Building, Room 218
657 Second Avenue N.
Fargo, ND 58108-3086
701/239-5131

**Ohio**
1111 Superior Ave., Suite 630
Cleveland, OH 44114-2507
216/522-4180

2 Nationwide Plaza, Suite 1400
Columbus, OH 43215-2542
614/469-6860

525 Vine St., Suite 870
Cincinnati, OH 45202
513/684-2814

**Oklahoma**
210 W. Park Ave., Suite 1300
Oklahoma City, OK 73102
405/231-5521

**Oregon**
222 SW Columbia Street, Suite 500
Portland, OR 97201-6605
503/326-2682

**Pennsylvania**
Allendale Square, Suite 201
475 Allendale Road
King of Prussia, PA 19406
610/962-3800

100 Chestnut Street, Suite 309
Harrisburg, PA 17101
717/782-3840

960 Penn Avenue, 5th Floor
Pittsburgh, PA 15222
412/644-2780

Penn Place
20 N. Pennsylvania Avenue
Room 2327
Wilkes-Barre, PA 18703-3589
717/826-6497

**Puerto Rico**
Citibank Bldg.
252 Ponce de Leon Ave., Suite 201
Hato Rey, PR 00918
809/766-5572

**Rhode Island**
380 Westminster Mall, 5th Floor
Providence, RI 02903
401/528-4584

**South Carolina**
1835 Assembly Street, Room 358
P.O. Box 2786
Columbia, SC 29202-2786
803/765-5132

**South Dakota**
110 S. Phillips, Suite 200
Sioux Falls, SD 57102-1109
605/330-4231

**Tennessee**
50 Vantage Way, Suite 201
Nashville, TN 37228-1550
615/736-5881

**Texas**
4300 Amon Carter Blvd.
Dallas, TX 76155
817/885-6500

606 N. Carancahua
Corpus Christi, TX 78476
512/888-3331

10737 Gateway West, Suite 320
El Paso, TX 79935
915/540-5676

222 E. Van Buren Street, Suite 500
Harligen, TX 78550
512/427-8625

9301 Southwest Freeway
Houston, TX 77074-1591
713/773-6500

1611 10th Street, Suite 200
Lubbock, TX 79401-2693
806/472-7462

727 E. Durango
San Antonio, TX 78206
210/472-5900

**Utah**
125 South State Street, Room 2237
Salt Lake City, UT 84138-1195
801/524-3209

**Vermont**
87 State Street, Room 205
P.O. Box 605
Montpelier, VT 05601-0605
802/828-4422

**Virginia**
1504 Santa Rosa Rd., Suite 200
Richmond, VA 23229
804/771-2400

**Virgin Islands**
3800 Crown Bay
St. Thomas, VI 00802
809/774-8530

3013 Golden Rock
St. Croix, VI 00820
809/778-5380

**Washington**
1200 Sixth Ave., Suite 1700
Seattle, WA 98101-1128
206/553-7310

W. 601 First Avenue, 10th Floor East
Spokane, WA 99204-0317
509/353-2810

**West Virginia**
168 West Main Street, 5th Floor
P.O. Box 1608
Clarksburg, WV 26301-1608
304/623-5631

550 Eagan Street, Room 309
Charleston, WV 25301
304/347-5220

**Wisconsin**
212 E. Washington Avenue
Room 213
Madison, WI 53703
608/264-5261

Henry S. Reuss Federal Plaza
310 W. Wisconsin Avenue, Suite 400
Milwaukee, WI 53203
414/297-3941

**Wyoming**
Federal Building
100 East B Street, Room 4001
P.O. Box 2839
Casper, WY 82602-2839
307/261-6500

## Small Business Development Centers (SBDCs)

Following are various SBDCs.

**Alabama**
University of Alabama at
Birmingham
1717 11th Avenue South, Suite 419
Birmingham, AL 35294
205/934-7260

**Alaska**
University of Alaska, Anchorage
430 W. 7th Avenue, Suite 110
Anchorage, AK 99501
907/274-7232

**Arizona**
Arizona SBDC Network
2411 W. 14th St., Room 132
Tempe, AZ 85281
602/731-8720

**Arkansas**
University of Arkansas
100 South Main Street, Suite 401
Little Rock, AR 72201
501/324-9043

**California**
CA Trade & Commerce Agency
Small Business Development Center
801 K Street, Suite 1700
Sacramento, CA 95814
916/324-5068

**Colorado**
Small Business Development Center
Office of Business Development
1625 Broadway, Suite 1710
Denver, CO 80202
303/892-3809

**Connecticut**
University of Connecticut
2 Bourn Place, U94
Storrs, CT 06269-5094
203/486-4135

**Delaware**
University of Delaware
Purnell Hall, Suite 005
Newark, NJ 19716
302/831-1555

**District of Columbia**
Howard University
Small Business Development Center
2600 Sixth Street, Room 128
Washington, DC 20059
202/806-1550

**Florida**
University of West Florida
Florida SBDC Network
19 W. Garden St., Suite 300
Pensacola, FL 32501
904/444-2060

**Georgia**
University of Georgia
1180 E. Broad Street
Athens, GA 30602
404/542-6762

**Hawaii**
Hawaii SBDC Network
University of Hawaii at Hilo
523 W. Lanikaula Street
Hilo, HI 96720
808/933-3515

**Idaho**
Boise State University
College of Business
1910 University Drive
Boise, ID 83725
208/385-1640

**Illinois**
Department of Commerce & Community Affairs
620 East Adams Street
Springfield, IL 62701
217/524-5856

**Indiana**
Indiana SBDC
One North Capital, Suite 420
Indianapolis, IN 46204
317/264-6871

**Iowa**
Iowa SBDC
Iowa State University
Chamberlain Building
137 Lynn Avenue
Ames, IA 50010
515/292-6351

**Kansas**
Wichita State University
1845 Fairmont, 21 Clinton Hall
Wichita, KS 67260-0148
316/978-3193

**Kentucky**
University of Kentucky
225 Business and Economics Building
Lexington, KY 40506
606/257-7668

**Louisiana**
Northeast Louisiana University
College of Business
University Drive
Monroe, LA 71209
318/342-5506

**Maine**
University of Southern Maine
93 Falmouth Street
Portland, ME 04104-9300
207/780-4420

**Maryland**
University of Maryland
7100 Baltimore Avenue
College Park, MD 20740
301/403-8300

**Massachusetts**
University of Massachusetts
205 School of Management
Amherst, MA 01003
413/545-6301

**Michigan**
Wayne State University
2727 Second Avenue
Detroit, MI 48201
313/964-1798

**Minnesota**
Dept. of Trade and Economic Development
500 Metro Square
121 Seventh Place East
St. Paul, MN 55101-2146
612/297-5770

**Mississippi**
Small Business Development Center
Old Chemistry Building, Suite 216
University, MS 38677
601/232-5001

**Missouri**
MO SBDC
University of Missouri
300 University Place
Columbia, MO 65211
314/882-0344

**Montana**
Helena SBDC
Montana Department of Commerce
1424 Ninth Avenue
Helena, MT 59620
406/444-4780

**Nebraska**
University of Nebraska at Omaha
College of Business Administration Building
60th and Dodge, Room 407
Omaha, NE 68182
402/554-2521

**Nevada**
University of Nevada, Reno
College of Business Administration
Room 411
Reno, NV 89557
702/784-1717

**New Hampshire**
University of New Hampshire
108 McConnell Hall
Durham, NH 03824
603/862-2200

**New Jersey**
Small Business Development Center
Rutgers University
180 University Avenue
3rd Floor–Ackerson Hall
Newark, NJ 07102
201/648-5950

**New Mexico**
NMSBDC Lead Center
Santa Fe Community College
P.O. Box 4187
Santa Fe, NM 87502
505/438-1362

**New York**
State University of New York
SUNY Central Administration S-523
Albany, NY 12246
518/443-5398

**North Carolina**
University of North Carolina
333 Fayette St. Mall, Suite 1150
Raleigh, NC 27601-1742
919/715-7272

**North Dakota**
University of North Dakota
118 Gamble Hall, UND
Grand Forks, ND 58202
701/777-3700

**Ohio**
Small Business Development Center
77 South High Street
Columbus, OH 43226-1001
614/466-2711

**Oklahoma**
Southeastern Oklahoma State University
517 W. University
Durant, OK 74730
405/924-0277

**Oregon**
Lane Community College
44 W. Broadway, Suite 501
Eugene, OR 97401-3021
503/726-2250

**Pennsylvania**
University of Pennsylvania
The Wharton School
444 Vance Hall
Philadelphia, PA 19104
215/898-1219

**Puerto Rico**
University of Puerto Rico
Mayaguez Campus, Box 5253
Mayaguez, PR 00681
809/834-3590

**Rhode Island**
Bryant College SBDC
1150 Douglas Pike
Smithfield, RI 02917
401/232-6111

**South Carolina**
University of South Carolina
College of Business Administration
Columbia, SC 29208
803/777-4907

**South Dakota**
University of South Dakota
School of Business
414 E. Clark Street
Vermillion, SD 57069
605/677-5498

**Tennessee**
Memphis State University
Building 1, South Campus
Memphis, TN 38152
901/678-2500

**Texas**
Dallas SBDC
Bill J. Priest Institute for Economic Development
1402 Corinth Street
Dallas, TX 75215
214/860-5831

**Utah**
University of Utah
8811 South 700 East
Sandy, UT 84070
801/255-5991

**Vermont**
Vermont SBDC
Vermont Technical College
P.O. Box 422
Randolph, VT 05060-0422
802/728-9101

**Virginia**
Virginia SBDC
Department of Economic Development
901 East Byrd
Richmond, VA 23206
804/371-8253

**Virgin Islands**
University of the Virgin Islands
P.O. Box 1087
St. Thomas, VI 00804
809/776-3206

**Washington**
Washington State University
Johnson Tower 501
Pullman, WA 99164-4851
509/335-1576

**West Virginia**
West Virginia SBDC
950 Kanawha Blvd. East
Charleston, WV 25301
304/558-2960

**Wisconsin**
University of Wisconsin
432 North Lake Street, Room 423
Madison, WI 53706
608/263-7794

**Wyoming**
University of Wyoming
P.O. Box 3622
Laramie, WY 82071-3622
307/766-3505

## Small Business Resource Websites

The Internet's World Wide Web is an amazingly useful tool for starting and running your business. You can do much of your business research, planning, problem solving, and interacting simply by traveling around the Web. Use it to get in touch with government agencies, trade associations, and potential lenders and investors; to get marketing and legal advice; to communicate with other entrepreneurs; and to reach your customers. The resources gathered here are some of the ones of particular interest to small businesses and entrepreneurs.

### Advertising

Commercial Sites Index–www.directory.net

Guide to Electronic Commerce–e-com.iworld.com

Internet Market Research–www.ora.com/info/research/

MouseTracks marketing resources–nsns.com/mousetracks

Trade Show Central–www.ts.central.com

### Commercial Enterprises

Convenience Store Resource Center–www.c-store.com

Dun & Bradstreet–www.dnb.com

The List Store–www.liststore.com

Thomas Register–www.thomasregister.com

### Competitive Information

Avenue Technologies–www.avetech.com/avenue

Hoover's Online–www.hoovers.com

### Employees

ADA InfoNet–www.usa.net/ada_infonet

Employee Relations Web Picks–www.nyper.com

F.E.D.–Business Resource Library–Employees–www.fed.org/library.html

Occupational Safety and Health Administration (OSHA)–www.osha.gov

**Finance**

ACENET–www.sba.gov/advo/acenet.html

Accounting Tips for Government Contractors–www.ccas.com/ccastips.html

America's First Business Funding Directory–www.businessfinance.com

FinanceNet–www.financenet.gov

Financing–www.kcilink.com.brc/financing

SBA: Financing Your Business–www.sbaonline.sba.gov

**Franchising**

Franchise Handbook–www.franchise1.com

The Franchise Network–www.ifis.com

Franchise Update On-line–www.franchise-update.com

FranInfo–www.franinfo.com

**General Business Information**

Big Book–www.bigbook.com

Business Resource Center–www.kcilink.com/brc

Business Research in Information and Technology–www.brint.com

EiNet Galaxy–www.einet/galaxy/business-and-commerce.html

E-land–www.e-land.com

Information Services for Small Business Owners–www.lowe.org

Insurance Information Institute–www.iii.org

Microsoft Small Biz–www.microsoft.com/smallbiz

Mystery Shoppers Network–www.nwscape.com/shoppers

National Business Resource Guide–mitc.org/mbinet/guide.html

Patent Info–www.sccsi.com/davinci/patentfag.html

Sample Business Plans–www.palo-alto.com

Small and Home-based Business Links–www.bizoffice.com

Small Business Resource Center–www.webcom.com

US Business Advisor–General Business–
www.business.gov/business

World Class Supersite–web.idirect.com

**Government Contracting**

Commerce Business Daily Today–
www.ld.com/cbd/today/index.html-ssi

Federal EDI Home Page–snad.ncsl.nist.gov/dartg/edi/fededi.html

Government Contract Resource Center–www.govcon.com

Overview of the Federal Market–
www.fedmarket.com/overview.html

Procurement Assistance Jumpstation–
www.fedmarket.com/procinet.html

US Business Advisor–Doing Business with Government–
www.business.gov/doingbusiness.html

**International Trade**

Business Monitor Online–www.businessmonitor.co.uk

ExportNet–www.exporttoday.com

Infomanage–International Trade–
infomanage.com/international/trade

International Trade Administration–www.ita.doc.gov

International Trade Centre–www.unicc.org/ite/itcinfo.html

International Trade Resource and Data Exchange–www.tpusa.com

List of Federal Export Programs–www.doc.gov/ita/prog4.html

STAT-USA/Internet Trade and Export Information Subject Listing–www.stat-usa.gov

Tips to help you export more successfully–www.dbisna.com

Trade Information Center–www.ita.gov.tic/

UNIBEX–www.unibex.com

United Nations Trade Point Development Centre–
www.unicc.org/untpdc/welcome.html

**Legal**

Basic US Patent, Trademark, and Copyright Information–
www.f-plc.edu/tfield/ipbasics.html

Copyright Clearance Center–www.copyright.com

The Copyright Website–www.benedict.com

Court TV Small Business Law Center–
www.courttv.com/legalhelp/business

Findlaw–www.findlaw.com

Legal Information Institute–www.law.cornell.edu/lii.table.html

Limited Liability Company Website–www.hia.com/hia/llcweb

The WWW Virtual Library –Law–
www.law.indiana.edu/80/law/lawindex.html

**Marketing**

Marketing for Today's Small Business–
www.digitalstore.com/marketing/mstern/index.html

Sales and Marketing Management Magazine Online–
www.smmmag.com

Sample Marketing Plan–www.palo-alto.com/printpre.html

The 6 Ps of Service Business Marketing–
www.actionplan.com/6psmarket.html

**Organizations**

American Home Business Association–www.homebusiness.com

American Institute of Small Business–
www.accessil.com/aisb/home.html

American Society of Women Entrepreneurs–
www.membership.com/aswe

Better Business Bureau–www.bbb.org/

Chambers of Commerce Directory–
www.chamber-of-commerce.com

HOAA (Home Office Association of America)–www.hoaa.com

Idea Cafe: The Small Business Gathering Place–www.ideacafe.com

National Business Incubation Association–www.nbia.org

National Small Business Development Center Resource Center–www.smallbiz.suny.edu

National Small Business United–www.nsbu.org

SBIR and STTR Resource Centers–www.seeport.com/sbir/resources.html

SOHO America (Small Office Home Office)–www.membership.com/soho/

Women Biz–www.frsa.com/womenbiz

**US Government Resources**

Federal Trade Commission–www.ftc.gov

Federal Web Locator–www.law.vill.edu/fed-agency/fedweb.exec.html

FedWorld Information Network–www.fedworld.gov

Internal Revenue Service–www.irs.ustreas.gov

Minority Business Development Agency–www.mbda.doc.gov

National Technology Transfer Center–www.nttc.edu/

Office of Minority Enterprise Development–sss.sba.gov/med/

Office of Women's Business Ownership–www.sba.gov/womeninbusiness/

Social Security Administration–www.ssa.gov

US Business Advisor–www.business.gov

US Census Bureau–www.census.gov

US Copyright Office–lcweb.loc.gov/copyright/

US Department of Commerce–www.doc.gov

US Department of Labor–www.dol.gov

US Department of the Treasury–www.ustreas.gov

US Environmental Protection Agency–www.epa.gov

US Government Information Sources–www.nttc.edu/gov_res.html

US Patent & Trademark Office–www.uspto.gov

US Postal Service–www.usps.gov/busctr/

US Securities and Exchange Commission–www.sec.gov

US Small Business Administration–www.sbaonline.sba.gov

# Index


A

accountants, 72, 228–29
accounting equation, 84
accounting programs, 73
advertising, 156–75
  agencies, 210, 229
  budget, 172–74
  E-mail, 169
  flyers, 169
  institutional, 157
  media, 157–67
    direct mail, 164–66
    Internet, 167–69
    magazines, 160–61
    newspapers, 158–59
    outdoor, 166–67
    radio, 161–62
    television, 162–64
    Yellow Pages, 166
  product, 166
  specialty, 169
  theater-screen, 169
American Association of Franchisees & Dealers, 224
American Institute of Certified Public Accountants, 229
angels, 104
assets, 85
attorneys, 229–30
autocratic management, 146–47

B

balance sheet, 83–86
bankers, 230
banks, 99
bar codes, 118
Ben & Jerry's, 154
Board of Directors, 54
bondholders, 99
building evaluation sheet, 46
Bureau of Export Administration, 206
burglary and robbery insurance, 196–97
business, going into checklist, 10–15
business interruption insurance, 194–95
business ownership, 1–5
  advantages, 1–2
  disadvantages, 2
business plan, 16–26
  executive summary, 20–21
  outline, 19–20
business tax and permit, 58
buying a business, 8–10

C

capital, investment, 49–50, 54, 84–86
capital, sources of, 96–104
captive pricing, 130
carrying costs, inventory, 113–14
Center for International Research, 207
Certified Development Companies, 102
Chambers of Commerce, 230
characteristics of business owners, 3
colleges and universities, 231
Commerce, Department of, 63, 231
commercial parks, 34
communication, 178–79
compensation, employee, 143
competition, 122–23

complaints, handling, 184–85
consumer protection regulations, 61
copyright office, 66
copyrights, 63, 66–68
corporate charter, 53
corporate culture, 153–54
corporation, 53–56
cost of goods sold, 86–88
credit, 6 C's of, 99–100
credit unions, 100
crime insurance, 196–97
crime prevention, 196–99
customer relations, 182–86
customer service checklist, 187–88
customers, 35, 41, 122–23
cyberspace, 35

D

delegation, 149–50
demand items, 41
democratic management, 147
demographics, 28, 221
Department of Commerce, 63, 205–06, 231
Department of Fair Employment, 139
Department of State, 207
direct mail advertising, 164–66
direct public offering, 98–99
discounts, 116–17
displays, 41–42
dormant partners, 52
double-entry accounting, 73
downtown business district, 31
Dun and Bradstreet, 95

E

economic development offices, 232
elasticity, price, 127
employer identification number, 61–62
exit interview report, 143–44
expenses, 68, 74–77, 87–88, 95
  automobile, 76–77
  business, 74–76
  entertainment, 77
  home business, 74–76
exporting/importing, 212–13
export management companies, 211

F

Federal Trade Commission, 61, 232
fictitious business name statement, 58–59
fidelity bonds, 195–96
finance companies, 103
financial ratio checklist, 93
financial statements, 83–93
  liquidity ratios, 89–91
  ownership ratios, 92
  profitability ratios, 91–92
financing checklist, 111–12
fire insurance, 191–92
Foreign Agriculture Service, 208
foreign licensing, 213
franchising, 216–26
  advantages, 217–18
  agreement, 219–22
  checklist, 224–25
  defined, 216
  disadvantages, 218–19
  evaluating, 223–24
  opportunities, 222–23
free-rein management, 147

G

General Foods, 30
general partners, 51
geographic information systems (GIS) mapping, 36
glass insurance, 195
goals, 5–7
government agencies, 231–34

Government Printing Office, 232
gross margin, 87–88

H

highway access, 34
home location, 31

I

impulse items, 41
incentives, 150–53
income statement, 83, 86–88
income taxes, 48, 50, 55–56
incubator, business, 34–35
industrial parks, 34
institutional advertising, 157
insurance, 189–200, 235–36
  agents, 235–36
  automobile, 193–94
  business interruption, 194–95
  checklist, 200
  crime, 196–97
  fidelity bonds, 195–96
  fire, 191–92
  glass, 195
  liability, 192–93
  marine, 193
  personal, 197
  workers' compensation, 194
Internal Revenue Service, 232–33
  tax publications, 238–39
International Franchise Association, 224
international marketing, 201–15
  checklist, 215
  evaluating foreign markets, 202–04
  publications, 211
  software/databases, 211–12
  sources of information, 205–12
  strategy, choosing your entry, 212–14
  websites, 212
International Trade Administration, 206, 233
Internet advertising, 167–69
Internet marketing tips, 169
Internet websites, 212, 251–55
inventory, 113–21
  carrying costs, 113–14
  checklist, 120–21
  economic order quantity, 116–17
  optimum level, 113–14
  perpetual, 115
  physical count, 115
  reorder point, 116
  shrinkage, 119–20
  turnover, 117–18
investment, initial, 94–95

J

job application form, 137–38
job description, 134–35
job evaluation, 142–43
job interview, 137–40
job orientation, 141
job training, 142
joint venture, 52–53, 213–14
just-in-time (JIT) management, 119

K

key personnel insurance, 197

L

layout, 40–41
leader pricing, 128
leadership checklist, 154–55
legal structure, 47–57
liabilities, 84–86
liability insurance, 192–93
libraries, 236
licenses, 58–61

limited-liability corporations, 57
limited partnerships, 51–52
liquidity ratios, 89–91
location, 27–37
  choosing the community, 27–30
  choosing the site, 30–35
  site evaluation, 36–37
  traffic count, 35–36

## M

magazine advertising, 160–61
major street locations, 33
management, 146–50
management and marketing consultants, 236–37
management by objectives (MBO), 143
management styles, 146–49
  autocratic, 146–47
  democratic, 147
  free-rein, 147
manufacturing, 39, 43
marine insurance, 193
marketing information sources, 205–12
marketing mix, 128–29
marketing research, 204–05
marketing research firms, 210
markup, 125–26
media kit, 172
merchandise turnover, 117–18
motivation, 150–52
Mrs. Fields Cookies, 118, 154
multinational expansion, 214

## N

National Business Incubation Association, 35
National Retail Merchants Association, 41
net income, 87
newspaper advertising, 158–59
nominal partners, 52

## O

objections, handling, 180–81
occupational license, 60–61
order quantity, economic, 116–17
Organization of Economic Cooperation & Development, 209
outdoor advertising, 166–67
ownership ratio, 92

## P

partnership, 49–52, 56, 98
partnership agreement, 49–50
patents, 63
pegboard recordkeeping, 74
penetration pricing, 129
perpetual inventory, 115
personal financial statement, 107–08
personal insurance, 197
plan, business, 16–26
planning checklist, 25–26
planning, guidelines for successful, 23–25
press release, 170–71
price bundling, 130
price checkers, 124
price lining, 129
pricing, 122–32
  markup, 125–26
  methods, 124–25
  strategies, 126–27
  strategy checklist, 131–32
product advertising, 157
product life span, 128
profitability ratios, 91–92
Profit and Loss Statement, 86–88, 110
profit objectives, 128
promotional pricing, 130
promotional strategy checklist, 174–75

prospects, good 176–77
psychographics, 28–29, 221
publicity, 169–70
purchase discounts, 117

R

radio advertising, 161–62
ratios, 87–93
recordkeeping & taxes, 161–62
  checklist, 80–82
recruitment of employees, 125–37
regulations, 57–62
retailing, 39, 41–42, 94–95
  initial investment, 94–95
  layout, 40–44
  looks, 38–40
risk management, 189–91
Robert Morris Associates, 95

S

S corporation, 57
sale, closing the, 181–82
sales, net, 87
sales presentations, 178
savings and loan associations, 100
secret partner, 52
seller's permit, 60
selling, 176–82
selling process, 176–82
  approach, 178
  closing, 181–82
  follow-up, 182
  handling objections, 180–81
  presentation, 178
  prospecting, 176–77
services, 39–40, 44
shopping center, 31–33
side street locations, 33–34
silent partners, 52
single-entry accounting, 74
site evaluation checklist, 36–37
skimming pricing, 129
Small Business Administration (SBA), 101–03, 105–10, 207, 233–34, 239–47
  loan application, 101–03, 105–10
  offices, 242–47
  publications, 239–41
Small Business Development Centers, 235, 247–51
Small Business Investment Companies (SBIC), 101–03
Small Corporate Offering Registration (SCOR), 98–99
sole proprietorship, 47–49
staffing, 133–45
  checklist, 145
  steps in employment process, 133
Standard Rate and Data Service, 160
stockholders, 53–54, 98
strategies, pricing, 123, 129–31
structuring the business checklist, 69–70
supplier credit, 103

T

tax(es), 48, 50, 55–56, 74–80
telephone book advertising, 166
television advertising, 162–64
temporary help services, 237–38
time-period pricing, 130
trade associations, 237
trademarks, 63–65
traffic count, 35–36
training, 142

U

Uniform Code Council, 119
United Nations, 209
United Parcel Service, 119
U.S. Customs Service, 208

U.S. & Foreign Commercial Service, 206
U.S. Travel & Tourism Administration, 207
universal product code (UPC), 118

### V

value-added pricing, 130
venture capital firms, 103–04

### W

websites, 212, 251–55
workers' compensation insurance, 194
World Bank, 209
World Trade Center Association, 209

### Y

Yellow Pages, 166

### Z

zoning restrictions, 58, 60